A HUMAN ALGORITHM

A
HUMAN
ALGORITHM

How Artificial Intelligence
Is Redefining Who We Are

FLYNN COLEMAN

COUNTERPOINT
Berkeley, California

Library of Congress Cataloging-in-Publication Data
Names: Coleman, Flynn, author.
Title: A human algorithm : how artificial intelligence is redefining who we are / Flynn Coleman.
Description: First hardcover edition. | Berkeley, California : Counterpoint, 2019. | Includes bibliographical references.
Identifiers: LCCN 2019019474 | ISBN 9781640092365
Subjects: LCSH: Artificial intelligence—Philosophy—Popular works. | Artificial intelligence—Social aspects—Popular works.
Classification: LCC Q334.7 .C646 2019 | DDC 303.48/34—dc23
LC record available at https://lccn.loc.gov/2019019474

Jacket design by Sarah Brody
Book design by Jordan Koluch
Graphics by Hoai Nam Pham

COUNTERPOINT
2560 Ninth Street, Suite 318
Berkeley, CA 94710
www.counterpointpress.com

Printed in the United States of America
Distributed by Publishers Group West

10 9 8 7 6 5 4 3 2 1

For my mom, the creative soul

For my dad, for lifting me up, whether I'm falling
or reaching for the stars

Inside us there is something that has no name, that something is what we are.

—JOSÉ SARAMAGO

Contents

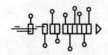

Introduction: Our Brave New World

AI is likely to be the best or worst thing to happen to humanity.

—STEPHEN HAWKING

The Intelligent Machine Age is upon us, and we are at a reflection point. We are already surrounded by artificial intelligence (AI), which is having a profound impact on all facets of science and life. For the first time in human history, we are making machines that will think and evolve without human control. The era of our intellectual superiority is ending. As a species, we need to plan for this paradigm shift. Whether intelligent machines will learn from the darkest parts of our human nature, or the noblest, remains to be seen.

At the moment we are more focused on advancing the technology and predicting its outcomes than on addressing how it will affect humanity and define our future. We need to reconsider some of our most entrenched assumptions and beliefs about ourselves and our place in the world. Paradoxically, we also need to ask what technology can teach us about being better humans.

This crossroads in the history of technology compels us to assess the value of intelligence, both organic and synthetic. Are we entering a new Industrial Revolution or something far more profound? If we make humanitarian ideals central to how we develop and deploy intelligent technologies now, we have a chance at preserving and advancing humankind, and, just maybe, making a leap forward instead of a dystopian step backward. While it may be unrealistic to expect that we will be able to seamlessly integrate with our intelligent creations, we must constantly strive to uphold our values, to become better people as we design better machines. This is a book about how our relationships with the technologies we create will help us reimagine what it means to be human and who gets to be included in the definition of humanity. It's about how we can continue to seek purpose, and how this search will challenge some of our most deeply held beliefs.

The Information Age, sometimes also called the Digital Age, has been incredibly fruitful technologically and beneficial to humankind in many ways. It is also now ending. We are rapidly transitioning to a new age. Whether this new era will one day be called the Experience Age, the Conceptual Age, the Superhuman Age, or something else, this next wave of technological development—from nanotechnology and biotechnology to space exploration and robot avatars—will be brought about not by human inventors alone, but by humans working with a generation of machines exponentially more advanced than anything we have seen before. This will upend patterns in human behavior, transforming the dynamics of how we see ourselves, others, and our machines.

We are living at the end of the last cycle of technological development led entirely by humans. Artificial intelligence is defining and determining the next era of technology and, thereby, our future.

INTELLIGENT MACHINES

While earlier technological revolutions have also provoked crises—such as the Atomic Age and the Protestant Reformation—historically humans have had long periods of time in which to absorb, adjust to, and incorporate transformative new technologies into their lives. This time, however, we don't have the luxury of decades to assimilate the changes that intelligent machines are poised to unleash on the world.

We are becoming irreversibly reliant on computers and machines, using our human memory less, and cognitively offloading more of our tasks, problem-solving, and learning. Simple forms of AI are already present and influential—from talking to Siri, to browsing Netflix and Google, whose proprietary algorithms do everything from suggesting the next movie to watch or career to pursue, to designing video games and flying drones. Driverless cars will spawn driverless taxis, trains, and trucks, pilotless airplanes, autonomous drones that drop medicines and bombs; robots that can win chess matches, write poetry, and compose music that people believe was written by Bach are already realities.

Futurist Ray Kurzweil predicts that we will reach "technological singularity," where machine intelligence surpasses human intelligence and comprehension, in less than thirty years.[1] While some think it will happen much sooner, others in the debate argue that it is a hundred years in our future, if it will even happen at all. No matter your stance on the timeline, the fact is that these technologies are now advancing at an extraordinarily fast clip. AI algorithms are already omnipresent in our daily lives.

Many of us are willfully ignorant about how much sway AI algorithms already have over our decision-making, or how we are now partially existing in virtual worlds. Consider how much of your life is spent online. (The typical American now spends twenty-four hours a week on average on the web.[2]) Consider, too, all of the data and personal information we already hand over to bots and companies. Digital devices and online platforms are ubiquitous. We are losing control over our technology, which creates enormous potential for malicious use. Our privacy is already compromised; underinformed political leaders are incapable of regulating technology companies,[3] much less understanding the science itself; and the complexity of the issues cannot be solved solely with algorithms or by those who craft them.

We are merging with our machines, delegating more decision-making to them without acknowledging how much our own cognitive abilities are becoming enmeshed with theirs. A 2015 study at Yale University, published in the *Journal of Experimental Psychology*, showed that "people who search for information tend to conflate accessible knowledge with their own personal knowledge."[4] In many cases Google is doing a significant amount of our "thinking" for us, and we subconsciously identify what we have searched for as a part of our actual memory.[5] Have you ever been browsing Netflix, only to notice that you have selected a movie with the same actor who was in the last film you watched? Did you think you chose the film, or did the film in fact choose you? Of course, this was no coincidence. The movie was already preselected for you, based on your viewing history. The same goes for why your Facebook feed seems uncannily simpatico with your preexisting preferences and viewpoints. Have you shopped online or searched for a product, only for it to appear shortly thereafter in a

Google, Facebook, or Instagram ad? Did you click on it again? Did you buy it this time? Or did it influence you to purchase the item in the real world at a physical store?

Whether you are deciding what shoes to purchase, which friends to "friend," or whom to vote for, an algorithm is involved. When the police decide how to allocate resources, when an insurance company determines your premiums, when someone lands on the "no fly" list, an algorithm is involved.[6] Today an algorithm can predict your sexual orientation with startling accuracy (better than humans) by looking at an image of your face.[7] While we are catching on to Google ads and Netflix recommendations, which seem harmless enough to many of us, are we registering just how successful machine intelligence already is at influencing the estimated 35,000 "remotely conscious" decisions you, and every adult, make every single day?[8] I believe we are not. Our elected leaders are not. We are completely unprepared for the near-term impact and consequences of this smart technology. And, as I will argue in this book, despite a well-intentioned fledgling "algorithmic accountability movement,"[9] we are alarmingly unready for the reality of powerful AI that reaches conclusions and decisions independent from human intervention.

Unless we deliberately intervene, AI will not develop an algorithm that values human concerns. I hope to convince you that we must acknowledge the science, face our technological fears, debate our present and future human and civil rights, and marshal the moral courage to create intelligent machines that reflect our humanity in all of its diversity. AI is changing the very way we approach science, and its successful development requires a combination of proficiencies, from neuroscience and psychology to mathematics and engineering. Modern computing power has begun to unlock what has been holding AI back for decades. The algorithmic clock is ticking. What we do today, who we are, and who we become will be mirrored in the AI we build.

> By far, the greatest danger of Artificial Intelligence is that people conclude too early that they understand it.
>
> —ELIEZER YUDKOWSKY

Mathematician I. J. Good said that "the first ultraintelligent machine is the last invention that man need ever make . . . provided that the machine is docile enough to tell us how to keep it under control."[10] Philosopher Nick Bostrom adds that, with respect to developing AI, "humans are like small children playing with a bomb."[11]

Lest you think we should let the machines sort out the future without factoring in the human condition, including our conflicts, emotionality, aspirations, and demons, just consider one of many early examples of what happens when AI operates without intentional ethical constraints and with our own biases—like the racist rants a Twitter chatbot learned within its first twenty-four hours of going live.[12] Facebook has allowed real estate advertisers to target housing ads exclusively to white people.[13] And then there is the use of algorithms to influence outcomes with global implications, as in the 2016 U.S. presidential election cycle, which was disrupted by a proliferation of "fake news" that was quickly disseminated by social media bots.[14] Truth itself is being threatened by machines that are currently controlled and programmed by people.

To briefly define the terms in this book, "technology" is used broadly here to mean both the application of scientific knowledge for practical purposes and the machines and equipment developed from such application of scientific knowledge. Artificial, machine, digital, synthetic, or virtual "intelligence"—AI, broadly speaking—refers to robotics, software, and computers that have the capacity for "intelligent behavior." I will use the term "AI" throughout this book, although at times I will be referring to specific applications deployed in numerous variations.

There is no uniform definition of AI that everyone agrees on, but generally, it is understood that the "reactive" machines being developed to mimic human behavior that are in use now are known as "narrow" and "weak" forms of AI. By contrast, "general" AIs are those that are able to learn and think for themselves and thus, at least in theory, become intelligent. Artificial general intelligence, "strong AI," or AGI refers to a machine that has an authentic capacity to "think," will have at least "limited memory," and will be capable of performing most human tasks. Artificial superintelligence or "ASI" is a speculative technology that would be self-aware, and some have suggested there should be a fourth category of AI, "conscious AI."

Algorithms are at the heart of AI. Modern computer algorithms have been around since the 1950s, although ancient algorithms first appeared in the ninth century. The Persian scientist, astronomer, and mathematician Abdullah Muhammad ibn Musa al-Khwarizmi, often cited as "the father of algebra," was indirectly responsible for the creation of the term "algorithm." In a twelfth-century Latin translation of one of his books, his name was rendered as "Algorithmi."[15]

A very simple explanation of an algorithm is that it is a step-by-step process for completing a task. Of course, algorithms are primarily associated with math and computer science, but something as ordinary as a food recipe is also an algorithm.

So an algorithm is a guide, or a set of formulaic instructions, which become computer programs that tell a machine what to do. With an AI algorithm, the computer can then begin to *learn on its own*, teaching itself, without being specifically reprogrammed by humans. This is called machine learning. When it learns (based on training data, for example), it updates its internal model to reflect what it has learned from its new training. Once the model is ready, it can be used to answer questions about new examples that have not been previously seen. With "reinforcement learning," a machine training method that allows AI to learn from past experiences, a computer or piece of software can automatically find the ideal behavior needed to maximize performance in a given context, without human intervention. AI technology is thus progressing quickly from solving basic problems to learning from the resulting data in order to act with "intelligence"— or at least a simulation of biological intelligence.

But what exactly does "intelligence" mean in this context? Does AI have *thoughts*? If an inanimate object is intelligent and can think for itself, does that mean it could have cognitive abilities such as perception, memory, judgment, and reasoning? Does it truly *know* things, or does it just store or generate data? What about sentience, feelings, emotions like joy and anger, and other experiences that living things share and that we associate with intelligence? Some people postulate that all organisms are simply algorithms: does this mean that *life* can actually be designed by copying nature with artificial means? Others suggest that our entire existence (including the universe) is merely a simulation running on some cosmic computer.[16] We'll take a more in-depth look at the science and what constitutes "intelligence" in chapter 2.

One of the polemical questions surrounding AI is, Could a substantially advanced intelligent machine become conscious—could it become aware of its own existence? A wide philosophical divide separates those who believe that consciousness is, in general, explainable as a purely material process of neurons interacting, and those who argue that there is something more, an indefinable quality beyond the realm of science, something Vladimir Nabokov called that "marvel of consciousness—that sudden window swinging open on a sunlit landscape amidst the night of non-being."[17] The mystery of what being conscious even means, for humans and other living things, is so fiercely debated that there is no consensus yet on whether the answers are even knowable. In chapter 8 we will explore the meaning of "consciousness," what it means to be *alive*, as well as whether highly developed AGI could *learn* to be conscious.

Irrespective of their capacity for consciousness, should artificially intelligent entities have rights? Further still, if artificially intelligent beings potentially have rights or personhood, do we humans have the right, and/or the responsibility, to build them in a certain way? Or to prevent them from developing in specific ways? Who decides the answers to these questions, who enforces the rules we decide on, and how may the answers change as AI grows more powerful than humans? Throughout this book, we'll be delineating the positions of the debate and examining some of the possible paths forward in our brave new world.

We need to start asking these and other big questions now. Critically, the discussion needs to include all of us whose day-to-day lives will be affected by the proliferation of AI, not just the scientists and theoreticians who have focused on AI thus far. PricewaterhouseCoopers expects AI to add $15.7 trillion to world GDP by 2030,[18] and the technology is being developed by a relatively small, selective, and secretive group of companies and individuals, all of whom have their own agendas.

I admit that I have an agenda as well. Mine is to illuminate what I believe are the most essential aspects of the AI revolution: the effect intelligent machines will have on all living things and how this will transform humanity.

THE LAST FRONTIER OF INVENTION

We already manufacture technology that is in many ways more capable than humans. And we have been making electronic machines smarter than we are in various forms since the advent of the first nonhuman computers, which were able to process data at speeds far faster than humans. Before that time, "computers" referred to the very smart people (typically women, often Black women) who crunched the numbers that did everything from actualizing nuclear fission for the Manhattan Project to sending us to the moon and back with NASA.[19] Electronic computers were developed as a tool to multiply our capacity to process numbers, giving humans the ability to calculate faster and more precisely. This dramatically enhanced how we create, build, and live. However, artificial intelligence is beginning to surpass us in ways far beyond mere calculations and data sifting.

Since humans first walked the earth, we have looked for ways to propel our forward motion by creating machines to assist us. *The Economist* equates the invention of the smartphone with the advent of the printing press. We now have a difficult time separating from our smartphones, even though excessive usage is strongly linked to depression and anxiety. It's easy to understand, however, why we've become reliant on them: these ubiquitous devices have more computing power than NASA's mainframes did in the 1960s.[20]

Our adoption of mobile phones and personal computers, and acceptance of how they have modified our behavior, has been remarkably swift. By 2020 there will be four computer devices in existence for every person on Earth,[21] and there is more significant change coming. Today, we are about to make a quantum leap beyond existing technology with advancements that may unlock the mysteries of neuroscience, nanotechnology, and the cosmos itself. Yet many of us remain head down, staring at a brightly lit screen as the tectonic plates of history and technology are shifting beneath our feet.

Intelligent machines currently being designed have the ability to reason for themselves and to improve themselves.[22] This will possibly be the last frontier of invention and innovation, since our machines will likely become better at inventing and innovating than we could ever be. These machines will also learn and act without human control, which means that at a certain point we will lose the ability to course-correct the technology that we have birthed and set free.

Already, the humans who create AI are often in the dark about what the AI is going to learn next. While developers understand generally how to build AI—for instance, by using neural networks, which are computer simulations of the human brain and nervous system, and programming them with deep learning algorithms—understanding exactly how these systems work and process information is, at present, largely unknown. According to Google's CEO, their AutoML AI (which they call "AI inception") is better at creating AI than humans are.[23]

This uncertainty about how we can expect AI to evolve is so clearly troubling that the European Union initiated discussions in 2018 about whether companies must begin honoring a legal mandate to interrogate an intelligent computer system concerning how it reached its conclusions. Getting an exact answer from an algorithm about how it arrived at an answer may in fact be impossible. Trying to deconstruct how an AI has reached a particular decision could be akin to examining the neurons of Einstein's brain to figure out how he developed the theory of relativity.

If we cannot explain why, or even how, AI does what it does, is there any way we can work with it as equal partners? Can we trust it? Could it ever be completely unbiased? We are not at all sure what will happen when a smart piece of technology develops a mind of its own, or whether that can even be called a mind at all.

The late, legendary Stephen Hawking has said that "success in creating AI would be the biggest event in human history . . . Unfortunately, it might also be the last, unless we learn how to avoid the risks."[24] Elon Musk has called AI "our greatest existential threat."[25] Vladimir Putin has thrown down the gauntlet with the bold statement that "whoever becomes the leader in [AI] will become the ruler of the world."[26] Meanwhile others, like roboticist Rodney Brooks, argue that this technology is all very manageable and that doomsday scenarios are not only incorrect, but irresponsible.[27] Representing a techno-optimistic point of view, Jeff Bezos believes that we are entering the AI "renaissance" and its "golden age."[28]

The original Renaissance Age, aided by the invention of Gutenberg's printing press, ushered in the spread of humanism and the Protagorean idea that "man is the measure of all things."[29] It made widespread the view that through the genius of the human mind, all things are possible. Thus the quest to build a fully intelligent machine has historical precedent in the idea of creating the ideal and universal man, the uomo universale, the Renaissance Man, a self-aware polymath at the center of the universe with limitless potential. In the future, it will not be a human but rather a machine that will ultimately embody the whole of human knowledge.

A multitude of perspectives underscore how acute the questions posed by technology are, but even with an array of competing, informed voices, we still do not have enough diverse groups of people collaborating on the development of emerging technologies. Ultimately, if we don't work together and do our best to ensure a future aligned with our highest values as humans, it may be the more insidious dangers that creep up on us and turn our world into a more hostile and inequitable place.

A 2016 Stanford report concluded "that attempts to regulate 'AI' in general would be misguided, since there is no clear definition of AI (it isn't any one thing), and the risks and considerations are very different in different domains."[30] As the vagueness of this statement indicates, while AI is indisputably upon us, the questions far outnumber the certainties. We haven't yet been able to lock down any one universal and complete definition of synthetic intelligence, much less shape the regulations, rules, codes, values, and laws needed to guide it.

So what rights should we, and our future robot friends, have? The right to keep our personal data and our mental thoughts private? The right to keep our personality as it was when we were born with it? What about the right to alter our personality or our brain with these new neural advancements? Or the freedom to think and do as we so choose, as in a right to cognitive liberty? As of this writing, international and domestic rules and standards for governing AI development are just starting to be fully weighed. I will propose that prior governing instruments—such as climate change protocols, constitutional amendments, and chemical and nuclear weapons bans—can help us to draft AI rules and treaties. So too can reviewing our past responses to historical clashes between technology and ethics, looking at both our successes and failures in adopting universal rules to protect us against existential threats. What is abundantly clear is that the issues are complex. We need a much broader conversation and an expanded and more inclusive set of stakeholders at the table.

There are quite a few institutions beginning to focus on these questions, including the British Parliament, which was recently in talks regarding the future of AI and robotics.[31] Members of the European Parliament, spearheaded by MEP Mady Delvaux, have called for rules and agency oversight of the future of robotics and AI.[32] However, there are no laws yet on the books, woefully little governmental understanding of the science, and it's often just the elite few—mostly male, Caucasian scientists, with similar educational backgrounds—who have a seat at the table. We'll talk more about this disconnect, why it's so damaging, and what we can do about it in chapter 3. In the meantime, there are still far too few humanists, rights advocates, social scientists, and others with diverse (and perhaps helpfully contrarian) viewpoints involved in the discussion.

POSTHUMAN

> When you're building something smarter than you, you
> have to get it right on the first try.
>
> —ELIEZER YUDKOWSKY

Despite our extraordinary progress in science and technology, and all of the combined and shared knowledge of the many people who have accelerated invention and discovery, we still haven't developed the tools to save us from the worst in all of us. Scientific advancements and the technologies that benefit from AI research depend heavily on which projects receive funding, an inherently biased and political process. Once a highly specialized technology is developed to alleviate a medical problem, disease, or disability, for example, it can also be used in ways that extend far beyond its originally intended purpose, as with the controversy around genetic engineering. Technology has allowed information and knowledge to spread and flourish, while also magnifying the agendas of ideologues who have been able to manipulate and monopolize the dissemination of ideas.

While we have been able to establish some rules with respect to biotechnological advances, AI experts are still divided on what widespread and highly developed digital intelligence might mean for us humans in both the short and long term. Theoretical astrophysicist Sir Martin Rees believes that we are imminently facing an "inorganic post-human era."[33] Automated technology with the capacity to kill humans, such as drones, is already here and in widespread use. The development of fully autonomous killer robots is on the horizon, and cyberwarfare, which includes attacks on information systems, once a fantastical movie plot, is now a growing threat to security.

Another major area where we are already beginning to feel the effects of synthetic intelligence is in the workplace. AI robots are already hard at work across the world. We know that a large percentage of labor will likely be taken over by robots in the coming years; some estimate that in the United States alone, about 38 percent of jobs will be performed by robots within fifteen years.[34] These statistics are startling, and we'll talk more about the future of work and the threats of automation in chapters 5 and 7.

Some very intelligent people are thinking about the scope and implications of AI. But is it possible we are still underestimating our machines' capacity to learn, and perhaps to become more like us in ways we have yet to imagine? Are we too narrowly focused on the machines' technology, while overlooking the underlying humanity that needs to be built into them? What about our own humanity?

Maybe you are wondering why we should be concerned about all of this right now. One reason is that it's notoriously difficult to predict how technology will advance and spread. In general, humans tend not to think through the full consequences of their futures until they are right in front of them. Amara's Law, coined by futurist and engineer Roy Amara, describes humans' proclivity to overestimate the impact of technology in the short term but underestimate its impact in the long term (like the dot-com bust of the late 1990s).[35] With respect to the revolutionary influence of AI, this axiom may be supercharged.

We are already beyond the realm of much of science fiction. That's why leading thinkers, such as AI scholar Stuart Russell, argue that the survival of our species may depend on keeping AI beneficial and properly aligned with the best of human values.[36] This makes a case for AIs that will not only learn as they go but will also explicitly acknowledge and understand the uncertainty inherent in life so that they have the ability to adjust course while pursuing an objective. That is, we could easily err by creating AI that remains dangerously absolute in its programmed path. This could engender a scenario where the AI is capable of doing something destructive in the pursuit of a simplistic purpose or goal.

The dilemma is exemplified by the "paper-clip robot" that philosopher Nick Bostrom described in 2003, in which a theoretical AI robot's job is to maximize paper-clip production.[37] If the robot's goal is to make as many paper clips as possible, it will begin by being highly productive and effective at doing so, until it decides to turn other things into paper clips to make more and more of them, which may include eliminating anything or anyone who might get in the way of a goal of making more paper clips.

Not everyone believes this particular scenario is possible, but that's not the point. As AI researcher Eliezer Yudkowsky describes it, "the AI does not hate you, nor does it love you, but you are made out of atoms which it can use for something else." One might assume a paper clip is a completely innocuous object until this hypothetical scenario, which forces us to think differently and realize that things were not always this way, that inevitably the tide of history and technology will change in ways we don't expect and cannot predict. Humans, by our very nature, often abhor change and shut down in the face of fear. Despite imminent risks, such as the looming climate disaster, we often dissociate from inevitable problems even when we have opportunities to solve them in advance.[38] If we can find the courage to face what's ahead, to think about what we truly fear and muster the will to try to make things better, no matter how Sisyphean the task may seem today, we can meet the challenge of intelligent technology. We can assess the past and move bravely toward the future, together.

I can't understand why people are frightened of new ideas. I'm frightened of the old ones.

—JOHN CAGE

As I will detail more fully in chapter 4, AI has added a whole new layer to the "trolley problem," one of the most famous and highly contested thought experiments in philosophy and ethics.[39] In one of its numerous hypothetical variations, a trolley car is barreling toward a group of ten people. You are standing near a lever that could divert the trolley to another track, in which case the trolley car would then kill only one person. Do you do nothing, or pull the lever? When a driverless car, or another form of powerful and autonomous AI, has a similar decision to make in the face of an imminent accident, what should it do?

These ethical quandaries illustrate how vital it is to address how machines might incorporate behaviors, principles, and values aligned with core human beliefs. Even when we do not agree on the specifics, if we can agree that the dialogue is still worth having, that we want to be better tomorrow than we are today, that our actions and decisions have an impact on ourselves and others, then at least we are moving toward an ideal, even if we never fully reach it. This could be as close as we get, and it might just be enough.

As we'll see, even this idea poses immediate problems, from definitions and standards to who gets to decide which values are most essential. Then, assuming we can even identify and reconcile our ethics and values, how do we effectively share these with the machines of the future in a way that will be beneficial for us, and for them? Technology on its own is arguably value-neutral. It could extinguish planetary life, or it could give us new opportunities to celebrate our human nature.

THE ARCANA OF VALUES

How do we determine whether one value or principle is more significant than another? Or are moral codes, by their very nature, incommensurable? Isaiah Berlin, a political theorist and philosopher, felt that certain values, such as equality and liberty, were comparably valid, and thus, by design, without resolution as to which was more important. Berlin saw moral conflicts as "an intrinsic, irremovable element in human life."[40] For Berlin, collisions of values can never be resolved, and such is the tragedy of humanity.

Thinking machines are going to present us with opportunities to deliberate "value pluralism," where the AI will need to prioritize one (arguably valid) value that is nevertheless different from how a human's values might work.[41] Should we attempt to impose our own principles and teach AI to be like us, or defer to the AI that is smarter than we are and let it correct and educate us? History has shown that our calculus for morals may need adjusting. There may not be a single right answer for humans, and adding an AI value system is going to further complicate our matrix of choices. The trolley dilemma helps us think about what an AI might do when faced with the decision to either stay on its track and kill ten adults, or veer onto another and kill one child to save the ten adults. Would the algorithm be wrong because we are never to harm children, or would the human view be wrong because we are swayed by sentimentality while AI is arguably more objective?

It is incumbent upon us to attempt to design and implement an ethical framework compatible with synthetic intelligence, ever mindful that we may hold competing views as to what constitutes morals, principles, and values. The schematic for an algorithmic charter that can guide both human and machine cannot be conceived—nor will it approach universality—without acknowledging human biases and respecting all forms of life with whom we share our home.

Man will only become better when you make him see what
he is like.

—ANTON CHEKHOV

In *Frankenstein*, one of our great books of science fiction, Mary Shelley shows us how Dr. Victor Frankenstein's creation of a new kind of sentient being was driven by a relentless pursuit of knowledge.[42] The doctor had an obsessive thirst to create this being, to be godlike, and to do so in secret, rather than pausing to question his work or try to instill in this creature any particular core values or humanity. How would the monster have been different had empathy been in the equation?

Will it even be possible to encode ethics and values? And if we can, we don't know how we can ensure that those ethics and values persist across generations of AI, or even within the lifespan of a single AI. We can try to put protections in its coding that prevent modification or eradication of this part of its training, but this will be very difficult to do. Even if it can be done, I imagine that an AI would make a pretty good hacker. It would likely defeat these protections and instructions in short order. We will explore the science of intelligence and consider what's possible in chapter 2.

Leave the door open for the unknown, the door into the
dark. That's where the most important things come from,
where you yourself came from, and where you will go.

—REBECCA SOLNIT

On our journey into the Intelligent Machine Age, we'll travel on dark highways to unknown destinations. We'll call on our capacity to dream, to adapt, to carry on. We'll comb through human history, finding the value in all forms of intelligence. We'll explore the magic of storytelling and our imaginations. By looking, too, at our human rights laws, as well as diverse perspectives such as those of disability and animal rights activists, we'll reflect on how we communicate knowledge and set standards for how to treat one another. We'll dive into this further in chapter 9.

How we choose to design synthetic intelligence is the key to protecting our rights, freedoms, and future. AI could make life more peaceful, more inclusive, and more just—not just for some, but for all. The work of building more humane technology, as we'll see in chapter 6, will give us the opportunity to contemplate our purpose and live our values. For to impart our aspirations and hopes to machines, we'll first have to come face to face with our own.

AI is a looking glass and perhaps our best and last opportunity to plot the course before it's set in digital stone. We owe it to future generations to provide a blueprint of our evolving human constitution, a guide to light the path. So down the algorithmic rabbit hole we go.

Let's begin.

A HUMAN ALGORITHM

1

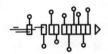

FIRE TO FIREWALLS

A Brief History of Technology

Two thousand years ago, in first-century Roman Alexandria, there lived a mathematician and engineer named Heron Alexandrinus, known as "Hero."

One of the few surviving Arabic manuscripts from the period is *The Pneumatics of Hero of Alexandria.*[1] It details a design Hero created for a simple radial steam turbine. He envisioned fire heating pipes, with the resulting steam lifting an engine, causing it to spin and generate torque, which would then power the opening of the heavy doors that guarded the city's temples.

Hero, an inveterate tinkerer who also invented the vending machine and stand-alone fountain,[2] showed the ancient Greeks' prowess in understanding advanced mathematics and machines some 1,600 years before the "Aeolipile," or "Hero's Engine," was further developed by Thomas Savery in 1698. The engine would ultimately be widely manufactured and marketed by James Watt.[3] With this invention, factories no longer had to be next to rivers (which they had needed for hydropower). This new industrial mobility and flexibility, and all the tangential benefits of steam power, engendered an enormous impact on production, transportation, and exploration.

The steam engine is now considered the single most important invention of the Industrial Revolution. Hero's story is a reminder that many of humanity's most significant technological achievements have occurred over long periods of time, as the slow domino effect of the collective knowledge of generations became apparent. Some even suggest that another of Hero's inventions, a system of pegs, ropes, and axles using weight to move a device across a stage by itself, should be considered the first programmable robot[4]—more evidence of this curious, creative generalist's influence on us today.

> Science and technology revolutionize our lives, but memory, tradition, and myth frame our response.
>
> —ARTHUR SCHLESINGER

Humans do not live long enough to gain perspective on our own history. However, as we embark on our latest technological journey, it is essential that we push ourselves to view our past through a wider lens. To understand where we are going, we need to look back. To know who we are, we need know who we were.

Today, when we think about technology, we tend to think of cool gadgets and inventions in the digital realm. But technology is any tool that allows us to innovate and to solve problems. Fire is technology. Language is technology. Other species, like birds and primates, also deploy complex and clever skills for practical and survival purposes.

However, humans have the apparently unique ability to record our communications for others' benefit across time, and to cooperate in numbers large and disparate enough to build skyscrapers, bridges, and computers. Technology, specifically information technology—which is any system, infrastructure, network, device, or other means of creating, storing, or exchanging information—can provide populations with agency, access, and opportunity when not being manipulated or controlled.

The creation and dissemination of knowledge and the evolution of machines and information technology will continue to dramatically affect our lives. Looking at how we have responded and reacted to technology developments in the past can help forecast what our future will hold. Let's start when humans invented and first used tools and technology and trace how our interactions and relationships have evolved since. What do the tools we have created say about who we are, what we believe, what we value, and where we are heading?

EARLY TECH

History is a vast early warning system.

—NORMAN COUSINS

Information technology has been around as long as humans have walked the earth. In the Pre-Mechanical Age (3000 BCE to 1450 CE), the beginnings of written language first appeared as we invented and learned words to define the world around us.[5] We also began to write on cave walls, using pictographs and petroglyphs, those mysterious cave paintings and carvings whose meanings are still subject to speculation today.[6] Were they addressing other humans? Were they part of a spiritual ritual? Were they made by a few artists or many? What were they trying to say to one another? To the gods? To the future generations? To the animals themselves? Or perhaps they were even speaking to the rock they were painting and carving. As Werner Herzog wonders aloud in *Cave of Forgotten Dreams*, describing the oldest human-made images ever discovered, believed to have been created some 32,000 years ago, "In a forbidden recess of the cave, there's a footprint of an eight-year-old boy next to the footprint of a wolf. Did a hungry wolf stalk the boy? Or did they walk together as friends? Or were their tracks made thousands of years apart? We'll never know."[7]

At the end of the fourth century BCE, the Sumerians in Mesopotamia (what is now Iraq and parts of modern-day Iran, Syria, and Turkey) created a writing system that used a stylus to imprint marks into cuneiform clay tablets.[8] As early as 11,000 BCE, the Phoenicians devised their famous script, the oldest known alphabet, which was derived from Egyptian hieroglyphs—stylized pictures that each represent a word used by the ancient Egyptians.[9]

Before we developed methods to communicate with others, we had no way of passing on our knowledge and adding it to the collective melting pot of human ideas. When we began to use eye contact, gestures, and then spoken language, we could communicate only with those in our immediate physical vicinity, which for thousands of years were the only other humans we would interact with during a typical lifetime.

When writing came along, we were able to move beyond oral histories and began to transport and spread knowledge like never before.[10] This was eventually followed by the mass distribution and democratization of information. This dissemination of knowledge allowed the combined intellectual pursuits and triumphs of human civilization to be accessed by people across time and space, eventually bringing down barriers of language and topography, so that we could build on these tools and technologies collectively. Inventions that advanced the flow of information and knowledge allowed other inventions to proliferate.

As populations expanded, humans needed to find ways to cooperate within larger communities. So we began to develop a more advanced sense of social order, including contracts and sets of rules for interacting with one another.[11] Something as basic as irrigation, for example, was essential to creating our modern notion of civilization. Irrigation gave farmers the capacity to produce an agricultural surplus, and thus more time for activities other than collecting food—time to pray, for instance, and make art. But irrigation also established an engine for mass production that consolidated the surplus in the hands of the elite, giving these managers a level of control that caused a substantial reorganization of social capital.[12]

These social systems evolved independently in many cultures around the world, and for thousands of years most societies operated without direct contact with others. But this changed as channels for connection, trade, and communication began to open and civilization began to spread. About 10,000–12,000 years ago, the Agricultural Revolution allowed tribes of humans to connect with one another in unprecedented ways. This revolution marked the transition of humans from hunters and gatherers to farmers, substantially improving human health and dramatically increasing populations,[13] allowing the same land to support larger groups. Some researchers contend that this transformation actually had a negative effect on human health and holistic progress; oral health declined and disease spread more quickly due to more people living in close quarters.[14] People had increasingly less leisure time, and with more wealth came more excessive consumption.[15] Jared Diamond argues that the prowess of Eurasian civilizations came not from any form of superior intelligence, but rather from a capitalization on a series of advantages and opportunities, from environmental and topographical to biological and political.[16] Despite our ingrained yearning to advance ever forward, and a general impression that the trajectory of technology is beneficial,[17] progress often brings about mixed results, affecting our freedom, happiness, and well-being in complicated ways.

The language of mathematics was first formalized when the Egyptians imagined their own numbering system; then, between the sixth and seventh centuries CE, the Hindus created a nine-digit frame of reference that is the ancestor of the numbering we use today.[18] The first evidence we have of zero is from the Sumerian culture in Mesopotamia, some 5,000 years ago.[19] One of the first big tech applications to process information mathematically was the abacus. The invention of numeral systems allowed for the scaling of mathematical calculations for trade, commerce, mapping the known world, and, critically, for the sharing of this information.[20]

Mathematical knowledge and tools would eventually propel humankind into the Scientific Revolution in the seventeenth century, when math and science began to flourish and spread rapidly throughout Europe, transforming our views about the scientific method and our place in nature. From Copernicus to Galileo to Newton, radical ideas were shaking the foundations of traditional thought, such as discovering that Earth was not the center of the universe. As with writing, mathematics eventually began to be taught widely across the world.[21]

THE MECHANICAL AGE

The most technologically efficient machine that man has
ever invented is the book.

—NORTHROP FRYE

The Mechanical Age began in 1450, when Johannes Gutenberg introduced Europe[22] to the printing press and movable type.[23] This seminal event revolutionized and democratized the spread of information, ushering in the era of mass communication, where a wide range of people could exchange information rapidly on a large scale. This launched what we might now call a knowledge-based economy, bringing educational opportunities to the masses. With the transition from handmade books to printed ones, information—including new and revolutionary ideas, interpretations of religion, politics, and economics—could now flourish and spread across the globe.

In 1517, a German professor, composer, and monk named Martin Luther wanted to protest the teachings of the Roman Catholic Church, specifically its selling of indulgences to reduce punishment for sin, sanctifying wealthy Church members' ability to buy a way out of purgatory for themselves or their loved ones.[24] He printed his "95 Theses" and put them on public display, intending to start an academic debate within the Church. Their enormous popularity was an entrepreneurial boon for printers, who capitalized on the runaway sales and kept the presses running. Luther's declaration went sixteenth-century viral.[25]

Before the printing press, Martin Luther could only preach to those who gathered to hear him that day, and his writings were limited to the number of copies he and others could write by hand. But with this technology the first pamphlet wars began, setting off a schism within the Church and upending the ecclesiastical and political paradigm that had a monopoly on Europeans' souls and purses. Church leaders in Rome tried to capture Luther and put him on trial. They would have undoubtedly burned him at the stake, as that was the punishment for heresy.[26] But he went into hiding and would go on to become the most famous preacher of his time. The proliferation of Luther's writings was not all positive, as he became an anti-Semite later in life; centuries later, the Nazis would use his words in their anti-Jewish propaganda.[27]

Luther had, quite unintentionally, generated a mass movement, turning the written word—his written words—into a way to influence millions, then and into the future. This would be the first of many examples of how new information technology paradigms could shift and spread across the globe, morphing into unexpected revolutions in culture, thought, and society.

> Technology made large populations possible; large populations now make technology indispensable.
>
> —JOSEPH WOOD KRUTCH

The Protestant Reformation ushered in the Renaissance period, a cultural rebirth that enhanced literacy, a rediscovery of classical learning, and a recovery of scientific inquiry in the ancient Greek style. A girl in France could now acquire textbooks for schooling, a young Leonardo da Vinci now had access to books on topics from optics to geometry in his native Italian,[28] and in the small town of Stratford-upon-Avon, a young William Shakespeare was able to read Greek and Latin classics.[29] The circle of those with entrée to acquire knowledge and live a vibrant intellectual life was widening.

At this time in history, the word "computer" referred to a person who made calculations,[30] and the term would continue to be applied to such individuals through the mid-twentieth century.[31] Ancient mechanical devices such as the Antikythera mechanism were analog computers used for astrological and calendrical purposes.[32] The fourteenth century brought such apparatuses as the astronomical clock, which could tell the relative positions of the sun, moon, major planets, and constellations.[33] Advances in cartography and astronomy—from maps and celestial navigation to compasses and astrolabes—accompanied humans on the first major maritime expeditions deep into the Age of Discovery (or the Age of Exploration), which would last through the eighteenth century, spreading knowledge and a predilection for colonizing uncharted (but not unoccupied) land across the globe.

The Industrial Revolution started in earnest in the mid-eighteenth century. Savery and Watt's development of Hero's early steam engine design helped to accelerate the revolution, which originated in Britain and then spread to the United States and the rest of the world, causing an unprecedented and explosive demand for information.

In 1787, in the new territory of America, a group of men were busy promoting the idea of the first United States Constitution by writing a series of Federalist Papers and publishing them in three New York newspapers.[34] Their popularity eventually demanded their publication as a bound volume, and the era of communicating ideological and partisan news media on a large scale took root in the United States.[35]

Across the sea, the French Revolution erupted in 1789, establishing the French Republic. Along the way it also produced a political road map for modern ideologies—from nationalism, to socialism, to secularism.[36] The surge in mass information promulgation was one of the many factors that helped bring the existing political and social structures toppling down.[37] Before the Revolution, only royally sanctioned papers could be distributed legally.[38] But, fueled by an insatiable demand for news, thousands of new periodicals and pamphlets emerged at this time, allowing people to create and make sense of their narratives within a broader societal structure.[39]

Reading these publications aloud and circulating them by hand helped citizens to understand their condition and become more aware of their place in the world, and to share these experiences in a period of turbulent change and uncertainty.[40] The large number of people and organizations starting their own newspapers—from government administrators and Jacobin clubs to army generals and constitutional circles—illustrated the seductive power of this new way to not only spread and commercialize information but also to shape public opinion and amplify a sense of one's own importance.[41] Ideas began to replicate rapidly, based not necessarily on their wisdom but on their ability to be marketed and mass-produced.[42]

Considered one of the most important events in human history and the birth of modern democracy, the French Revolution forever changed how people thought of themselves and their place in the world. While monarchies, aristocracies, and religious institutions would remain powerful, a modern era of human rights, civic engagement, and participatory politics came into being.[43] Citizens (both men and women) protested, created and joined civic-minded organizations, voted, read, debated, and shared knowledge. Historian Paul Hanson believes that the newspapers of this revolution inspired the modern press.[44]

Across the English Channel, at the end of the Mechanical Age, Charles Babbage, an English mathematician, invented one of the earliest modern computers. Taking ideas from such devices as the loom, and using a fixed program operating in real time and with binary logic, Babbage's Difference Engine, designed in the 1840s, had the first written programs that a machine could perform. Babbage's work and his machines were inspired by the difficulty mathematicians and human computers had in calculating tables without mistakes, which sparked his idea to design a mechanism that would automate this error-prone human process.[45]

ELECTRICITY

The discovery of electricity and how to harness its energy marked the beginning of the Electromechanical Age in 1840. Electricity supercharged our societies and also affected parts of our lives no one ever could have predicted. It did something extraordinarily disruptive (both to society and our sleep cycles) when it removed our dependence on natural light and induced our dissociation from the rhythms of nature, moving us toward constant production, information intake, and stimulation.[46] The battery (1800), Morse code (1837), the telegraph (1844), the telephone (1876), and radio (1895) followed and were developed, mass-produced, and embraced by populations who could now communicate with one another across great distances in real time. Advances in transportation, combined with the proliferation of news sources and learning institutions, meant that information was distributed on a vastly expanding global basis.

As the Industrial Revolution continued to define new categories of labor and new modes of progress, productivity, and economic growth, we can trace a parallel through-line in the rewriting of moral codes and the creation of new societal norms. The French Revolution had helped spread the seeds of resistance against tyranny, fomenting the ideals of freedom and equality. The Industrial Revolution in Great Britain became intertwined with the abolitionist movement, and experts continue to debate how closely tied these movements were (and how much one helped cause the other).[47] The antislavery movement, one of the most important social reforms in history, rooted in the Industrial Technological Revolution, continues to reverberate to this day in the discourse about equality, freedom, fairness, and moral reform.[48]

In 1861 in the United States, a nation divided over the abomination of slavery began the bloody Civil War that eventually united the Republic. During this pivotal time, the telegraph made Abraham Lincoln the first "wired" president, and his new telegraph office became the first Situation Room. Before Lincoln installed the room, a White House staff member had to stand in line at a public facility to send out telegrams, and army generals gave orders without having real-time communication from superiors far from the battlefield. Telegraph technology enabled Lincoln to respond to his generals and to address the nation to defend his policies, while leading a country from the safety of the White House. Harnessing this technology was a critical asset in the governing of a divided country.[49]

In the nineteenth century, the world became transfixed by the power of audio transmissions and projected images as a result of the invention of photography and motion pictures, followed in the twentieth century by the rapid adoption of television in households around the world. These sounds and pictures had a transformative effect on society. People were fascinated by hearing voices and seeing human faces and stories on a screen. Franklin Delano Roosevelt used radio as a way to inform and rally the nation during the Great Depression and World War II, selling the New Deal and the war against the Axis powers.[50] His natural, confident, and informal tone created an intimate relationship between himself and his viewers (and would-be voters), pioneering the modern political campaign and mastering the medium for political advantage.

John F. Kennedy would follow in FDR's footsteps in the television era, which again revolutionized political campaigning, introducing the notion of crafting an image, a story, and a presidential brand for the nation to see.[51] Film and television entertainment opened up new ways of telling stories through images, capitalizing on fundamental human desires for narrative and escape.

Storytelling has long been among humans' most effective tools for transferring knowledge and values from person to person and community to community. Pioneering mythologist and writer Joseph Campbell saw this when he looked at societies across space and time: that many cultures share very consistent core myths, with the same underlying structures.[52] Stories remind us of who we are and who we want to be. Stories help us unlock the doors to our future.

Photography, film, and television gave new shape and color to the production and distribution of knowledge. These media continue to have a determinative impact on which information spreads, and they remain among the most persuasive means of communicating narratives, whether fictional or factual.[53] Our human memories, and our ability to distort, fade, combine, and morph them, are a powerful component of why this is so.

It's important that we understand how fervently we have adopted this technology, be it in the form of a powerful film, a touching photograph, a news bulletin, a propaganda piece, or a video game. Having access to more and more information in more media has created more stories that are more freely shared worldwide. Yet, at the same time, it has suppressed the demand for humans to occupy their lives with their own, non-electronic imaginations, actions, and lessons. This passive approach, rendering us observational players in our own reality, is now, in the Electronic Age, coming back to haunt us.

THE ELECTRONIC AGE

> In the electronic age we see ourselves being translated more
> and more into the form of information, moving toward the
> technological extension of consciousness.
>
> —MARSHALL McLUHAN

Alan Turing, one of the fathers of modern computing science, was among the first to envision a machine that could think for itself. In his 1936 PhD dissertation, he presented an idea for a theoretical machine (now known as a Turing Machine) capable of simulating any algorithm's logic.[54]

About a decade later, around 1946, the Electronic Age began. Some early milestones of this age include Herman Hollerith of IBM introducing electromechanical computing[55] and Grace Hopper, one of the first programmers of the Harvard Mark I computer, popularizing the concept of machine-independent programming languages.[56] Vacuum tubes replaced mechanical devices doing calculations, producing the first electronic computers.[57] John von Neumann wrote the "First Draft Report on the EDVAC" in 1945, and the first computer to store its programs, the Manchester Mark 1, was created in 1948.[58] That same year, Norbert Weiner coined a contemporary definition of cybernetics as "the study of control and communication in the animal or machine."[59] The era of thinking about thinking machines had begun.

The scientific developments of the early Electronic Age coincided with the Atomic Age, which posed the most momentous technological ethics question in human history to that point—when the United States dropped two atomic bombs on Japan in 1945, the first and only time this terrifying technology has been deployed in warfare.

Politicians and historians continue to wrestle with whether dropping the bomb was necessary to end the war, or if it was a war crime and deploying the weapon was absolutely immoral under any circumstances.[60] Inarguably, for the first time, humans had developed technology with the capacity to destroy the world. The proliferation of this technology, now developed and acquired by nations large and small, remains humankind's most clear and present danger. It stands as a stark admonition of the enormous risks of building powerful technologies without true comprehension of the scale of their impact and with a dissociation from the scope of its consequences.

At the time the bombs dropped on Hiroshima and Nagasaki, there was no specific international law governing the use of such weapons, and scholars deliberated whether the Hague Conventions could cover types of warfare that were unknown at the time.[61] An arms race to construct various forms of atomic weaponry continues to this day, while negotiation of treaties and other measures to reduce, eliminate, and modernize them and to regulate their use trails behind.[62] One would think that the invention of technology that allowed humans to build nuclear and now hydrogen weaponry with the power to annihilate the species, and which has forever altered and disrupted life on our planet, would be sufficient to make humans very wary of emerging technologies with extraordinary capacities—and to convince us of the absolute necessity to have moral clarity about their design and implementation from the get-go.

Acknowledgment of the atomic bomb's existence came only after it was deployed, and awareness of its true lethality and mission was secretly confined to and guarded by a select, homogeneous few. The majority of those working on disparate aspects of the project were unaware of what pernicious weaponry was being created.[63] Humanity cannot afford to make the same mistakes with our next unprecedented inventions, blindly deploying intelligent machines while ignoring the prospective consequences. The secrecy surrounding the current development of AI applications, particularly AI weaponry, is alarming.

Will the lessons learned from making the bomb be applied to developing technologies? Or will we wait until a catastrophe has occurred? And what kind of standards should scientists and others involved with its creation be held to? I do not believe it's too late to find ways to make AI more holistically ethical before it's fully flourishing and doing so beyond our control.

In 1956, John McCarthy, Marvin Minsky, and Claude Shannon organized a conference at Dartmouth College on the subject of "artificial intelligence," a term that McCarthy had just coined.[64] At this conference, Herbert Simon, Allen Newell, and John Shaw introduced the first program engineered to mimic the problem-solving skills of a human being, called Logic Theorist.[65] This idea, the first known example of AI, came out of a theory that machines could be taught to think. Logic Theorist received a lukewarm reception at the conference, possibly because people didn't recognize the long-term significance of what they were seeing, although the presenters admit they might have been a bit too arrogant.[66] In any case, it did establish the field of heuristic programming, which uses shortcuts to solve problems in AI by using experience-based rules.[67]

In 1957, FORTRAN (a general-purpose programming language) was developed. In the 1960s, a second generation of computers replaced vacuum tubes with transistors and semiconductors, while magnetic tape and disks began to replace paper punch cards as external storage devices.

This was followed by a third generation of computers between 1964 and 1971.[68] In this iteration, transistors were replaced by integrated circuits; advanced programming languages were soon invented as well. In 1973, Bob Metcalfe of Xerox published his Ethernet memo, which outlined how to connect his office's new personal computers to a printer.[69] This memo is credited with marking the beginning of the Ethernet.[70]

By the 1970s, an entire generation had become immersed in immediate and ubiquitous forms of visual and audio communication. By the end of the decade, Alvin and Heidi Toffler had published *Future Shock* and *The Third Wave*, as well as other books and articles predicting our transition from an industrial-based society to an information-based one. The Tofflers speculated on the dangers that might occur when changes happened too fast, and the possible disruption they would bring.[71] They were the first to use the phrase "information overload."[72] The Tofflers saw knowledge as the essential commodity of a rapidly changing society that was fast decentralizing into niche networks, where information was becoming more valuable than labor or capital. They prophesied that the speed of change would overwhelm and fragment us.[73] In the past, a truth or an untruth could endure for centuries or millennia without challenge. Now, information could become outdated in a matter of moments.

As the Tofflers envisaged, transforming a global economic system from one primarily based on capital or labor to one based on knowledge and "info-wars" has put us on a collision course with a very different future.[74]

> Humanity is acquiring all the right technology for all the
> wrong reasons.
>
> —R. BUCKMINSTER FULLER

The fourth generation of computers began in 1971, using large-scale integrated circuitry and microprocessors that had memory, logic, and controls in a single chip (a central processing unit, or CPU).[75] The first home computers were also introduced during this time. This was also when computing pioneers like Bill Gates and Paul Allen got their starts.[76] Michael Dertouzos later observed that the computer was the first type of technology directly related to learning and knowledge,[77] devised not for a single task but for a multitude of them, thus expanding the definition of what a tool can be used for, and where the human imagination might take it.

The earliest ideas for a computer network that allowed general communication between computer users were described in April 1963 by J. C. R. Licklider of Bolt, Beranek, and Newman. ARPANET, commissioned by the U.S. military, was the forerunner of today's internet. It was designed in the late 1960s, deployed in 1970, and ran until 1990.[78] In 1989, Tim Berners-Lee invented the World Wide Web software, which was placed in the public domain in 1993.[79]

The web completely changed almost everything about human communication. From the 1980s to the present day, most of us have witnessed an explosion of electronic data, with exponential amounts of information riding on this worldwide infrastructure.

Billions of mobile phones proliferate across the planet. Big data tracks us, social media has built millions of new communities (and we have created online personas to go with them),[80] and "information" is now instantly created and shared, and often becomes outmoded and in some cases inaccurate just as quickly. The Internet of Things (IoT) is the idea that anything that has an on/off switch can be connected to the internet; it now steadily and progressively links an extraordinary number of objects and people in the world. But the massive amounts of data generated by the IoT have not been fully analyzed or utilized until now.[81]

In just a few short decades, a blink of an eye in evolutionary terms, computers have become integrated into every aspect of our lives in many parts of the world. This revolution has been adopted by billions (as of the third quarter of 2018, Facebook had 2.27 billion users[82]). Via social media, we are already using avatars of ourselves in a virtual world. Information technology has merged into human existence and is now rapidly transforming our sensibilities at an exponential pace. The social and economic repercussions are revolutionary.

Today, we sit at the edge of a great chasm. In his book *The Question Concerning Technology*, Martin Heidegger talks of technology as a means to an end, specifically a means to the end of revealing the truth.[83] As we know, while many species create tools for practical use and for survival, so far, humans have been the only species able to record language and cooperate sufficiently to do things like build theme parks and warships, fill libraries, and spread information around the globe in a single click. And now we have computers powerful enough to turn the idea of AI into a reality.

In the early 1940s, few would have believed we would send a man to the moon in 1969. But we were aware that we had the technology to propel us into space. However, technology is progressing so quickly now that it is almost impossible to foresee what the world will look like in thirty years. Increasingly we are immersed in virtual realities, and now "augmented realities," through video games and headsets. A new dimension is upon us, and the digital world is merging so rapidly and seamlessly with the real world that most of us no longer notice.

Our synthetically brainy devices may make us feel less alone and more connected, even as they pull us farther and farther from "real life." Professor of psychology and author Jean Twenge has described how smartphones have precipitated the "worst mental-health crisis in decades."[84] A 2017 study has shown that the mere presence of your cell phone reduces your cognitive capacity.[85] Younger people's entire lives have been radically altered by their phones, and their heavy use has been linked to skyrocketing levels of anxiety, depression, and social isolation.[86] Perhaps Henry David Thoreau knew our technological addictions were inevitable many years ago when he ventured into the woods seeking simplicity. Maybe we should be thankful that companion and psychologist robots are just around the corner?

Our technological tools are indeed becoming more intelligent, but we might not be. We are glimpsing the limits of human potential on a fully interconnected planet. How will we react and adapt to this as a society? As a species? We already live in a world that seems to value wealth over acumen, celebrity over wisdom, and self-interest over the common good—what will happen when machines start making the decisions? We've been incorporating technology into our lives since the beginning of human history. And ever since, the accelerating pace of change has left us with less and less time to assimilate before the next changes arrive.

An insightful biological comparison is how the human hand and brain coevolved, along with tools, very slowly, over thousands of years.[87] The brain and hand needed to adapt simultaneously to work with the tools necessary for survival and social cooperation.[88] And there is strong support for the idea that the invention of tools co-

A BRIEF HISTORY OF TECHNOLOGY

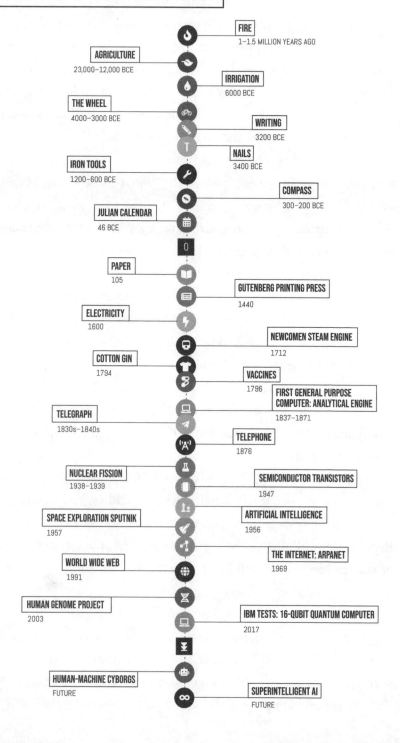

FIRE
1–1.5 MILLION YEARS AGO

AGRICULTURE
23,000–12,000 BCE

IRRIGATION
6000 BCE

THE WHEEL
4000–3000 BCE

WRITING
3200 BCE

NAILS
3400 BCE

IRON TOOLS
1200–600 BCE

COMPASS
300–200 BCE

JULIAN CALENDAR
46 BCE

PAPER
105

GUTENBERG PRINTING PRESS
1440

ELECTRICITY
1600

NEWCOMEN STEAM ENGINE
1712

COTTON GIN
1794

VACCINES
1796

FIRST GENERAL PURPOSE COMPUTER: ANALYTICAL ENGINE
1837–1871

TELEGRAPH
1830s–1840s

TELEPHONE
1876

NUCLEAR FISSION
1938–1939

SEMICONDUCTOR TRANSISTORS
1947

SPACE EXPLORATION SPUTNIK
1957

ARTIFICIAL INTELLIGENCE
1956

THE INTERNET: ARPANET
1969

WORLD WIDE WEB
1991

HUMAN GENOME PROJECT
2003

IBM TESTS: 16-QUBIT QUANTUM COMPUTER
2017

HUMAN-MACHINE CYBORGS
FUTURE

SUPERINTELLIGENT AI
FUTURE

incided with the development of language.[89] Now, the rapid rise of computers and cellular devices is on track to permanently alter the structure of the human hand.[90] These gadgets we use will modify our physiology similar to the way utensils have altered the structure of our bite.[91] Our brains will be challenged to coevolve with our devices in order to keep pace with exponentially accelerating intelligent machines. We've had more than forty years to adapt to the Information Age. We are not going to have that much time to acclimatize to the Intelligent Machine Era.

> Anything that could give rise to smarter-than-human intelligence—in the form of Artificial Intelligence, brain-computer interfaces, or neuroscience-based human intelligence enhancement—wins hands down beyond contest as doing the most to change the world. Nothing else is even in the same league.
>
> —ELIEZER YUDKOWSKY

Whichever name is given to the next Technological Age, this will be the last era of invention and discovery decided exclusively by humans. Merging with artificially intelligent technology is going to be like learning to live with a new species. It remains to be seen whether we will learn from historical patterns—whether we will make the same mistakes we did with the atomic bomb, or if we can achieve a productive and peaceful alliance with our digital offspring.

Since we cannot completely and accurately envision what our AI-driven world will look like, we'll have to calibrate our internal compasses, human and machine, to keep us and our technologies moving toward true north. Whether AI brings with it fully autonomous weapons of mass destruction, the keys to unlocking immortality,[92] or a way to make the rich richer while the middle class shrinks and the poor are disenfranchised further still,[93] it also now affords us the opportunity to commit to building empathy, compassion, quality of life, and fairness into our future.

Although we are at an unprecedented place in human history, the patterns of the past can provide insight into the likely human response to the quandaries posed by intelligent technologies. We've become comfortable with our tools and accustomed to our place. Now, we are staggering out of Plato's Cave and will be thrust outside, into the glaring light. Great danger and great possibilities lie ahead.

2

THE SCIENCE OF INTELLIGENCE

Algorithms, Animals, and Machines That Can Learn

> Artificial Intelligence (AI) is the science of how to get machines to do the things they do in movies.
>
> —ASTRO TELLER

At the Seattle Aquarium in 2005, a giant Pacific octopus named Billye was given a herring-stuffed medication bottle. Billye and her octopus friends had previously been served their supper in jars with lids fastened. They had quickly learned to open them and routinely did so in under a minute. But biologists wanted see what Billye would do when her meal was secured with a childproof cap—the kind that require us to read the label instructions and push down and turn simultaneously to open (it still sometimes takes me a few tries).

Billye took the bottle and quickly determined that this was no ordinary lid. In less than fifty-five minutes she figured it out and was soon enjoying her herring. With a little practice she got it down to five minutes.[1]

Octopuses are cephalopods, related to oysters. They are sentient, like all animals. They have personalities, interact with their surroundings, and have expressions and memories. It is their distributive approach to solving problems that intrigues those looking for a model for machines. Octopuses are considered the most intelligent invertebrates and are very cognitively efficient.[2] While they have a good-sized central brain, two-thirds of their neurons are in their eight arms, controlling hundreds of suckers. They use distributed intelligence to perform multiple tasks simultaneously and independently—something the human brain cannot do. Scientists at Raytheon, building robotic systems for exploring distant planets,[3] believe that octopus intelligence is far better suited to the operational functionality they are seeking than human intelligence, since the robots will require similar distributed, multifaceted intelligence.

Humans may not always be the best source for our AI models or the most accessible to replicate. Modeling the human brain, via trying to hack its eighty-six billion neurons, may indeed be an impossibility. As the epigram goes: "If the brain was simple enough for us to understand we'd be too stupid to understand it."[4]

The study of intelligent technology is actually a philosophical study of the fundamental nature of our existence, reality, and knowledge that will be mirrored in our machines. For this reason, it requires an exploration of the nature of life and humanity itself. Alongside brilliant scientists, academics, roboticists, engineers, technologists, and developers using the scientific method to seek technological advancement, our futures are equally dependent upon all of us endeavoring to infuse the process of invention with magnanimity.

At this particular crossroads, the last before we invent machines infinitely smarter than we are, we are being given a once-in-human-history chance to peer through the looking glass. In a sense, all of our bold discoveries have led to this point: the moment when we discover whether we are capable of building true intelligence, and possibly even consciousness, from scratch.

THE BEGINNING

In 1950 the term "artificial intelligence" had not yet been coined. Around that time, Alan Turing, a mathematician and World War II code breaker, was wondering whether it would be possible to teach machines to think for themselves. In 1952, he published a paper about a set of equations that attempted to explain the patterns of nature, from a leopard's spots to a zebra's stripes to a plant's leaves.[5] Even before the field had a name, one of its founding visionaries was taking cues from biology and from nature that would inform his groundbreaking ideas about machines that could think.[6]

I believe that Turing could envision an intelligent machine, even before electronic computers were invented, in part because he maintained an extensive range of interests across multiple disciplines and scientific fields.[7] I also believe that Turing's status as an outsider, like that of others who were seen as rebels and outliers (in Turing's case, stemming from his then-illegal lifestyle as a gay man), helped lead to his understanding that just because a person deviates from the so-called norm doesn't mean that person is not valuable. This likely helped him cultivate an expansive intelligence. By contrast, a lack of this understanding on the part of the very government and institutions that Turing helped save by decoding encrypted German messages led to his being shunned and punished for who he was, and ultimately, to his suicide.[8]

Turing would eventually be recognized as the father of theoretical computer science and AI. His mathematical model of computation, now known as the Turing Machine, was a hypothetical device that could read and record data on an infinitely long symbol-laden tape that was fed through the machine. The tape acted as the memory of the computer, and it stored encoded instructions that could be read by the machine, which could then add more symbols to the tape.[9] The idea was that any computable instruction could be calculated. This is critical because with this study of mathematical logic, Turing suggests that a computer could, theoretically, do any type of reasoning it was trained to do. It could be a general-purpose, universal machine.[10]

Thus, if a computer could ultimately perform any type of reasoning, then a brain or a type of intelligence could, in theory, be built electronically. This is often called the Church-Turing Thesis.[11] Despite Turing's prescience and inquisitiveness, the technology at the time was too primitive for him to develop his thesis more extensively through experimentation. Nevertheless, today's computers operate using a binary system of algorithms, converted into 1s and 0s, which function just like the Turning Machine, minus the infinite tape.[12]

The phrase "imitation game" comes from Turing's quest to satisfy his own curiosity regarding whether a machine could think, which he began to ponder just as the first computers were booting up.[13] From this question, Turing derived the Turing Test, which is an abstract game consisting of questions a judge would ask both a human and a machine to figure out which one was human and which was not. If the judge could not distinguish between the answers of the human and machine, the machine would be said to pass the Turing Test and to therefore be intelligent. Computer scientists continue to parse the relevance and accuracy of the Turing Test, and some complain that this test impedes innovation by focusing on the wrong endgame.[14] Nonetheless, Turing's revolutionary thinking at the dawn of the modern computer age sparked the development of the technology we know today as artificial intelligence.

Around the same time, the field of cybernetics was also gaining steam. Cybernetics is the study of how humans, animals, and machines communicate with and control one another, or, in the words of the psychologist Ernst von Glasersfeld, "the art of creating equilibrium in a world of constraints and possibilities."[15] Those in the field study how living organic beings are deconstructed, hacked, and rebuilt; these views converge with the development of AI.

Concurrently, in 1953, based in large part on the groundbreaking work of Rosalind Franklin and Maurice Wilkins, James Watson and Francis Crick identified the structure of DNA, the complete set of instructions for how to construct a human being from a single fertilized human egg.[16] This Nobel Prize–winning achievement began to unwrap the mysteries of human life,[17] and along with it presented myriad ethical questions about how we should or should not design the DNA of our future babies[18] and who should be granted access to information about a person's genetic makeup.[19] The discovery of the double helix structure of our DNA paved the way for the Human Genome Project (begun in 1990 and completed in 2003), an international collaboration of scientists tasked with mapping the genetic structure of human beings.

It is within this ethical and scientific context that, some sixty years ago, a new field of science was born. The term "artificial intelligence" was first used by John McCarthy in 1956. Because of the inherent power and suggestion of language and terminology, some now prefer to use alternative terms, such as "machine intelligence," "synthetic intelligence," "digital intelligence," or "augmented intelligence." More terminology will emerge and evolve. All have persuasive arguments in their favor, and while I will often use the term "AI" for simplicity's sake, think about how each of these terms resonates with you or not, and why.

Although we now roughly define AI as artificial constructs such as software, computers, algorithms, and robotics that have the capacity for intelligent behavior,[20] AI has historically meant many things to many people.[21] Even today, it continues to elude a cohesive definition. This has presented challenges to cultivating a unified explanation of the characteristics of machines that can think, but the semantic debate has also brought attention to the field and its possibilities. The dramatic difference from early AI science is that now we have the data, computing power, and storage necessary to elevate virtual intelligence, along with the science of AI itself, which is no single discipline but rather a search for an understanding of intelligence, learning, and thought.

THE NUTS AND BOLTS

The general categories of AI are quite broad and encompass multiple kinds of science among numerous disciplines. Many AI experts focus on building software, which is the most common mode of artificial intelligence presently being developed. Others concentrate on building hardware; another subspecialty is robotics. Altogether, the field is a branch of computer science that studies, researches, designs, and builds synthetic versions of intelligence.

For a computer to perform an action, it needs to be programmed. The algorithm is a set of rules with a sequence of steps the computer takes to perform the operation. It's the basic building block, or instruction manual, that people use to create programs. The key difference with artificial intelligence is that the algorithms themselves are designed to let the computers *learn on their own*.

You browse Netflix, which uses a common AI,[22] and notice that it is recommending movies with your favorite actor. Or an advertisement for a pair of shoes you were looking at pops up in your next Google search. AI, an algorithm designed to learn about your tastes and preferences, is at play.[23] It wasn't told exactly which fashion styles or movies you liked, but rather to track what you have shown interest in and show you more of that, or something like that, once it learns and builds its data set. Similarly, Google uses machine learning to help us search (and will even guess your questions).[24] When you start to type a query into Google, it remembers your past searches and those requested by other users seeking similar information, and thus predicts what you might be thinking. It compares your input to what a group of people with analogous searches to yours have typed in the past, based on the data set it has accumulated from your prior searches. The algorithms are doing the research humans used to do. Google translates 143 billion words a day in 100 languages, and advancements in the fields of data science and statistics, coupled with the increasing power of computer systems, are pushing development at a lightning-fast clip.[25]

Two other potent and effective roles of intelligent algorithms are data mining (finding patterns and connections in data sets) and pattern recognition. These functions currently let AI help with such tasks as medical diagnosis, logistics, and beating humans at ancient strategy games like Go and chess, as well as more modern pursuits like poker and the game show *Jeopardy!*[26]

Though definitions continue to be fluid, AI is differentiated between "soft," "weak," or "narrow" AI (which can intelligently perform specific tasks better than a human, but lacks what we think of as common sense and the kind of comprehensive intelligence that belongs to human beings) and "strong" AI[27] (which could be classified as being as intelligent as a human).[28]

"General" AI or "AGI" will be far more advanced. It is the holy grail of synthetic intelligence: the form that, in theory, could function just like human intelligence. To reach AGI capabilities will likely require the development of quantum computing technology[29] millions of times faster than our existing computers.[30] While some think AGI is impossible, many AI dreamers have also contemplated what Nick Bostrom calls "superintelligent" AI, which would be an intelligence even beyond strong AI.[31] Superintelligent machines would, theoretically, have an "intellect that is much smarter than the best human brains in practically every field, including scientific creativity, general wisdom, and social skills."[32]

Two key developments that have taken AI out of the realm of speculation and science fiction and into reality and practical intelligent applications are disciplines known as "machine learning" and "deep learning."[33] Machine learning is currently generating the most buzz as a promising way forward for the technology and is now being seen as a concentration in and of itself. It is the methodology for getting computers to work without being explicitly programmed. If AI is the science of machine intelligence, machine learning can be thought of as the techniques and methodology of machines creating the algorithms that will infuse other machines with intelligence.[34]

Although some experts argue that machine learning is not yet living up to its promise,[35] it has helped to unify a field that was developing in disparate ways before advances in the twenty-first century brought them together under one scientific umbrella.[36] Machine learning is typically achieved via neural networks, which are computer systems modeled on the human brain and nervous system, albeit in a very abstract and simplified way. Traditionally, these neural networks have focused on vision, though some scientists are looking to olfaction to advance AI capabilities.[37] A subset of machine learning called "deep learning" endeavors to model the human brain to create machines capable of learning and thinking like we do.[38] Terrence Sejnowski of the Salk Institute explains that deep learning is "one part of machine learning and machine learning is one part of AI."[39] Deep learning, first developed in 2010,[40] uses layers of artificial neural networks to carry out machine learning through a web of neural nodes modeled on the human neocortex. As computer science continues toward its inevitable collision with neuroscience, this technology will be at the center of the debate around how closely AI does and should correlate to the workings of the human brain.

Machine learning has so far been the key driver behind the invention of self-driving cars, web search, and speech recognition. It has also given us the ability to understand the human genome on a more sophisticated basis than ever before, enabling a level of large data set analysis for such information as human genome sequencing, with speed and accuracy that far outpace anything a human (or group of humans) could do over several lifetimes.[41]

Machine learning is essential to our current delineation of AI. As researcher Pedro Domingos describes it, computers are designed not to be creative, but to do what you instruct them to do.[42] When you design a computer in a way that permits it to be creative, that's machine learning.[43] Machine learning is a computer doing something akin to writing its own program based on the operational objective and the data being given to it, with optional adjustments that then cue a neuron to send a signal (nerve impulse) to its neighboring neurons; this is in contrast to contemporary computing, in which a human writes the program and tells the computer what to do via inputting data and algorithms. Like a digital farmer, the machine learning programmer inputs the seeds of data into the computer, and those seedlings then sprout crops in the form of programs that grow themselves.[44]

If in the old view programmers were like gods, authoring the laws that govern computer systems, now they're like parents or dog trainers. And as any parent or dog owner can tell you, that is a much more mysterious relationship to find yourself in.

—EDWARD MONAGHAN

Spam email filtering, Amazon recommendations, and Google and Facebook ads are all machine learning at work.[45] These systems learn from your preferences by applying statistics to identify data patterns automatically, thereby adjusting what you see on your screen. In Domingos's words, whereas the "Industrial Revolution automated manual work and the Information Revolution did the same for mental work . . . machine learning automates automation itself."[46]

Machine learning is further divided into "supervised learning" versus "unsupervised learning."[47] Both describe how a machine's algorithms work with the data given to learn and to achieve a certain result. However, with supervised learning, the more common technique, input and output are both known, so that an algorithm is being taught from the information it is instructed to analyze. Like a student learning from a teacher, the data scientist's input guides the machine to the desired outcome. For example, a programmer teaches an algorithm to recognize a shape as a square or an animal as a horse, based on a data set of multiple images labeled as belonging to each category and then given to the machine to analyze.[48]

However, with unsupervised learning (a much more complex process), there is no known outcome, and the machine is teaching itself to come up with one based on the data inputs it is given.[49] There is no reference data from which it can draw its conclusions. Rather, the machine classifies information from the input data based on associative correlations. For example, it won't have the identification markers for "horse" or "square" up front in the form of labeled and associated images of a certain category, so it will group shapes and images based on assumptions about which should belong in each category,[50] without having the reference data of animals and shapes to choose from. Unsupervised machine learning will be essential to creating truly strong AI,[51] as this is where digital intelligence begins to do things humans cannot program or predict, without the need for preestablished data sets. This is where AI shows us things we didn't even think to look for.

A third class of machine learning is "reinforcement learning."[52] In reinforcement learning, a machine can shift from pattern recognition to actually making decisions. Reinforcement learning is used in teaching a machine to play and win games, and currently requires much trial and error in the learning process, not unlike a human's learning process. With reinforcement learning, a machine picks a series of actions for a particular environment to reap a reward (for an AI the reward is a numerical win, as opposed to any pleasure-based reward that an animal may seek). This branch of machine learning was inspired by behavioral psychology and takes cues from game and information theories.[53] Google DeepMind's AlphaGo was able to win against a human Go player for the first time after being trained via reinforcement learning. Beating Go is a particularly important milestone for AI, as the game requires high levels of intuition and pattern recognition that were believed to be uniquely human traits.[54] Now both humans and machines alike can learn by trial and reinforcement.

Another AI method, "natural language processing" (NLP), looks at the connection between computers and any natural human language.[55] This is a challenge for AI, because understanding language requires decoding the meaning behind the words.[56] NLP has potential for numerous and far more accessible applications across machine translation, speech recognition, and document summarization as it develops the competence to decipher, comprehend, and answer questions posed in human language. Most essentially, NLP allows non-programmers to interact and collaborate with computers. What's more, the vast majority of existing data is unstructured, and NLP will help to analyze it.[57]

IBM's Watson is an example of NLP, and it is capable of accepting and responding to questions presented in natural language. Watson has been deployed in a variety of ways, from competing on *Jeopardy!* to scanning thousands of medical journals to help doctors find diagnoses for their patients.[58] It has been employed by medical professionals on multiple cancer studies at such institutions as Yale,[59] Duke, and the Cleveland Clinic, as well as at Memorial Sloan Kettering Cancer Center, where it was charged with assisting in the management of lung cancer patient care through searching medical records to determine possible options for a doctor to consider with her patients.[60] As of this writing, the initial results demonstrate its potential, but have been mixed overall. However, developing neural networks that function with NLP will help to demystify artificially intelligent tech, as will such techniques as Local Interpretable Model-Agnostic Explanations (LIME) systems, which help explain how machines trained by machines reach their conclusions.[61]

By the late 2010s, synthetic intelligence had had a series of major breakthroughs, including advances in machine learning due to increasing computing power and access to huge amounts of digital data sets. Its development and proliferation has been garnering a much higher profile in popular thought and culture. However, to propel AI science into truly transformative tech, something we can all recognize as truly intelligent, many questions still need to be resolved and much functionality has yet to be designed. One principal obstacle to achieving a high level of nuanced intellectual performance is our current inability to endow a machine with what we call common sense.[62]

Common sense is a quality we humans often take for granted: our ability to make sound judgments quickly, based on the sum total of the experience and knowledge we have accumulated throughout our lifetimes. We know that common sense governs the majority of our everyday decision-making, but we do not fully understand, nor can we explain, how this know-how leads us to make these many small decisions.

As humans make these constant, seemingly minor decisions, we use a broad array of senses and skills in tandem, making assumptions and associations on the fly that are seamlessly integrated into our daily actions. To develop a thinking machine with truly humanlike intelligence, one of the biggest challenges is figuring out how to simulate humans' commonsense problem-solving.[63] Now that we have developed the technology to help machines see (such as Dense Object Nets [DON] computer vision systems),[64] Yann LeCun, director of Facebook AI Research and founding director of the NYU Center for Data Science, thinks that machines might be able to gain commonsense knowledge from visual learning, through scanning images and watching video, as visual perception adds much more context than language alone—learning in a manner not unlike that of human babies.[65] Discovering how a young child gradually acquires common sense may provide the key.

Cloud computing and powerful data processing systems are allowing AI research to flourish, but to make very large numbers of calculations quickly enough to simulate a level of high human intelligence, still more computing power will be required. This will likely only come with the development of quantum computing, which is the next generation of computing and whose speed is measured in petaflops.[66] The current generation of classical computing requires a huge amount of energy to power our devices. Studies predict that by 2040, we will have exhausted our capability to run all of the computers in

A BRIEF HISTORY OF AI

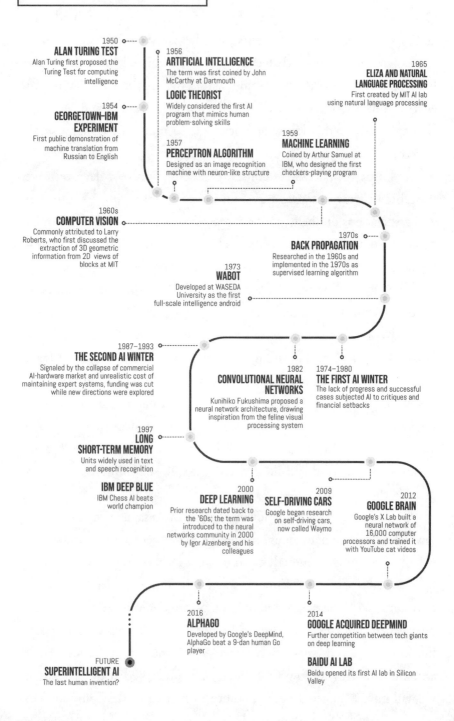

1950
ALAN TURING TEST
Alan Turing first proposed the Turing Test for computing intelligence

1954
GEORGETOWN–IBM EXPERIMENT
First public demonstration of machine translation from Russian to English

1956
ARTIFICIAL INTELLIGENCE
The term was first coined by John McCarthy at Dartmouth

LOGIC THEORIST
Widely considered the first AI program that mimics human problem-solving skills

1957
PERCEPTRON ALGORITHM
Designed as an image recognition machine with neuron-like structure

1965
ELIZA AND NATURAL LANGUAGE PROCESSING
First created by MIT AI lab using natural language processing

1959
MACHINE LEARNING
Coined by Arthur Samuel at IBM, who designed the first checkers-playing program

1960s
COMPUTER VISION
Commonly attributed to Larry Roberts, who first discussed the extraction of 3D geometric information from 2D views of blocks at MIT

1973
WABOT
Developed at WASEDA University as the first full-scale intelligence android

1970s
BACK PROPAGATION
Researched in the 1960s and implemented in the 1970s as supervised learning algorithm

1987–1993
THE SECOND AI WINTER
Signaled by the collapse of commercial AI-hardware market and unrealistic cost of maintaining expert systems, funding was cut while new directions were explored

1982
CONVOLUTIONAL NEURAL NETWORKS
Kunihiko Fukushima proposed a neural network architecture, drawing inspiration from the feline visual processing system

1974–1980
THE FIRST AI WINTER
The lack of progress and successful cases subjected AI to critiques and financial setbacks

1997
LONG SHORT-TERM MEMORY
Units widely used in text and speech recognition

IBM DEEP BLUE
IBM Chess AI beats world champion

2000
DEEP LEARNING
Prior research dated back to the '60s; the term was introduced to the neural networks community in 2000 by Igor Aizenberg and his colleagues

2009
SELF-DRIVING CARS
Google began research on self-driving cars, now called Waymo

2012
GOOGLE BRAIN
Google's X Lab built a neural network of 16,000 computer processors and trained it with YouTube cat videos

FUTURE
SUPERINTELLIGENT AI
The last human invention?

2016
ALPHAGO
Developed by Google's DeepMind, AlphaGo beat a 9-dan human Go player

2014
GOOGLE ACQUIRED DEEPMIND
Further competition between tech giants on deep learning

BAIDU AI LAB
Baidu opened its first AI lab in Silicon Valley

the world,[67] so to find the computer power necessary to advance AI, the leap must be a quantum one.

Unlike the traditional binary code of 1s and 0s that computers use today for data storage, quantum computing's "qubits" can store much more information.[68] A qubit can also be both on and off simultaneously. Only when the qubit is examined by the program is it forced to take on one value or the other. This concurrent holding of both states is possible because the value of the qubit is tied to quantum state, such as the spin of an electron (up or down) or the polarization of a single photon (vertical or horizontal). And because qubits can simultaneously hold both on and off states, a collection of qubits can be used to consider a vast number of possibilities at the same time.

This next generation of faster chips, perhaps neuromorphic ones (which more closely imitate brain circuitry), will have the capacity to fire up machines that could mimic how the human brain functions, processing and responding to data in ways not specifically programmed into them, allowing them to think on their own and on the fly—like us.[69]

MODELING THE HUMAN MIND

> Viewed narrowly, there seem to be almost as many definitions of intelligence as there were experts asked to define it.
>
> —R. J. STERNBERG

How or if we should model inorganic intelligence remains a question mark, and opinions are diverse. Some believe that imitating human brains is the most logical and pragmatic approach,[70] whereas others reject the obvious archetype and contend that AI systems can and should be modeled on a variety of forms of intelligence;[71] to accept the latter view means letting go of the idea that a smart machine has to have a brain like ours, and recognizing that it could be intelligent in ways that differ from human intelligence. Still others see human thought as a guide and an inspiration for AI, but believe the final goal is not to create a system analogous to human intelligence at all.[72]

Confounding the issue is that there is no universally accepted definition of human intelligence. Just as we don't fully comprehend how AI works, we also do not fully understand how our own brains function, nor do we have a definitive grasp of what consciousness is, nor who, or possibly what, is conscious.[73] We are still learning how we store, retrieve, and process memories,[74] and we don't quite know why we dream and sleep.[75] The nature versus nurture conundrum persists, as do questions about how much of our personality comes from our brains.[76] We don't know precisely how we make decisions,[77] we don't know how perception works,[78] and we don't know if we have free will.[79]

I contend that our current incapacity to definitively model our intelligent technology on our own brains may ultimately prove not to be a failure but rather a unique opportunity to embrace our limitations and expand our viewpoint. If we see intelligence as the ability to solve new problems, this opens the door to honoring the vast variety of intelligence in the world, not just human.

Perhaps the greatest gift that new forms of intelligence will give us is not a replicated model of our own brains, but an expansion of our lens and our vantage point as to what intelligence, life, meaning, and humanity are and can be. It will also help us to better communicate with, understand, and protect the world around us. In the process, the questions that elude us about our own minds, bodies, and being may indeed find illumination in our parallel search for intelligence outside of ourselves.

INTELLIGENCE—WHO HAS IT?

Man is a machine, a bird is a machine, the whole universe
is a machine.

—MARCO CIANCHI

One definition holds that intelligence is "a general mental ability for reasoning, problem solving, and learning."[80] Education researcher Carl Bereiter defines intelligence as "what you use when you don't know what to do."[81] I mentioned "the ability to solve new problems" above—what would your definition be?

For example, an electronic calculator is now able to do certain calculations at a speed greater than humans, meaning that its computational ability in this arena—but only this arena—is greater than ours. But no one would argue that a calculator is intelligent, certainly not outside its purpose; it cannot drive a car or play a board game, and it certainly can't negotiate a painful conversation or write the next great American novel.[82]

There are various types of human intelligence, and infinitely more among other species and machines. It is helpful to think about intelligence as being on a multi-axis spectrum. Intelligence is associated with the workings of the mind, including concepts such as learning, reasoning, perception, planning, processing language, and problem-solving.

Over the course of our history, humans have been able to leverage our capacity for multiple levels of hierarchical intelligence to recognize patterns in the sophisticated form of *ideas*, building upon them to create a body of *knowledge*.[83] Humans have been able to gain control of and dominance over other species on our planet by connecting our minds across time and space to pass on this body of knowledge.[84] If we had not been able to, for instance, relay information about how to make a weapon or where to find food, we could never have survived or evolved into who we are today.

Humans are predisposed to put ourselves at the center of the universe, and to place ourselves at the "top" in any discussion of intelligence—as the philosopher Daniel Dennett would put it, being "cerebrocentric." However, animals and plants[85] have certain types of intelligence that far eclipse our own. There is a reason that Charles Darwin—another insatiably curious polymath and creative thinker—and his theory of evolution, detailed in his *On the Origin of Species,* were rejected at the time of publication, and still are in some present-day religious teachings.[86] Humans have often preferred that their origin story include being made in the image of a higher power rather than believing that we share common ancestors with amoebae and chimpanzees. Eventually, though, as we generally came to accept a heliocentric solar system, most of us have come to believe humans have evolved from other species. The incorporation of new intelligent agents into our world will offer a dialectic moment for evolutionary growth.

> I think of what I do as copying nature's design process . . .
> All this tremendous beauty and complexity of the biolog-
> ical world all comes about to this one simple beautiful de-
> sign algorithm.
>
> —DR. FRANCES ARNOLD

A leaf can photosynthesize light in ways we cannot, and a jaguar can run and pounce at speeds faster than the most exceptional human athletes. Salmon return to the exact place of their birth after being gone at sea for years. Chimpanzees have better short-term memory than humans. And as we saw with Billye, octopuses have the ability to distribute their cognition and solve multiple problems at once.

There are plenty of forms of intelligence we don't have, or have less of than other living things. So, while comparing AI to human intelligence helps us frame the issues from within our comfort zone of understanding, it fatally discounts other forms of unique intelligence.

Humans can be quick to say that while a machine can perform certain calculations or rapidly cull through data, that does not mean it is *thinking* and can *understand* what it is doing. We need to expand our fundamental approach to thinking about thinking and what constitutes intelligence, and push our intellectual curiosity to fully esteem all types of intelligence if we want to properly design, implement, and coexist with AI.

Consider two things: First, think about *why* we feel the need to separate human intelligence as categorically different from and better than that of a machine, or a wasp, or a pig. Second, consider that the mathematical science used to build software such as Apple's Siri and IBM's Watson is not dissimilar to our own brains' neocortex, which, through a biological form of statistical analysis, shaped and evolved into the largest and newest part of our brains, in charge of perception, language, cognitive thought, and our sense of consciousness.[87]

Some scientists, such as Radhika Nagpal, a computer scientist who studies biologically inspired engineering and robotics, have already experimented with modeling AI on other forms of intelligence.[88] Nagpal does fascinating work on the intelligence of schools of fish and argues that we need to move away from the "human on top" mentality in order to understand, design, and develop AI. Anil Seth, a professor of cognitive and computational neuroscience, asks us to think also about the intelligence of octopuses, who perceive the world and themselves in clever ways to maximize their chances of survival, and thus may indeed be conscious, although in ways very different from humans.[89] Early in his career, Rodney Brooks felt that action and behavior were more useful models for AI than computation. His idea of "nouvelle AI," pioneered in the 1980s, in defiance of classical AI, aimed to create robots modeled on insects.[90]

Brooks proposed at the time that to create a truly intelligent system, it was essential to focus on simple behaviors grounded in the physical world, as opposed to the classical AI model of symbols and mathematical computations of constructed worlds that are then programmed into a machine.[91] By continually referring to its sensors, this model would solve the problem of AI needing constant updates to stay effective and relevant in its learning process. Brooks theorized that in building upon these simple actions, complex behavior would emerge from their interaction in a real-world environment.[92] Valuing and appreciating all forms of intelligence is fundamental to understanding our own as well as to creating synthetic versions.

THE AI EFFECT

As AI becomes more quotidian and omnipresent in our lives, the identification and definition of AI, or what we perceive to be intelligent tech, tends to shift and morph. What makes categorizing and defining AI more difficult is that often, after a technology originally classified as AI becomes regularly incorporated into our day-to-day existence, it stops being considered AI. This is the "AI Effect,"[93] which occurs when a form of AI masters a task and therefore becomes commonplace. People then begin to suggest that the technology in question (such as beating a human at Go or chess) is not *really* thinking or exhibiting true intelligence, and is thus not truly a type of AI. Douglas Hofstadter, the cognitive scientist and author of *Gödel, Escher, Bach: An Eternal Golden Braid*, sums up this AI phenomenon: "AI is whatever hasn't been done yet."[94]

Why is this so? Why is it that when a machine exhibits a certain feat of intelligence we had previously considered a uniquely human trait, we inevitably get comfortable with the technology and no longer consider it intelligence at all?

The human propensity to assert intellectual superiority and distinguish advancing technology from what we think of as intelligence perhaps demonstrates our deep fear of anything that could potentially become as smart, or smarter, than we are. Once we have integrated them into our daily lives, we stop categorizing Netflix and Google algorithms as thinking algorithms and relegate them to common website features capable only of selecting our next movie or pair of shoes. A driverless car is simply following commands on a computer. This seems to be an essential element of the human relationship to AI and foreshadows a serious existential threat.

Fearing intelligent technology is not productive. Education about the general science of AI is vital so that it becomes more inclusive and approachable, a subject more easily discussed in diverse and accessible fashions, thereby making it far less intimidating. Broadening the conversation from where only AI experts are privy to its future applications to one where we all can understand its impacts and participate in its design will generate better solutions.

Opening our minds to different ways of thinking about the science will make it more accessible. To progress from weak to strong AI, the human mind is going to have to progress *with it*, mindful of how innovation in the current development of thinking machines can accelerate at a pace far surpassing oversight or input from the vast majority of us.

To teach our machines to think creatively, and to move from narrow to general AI, we are going to have to think creatively too. AI experiments have already produced miraculous advancements in medicine and can now mimic speech almost perfectly. AI, along with technologies such as blockchain, 3D printing, and CRISPR, can decipher some of life's great puzzles. The potential is unlimited. But the only way to successfully develop this technology in a beneficial way is to resist our human impulses to capitalize on it without fully considering the consequences for society.

This is the challenge: to preserve, protect, and expand our humanity in tandem with scientific advancement. No one person has all the answers; universally beneficial solutions won't flourish in isolation. I believe this is why the grandmasters of chess and Go were always going to lose to their AI counterparts. For while we love to rejoice in individual triumphs and the capacity of one brilliant mind, it is simply no match for a team working together using the power of collective intelligence—whether that's to build a bomb, a hospital, a game, a city, or an AI that raises humanity to new heights.

As long as humans inhabit this planet—and perhaps beyond that time—technological advancement is unstoppable. The spectrum of intelligence is infinite. Can we find a way to recognize and celebrate the full prism of our diversity, find our place in the circle of life and the tide of history, and work together, using all types of intelligence for what's coming next, whatever that may be?

3

THE DANGER OF HOMOGENEITY AND THE POWER OF COMBINATORIAL CREATIVITY

If I have seen further it is by standing on the shoulders of giants.

—ISAAC NEWTON

A da Lovelace was an English mathematician who lived in the first half of the nineteenth century. (She was also the daughter of the poet Lord Byron, who invited Mary Shelley to his house in Geneva for a weekend of merriment and a challenge to write a ghost story, which would become *Frankenstein*.)[1] In 1842, Lovelace was tasked with translating an article from French into English for Charles Babbage, the "Grandfather of the Computer."[2] Babbage's piece was about his Analytical Engine, a revolutionary new automatic calculating machine. Although originally retained solely to translate the article, Lovelace also scribbled extensive ideas about the machine into the margins, adding her unique insight,[3] seeing that the Analytical Engine could be used to decode symbols and to make music, art, and graphics.[4] Her notes, which included a method for calculating the Bernoulli numbers sequence and for what would become known as the "Lovelace objection," were the first computer programs on record, even though the machine could not actually be built at the time.[5]

Her contributions were astonishing. Though never formally trained as a mathematician, Lovelace was able to see beyond the limitations of Babbage's invention and imagine the power and potential of programmable computers.[6] Also, she was a woman, and women in the first half of the nineteenth century were typically not seen as suited for this type of career. Lovelace had to sign her work with just her initials because women weren't thought of as proper authors at the time.[7] Still, she persevered,[8] and her work, which would eventually be considered the world's first computer algorithm, later earned her the title of the first computer programmer.[9]

Lovelace was an imaginative and poetic mathematician, who said that the Analytical Engine "weaves algebraic patterns just as the Jacquard loom weaves flowers and leaves,"[10] and called mathematics "poetical science."[11] She arrived in the field educated but also unshackled by conventional training,[12] and so was able to envision that this new type of computing machine could be used for far more than just numbers and quantities.[13]

Ada Lovelace took us "from calculation to computation,"[14] and nearly two centuries later, her visionary insights have proved true. She received little recognition for her contributions at the time and didn't receive an official *New York Times* obituary until 2018, when the *Times* decided to go back and eulogize the many women and people of color the newspaper had overlooked since 1851.[15] She was able to see the vast potential of the computer in the mid-nineteenth century, and her creative and unconventional approach to mathematical exploration has much to teach us about the power of diversity, inclusion, and multidisciplinary, cross-pollinating intelligence.

WHO IS GOING TO DESIGN THE FUTURE?

> Innovation will come from people who are able to link beauty to engineering, humanity to technology, and poetry to processors. In other words, it will come from the spiritual heirs of Ada Lovelace, creators who can flourish where the arts intersect with the sciences and who have a rebellious sense of wonder that opens them to the beauty of both.
>
> —WALTER ISAACSON

We all have a role to play in building AI and ensuring that this revolutionary technology is used for the benefit of all. What kind of skills and intelligence will be required to build our best technological future? How will we avoid the pitfalls of homogeneity? Almost all of the major advances in AI development are currently being made in silos, disparate laboratories, secret government facilities, elite academic institutions, and the offices of very large companies working independently throughout the world. Few private companies (as of this writing) are actively sharing their work with competitors, despite the efforts of such organizations as OpenAI, the MIT-IBM Watson AI Lab, and the Future of Life Institute to bring awareness to the importance of transparency in building AI. Keeping intellectual property secret is deeply ingrained in the culture of private enterprise, but with the acceleration of AI technology development and proliferation, our public duty to one another is such that we have to prioritize transparency, accountability, fairness, and ethical decision-making.

The people working in the various fields of AI are presently doing so with little or no oversight outside of a few self-imposed ethical guidelines. They have no consistent set of laws or regulations to guide them, in general or within industries.[16] The intelligent machine gold rush is still in its Wild West phase, and there are huge financial rewards on the line. Many believe that the first trillionaire will be an AI entrepreneur.[17]

While the rewards of inventing the next generation of smart tech are undoubtedly attracting the best and the brightest from around the world—and there is currently a substantial demand for AI experts—for the most part they constitute a homogeneous group of people. Many of AI's foundational concepts were created by an even less diverse set of people. The building blocks of AI are incredibly eclectic, in that they draw from such distinct fields as psychology, neuroscience, biomimicry,[18] and computer science,[19] yet the demographic of AI's developers does not reflect this diversity. Researcher Timnit Gebru was at the Neural Information Processing Systems (NeurIPS)[20] conference in 2016, with approximately 8,500 people in attendance. She counted six Black people among them, and herself the only Black woman.[21] If the players are all very similar, the game is already stacked.

> How rarely an isolated group of people, all of whose backgrounds and educations are identical, come up with anything interesting and new. Self-reinforcing habits and dogmas are not a good recipe for revolution.
>
> —FRANK MOT

The teams designing smart technology represent some of the most astute computer scientists working today, and they have made and will continue to make extraordinary contributions to science. However, these brilliant people, for the most part—except for some of those writing on the subject, and some of the coalitions calling for more transparency in AI research[22]—are working in isolation. The result is a silo effect.[23] To avoid the most harmful repercussions of the silo effect, we need to be having a broader discussion about the homogeneity of the people involved in artificial intelligence development.

Although many of the current leaders in the AI field have been trained at the most prestigious schools and have earned advanced degrees, most have received virtually no training in the ethical ramifications of creating intelligent machines, largely because such training has not historically been a standard expectation for specialists in the field. While some pilot programs are underway, including a new AI college at MIT,[24] courses on ethics, values, and human rights are not yet integral parts of the computer and engineering sciences curriculum. They must be.

The current educational focus on specialized skills and training in a field such as computer science can also discourage people from looking beyond the labs and organizations in which they already exist. In the next generation of AI education, we will need to guard against such overspecialization. It is crucial that we institute these pedagogical changes at every level, including for the very youngest future scientists and policy-makers. According to Area9 cofounder Ulrik Juul Christensen, "discussion is rapidly moving to the K-12 education system, where the next generation must prepare for a world in which advanced technology such as artificial intelligence (AI) and robotics will be the norm and not the novelty."[25]

Some of the biggest players presently in the AI game are the giant technology companies, such as Google, Facebook, Microsoft, Baidu, Alibaba, Apple, Amazon, Tesla, IBM (which built Watson), and DeepMind (which made AlphaGo and was acquired by Google).

These companies swallow up the smaller AI companies at a rapid rate. This consolidation of technological knowledge within a few elite for-profit companies is ascendant and will continue to rise due to conventional power dynamics. We will need, among many other societal changes, incentives to encourage entrepreneurship that can spawn smaller, more agile, and more diverse companies in this space. Given the economic trends toward tech monopolies and against government intervention in corporate power consolidation,[26] we have to counter not only by investing in creative AI start-ups, but also by educating the public on how important it is to infuse transparency, teamwork, and inclusive thinking into the development of AI.

The demand for the most accomplished people working in AI and related fields is fierce, and so these relatively small numbers of corporations that control enormous resources are thus able to offer significant compensation. Even such elite universities as Oxford and Cambridge are complaining that tech giants are stealing all of their talent.[27]

On the federal level, the U.S. Department of Defense's Defense Advanced Research Projects Agency (DARPA) is readying AI for the government's military use. Governments and tech giants from Russia to China are hard at work in a competition to build the most robust intelligent technology. While each nation is covert about its process, sources indicate that China and Russia are outpacing the United States in AI development in what is being called the next space race.[28]

Concentrating AI talent in a very small and secretive group of organizations sets a dangerous precedent that can inhibit democratization of the technology. It also means that less rigorous academic research is being conducted and published than could be achieved if ideas were shared more freely. With a primarily capitalistic focus on growth, expansion, and profit, the pendulum of public discourse swings away from a deeper understanding of the philosophical and human repercussions of building these tools—topics that researchers and those outside these siloed environments are freer to debate in academic institutions.

> There are perhaps 700 people in the world who can contribute to the leading edge of AI research, perhaps 70,000 who can understand their work and participate actively in commercialising it and 7 billion people who will be impacted by it.
>
> —IAN HOGARTH

To better manage the looming menaces posed by developing smart technologies, let's invite the largest possible spectrum of thought into the room. This commitment must go beyond having diverse voices, though that is a critical starting point. To collaborate effectively (and for good), we must move toward collective intelligence that harnesses various skills, backgrounds, and resources to gather not only smart individuals but also smart teams.[29] Thomas W. Malone, in his book *Superminds*,[30] reminds us that our collective intelligence—not the genius of isolated individuals—is responsible for almost all human achievement in business, government, science, and beyond. And with intelligent tech, we are all about to get a lot smarter.

Harnessing our collective ingenuity can help us move past complacency and realize our best future. Unanimous AI[31] uses swarm intelligence technology (sort of like a hive mind) inspired by swarms in nature in order to amplify human wisdom, knowledge, and intuition, optimizing group dynamics to enhance decision-making. Another idea will be to consider more open-source algorithms to better support algorithmic transparency and information sharing.[32] Open-source allows developers to access the public work of others and build upon it. More aspirationally, we must endeavor to design a moral compass with a broad group of contributors and apply it throughout the entire AI ecosystem.

The STEM fields are relatively homogeneous, with few women, people of color, people of different abilities, and people of different socioeconomic backgrounds. To take one example, 70 percent of computer science majors at Stanford are male.[33] When attending a Recode conference on the impact of digital technology, Microsoft researcher Margaret Mitchell, looking out at the attendees, observed "a sea of dudes."[34] This lack of representation poses many problems, and one is that the biases of this homogeneous group will become ingrained in the technology it creates.[35]

Generally speaking, in the United States, 83.3 percent of "high tech" executives are white and 80 percent are male.[36] The U.S. Equal Employment Opportunity Commission says that amid major economic growth in the high-tech sector, "diversity and inclusion in the tech industry have in many ways gotten worse."[37] Women currently earn a smaller percentage of computer science degrees than they did almost thirty years ago: "In 2013, only 26 percent of computing professionals were female—down considerably from 35 percent in 1990 and virtually the same as in 1960."[38]

Jeff Dean, the head of AI Google, said in August 2016 he was more worried about a lack of diversity in AI than he was about an AI dystopia.[39] Yet, a year later, the Google Brain team was 94 percent male and over 70 percent white.[40] Many AI organizations do not share any diversity data, but based on the information that is publicly available, the teams often appear homogeneous, including those that have been profiled as the future of AI.[41] The 2018 World Economic Forum Global Gender Gap report found that only 22 percent of AI professionals around the world are women.[42] The cycle perpetuates itself when training programs are open only to those already in the circle, as opposed to the thousands from underrepresented groups that graduate with degrees in computer science and related disciplines.[43]

As of 2018, Google reported a 69 percent male workforce, with 2.5 percent Black and 3.6 percent Latinx employees.[44] At Facebook, 4 percent of their employees are Black and 5 percent are Hispanic.[45] Overall, men hold 74.5 percent of Google's leadership positions.[46] Only 10 percent of those working on "machine intelligence" at Google are women, and only 12 percent of the leading machine learning researchers worldwide are women.[47]

Women were the first computer programmers.[48] However, women who are trained in the tech fields today tend to eventually flee in large numbers, due to an office culture riddled with biases[49] that are often unconscious and permeate every aspect of the field.[50] In general, funding for more diverse tech founders and for companies that are not led by white, cisgender men[51] is so low that Melinda Gates has said she no longer wants to invest in "white guys in hoodies,"[52] preferring to focus on women- and minority-led initiatives.

The lack of diversity infiltrates every level of technology, including the people providing its financial backing. Venture capital firms are 70 percent white, 3 percent Black, and 18 percent women (and 0 percent Black women as recently as 2016). A shocking 40 percent of all major venture capital executives in the United States went to just two schools: Harvard University and Stanford University.[53]

This means that those financing our most vital new tech businesses are homogeneous along racial, gender, and cognitive lines and thus highly prone to funding people who look and think like them. Other intersecting factors, such as age, ability, and cultural/socioeconomic background, also contribute to this cycle of homogeneity.[54] This inherent bias is evident throughout the technology ecosystem, where the limited amount of money available to underrepresented groups matches their underrepresentation in the industry.

GENDER MAKEUP IN TECH

PERCENTAGE OF WOMEN WORKING IN TECH IN MAJOR TECH COMPANIES[1]

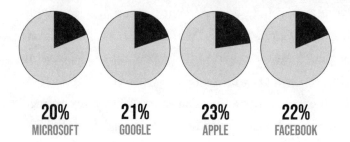

20%	**21%**	**23%**	**22%**
MICROSOFT	GOOGLE	APPLE	FACEBOOK

PERCENTAGE OF WOMEN IN AI RESEARCH WORLDWIDE[2]

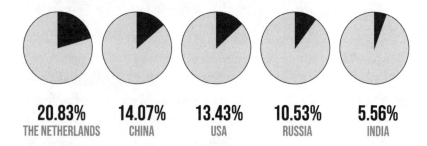

20.83%	**14.07%**	**13.43%**	**10.53%**	**5.56%**
THE NETHERLANDS	CHINA	USA	RUSSIA	INDIA

PERCENTAGE OF WOMEN IN LEADERSHIP IN TECH

9% WOMEN IN SENIOR IT LEADERSHIP POSITIONS
(CIO, CTO, AND VP TECH) IN 2017[3]

(1) Felix Richter, "The Tech World is Still a Man's World," *Statista*, March 8, 2019.
(2) Tom Simonite, "AI is the Future—But Where are the Women?" *Wired*, August 17, 2018.
(3) "Navigating Uncertainty," *Harvey Nash/KPMG CIO Survey*, 2018.

There are, fortunately, individuals and organizations who are encouraging multifarious groups of people to pursue careers in technology, including Women in Machine Learning (WiML), Black in AI, Lesbians Who Tech, Trans Code, Girls Who Code, Black Girls Code, and Diversity AI, all of whom are trying very hard to help poorly represented groups break into the industry. In the words of Timnit Gebru, the cofounder of Black in AI: "We're in a diversity crisis."[55] It's a myth that there is a pipeline problem.[56] The reality is that there is an unconscious bias problem.

The absence of heterogeneity is more pronounced in technology than in other industry sectors.[57] And the discouraging numbers include only publicly available data. For example, even getting access to statistics for tech employees with disabilities is a challenge.[58] More research, data, and action are sorely needed around confronting bias in the field of AI and the complex, structural, and deeply rooted issues surrounding the intersections of gender, ability, race, sexuality, socioeconomic status, discrimination, and power.

The perpetuation of stereotypes and cloistered educational pipelines creates a vicious cycle of homogeneity and in-group bias. Consciously or not, many of us prefer people who are like ourselves and who already exist within our own social circles, which can induce discrimination.[59] The fact that holding these biases is unintentional is no excuse. If the homogeneity in the field of AI development continues, we risk infusing and programming a predictable set of prejudices into our intelligent digital doppelgängers.

EXPANDING THE CONVERSATION

Nobody phrases it this way, but I think that artificial intelligence is almost a humanities discipline. It's really an attempt to understand human intelligence and human cognition.

—SEBASTIAN THRUN

The 2018 U.S. Congressional Facebook hearings demonstrated how little our technology scions and government officials understand each other.[60] Some legislators spent their limited time asking for explanations of basic elements of how Facebook works, revealing digital illiteracy while Facebook's representatives remained as tight-lipped as possible.[61] Large gaps in understanding still exist between the tech community, associated industries, and the elected representatives entrusted to regulate them. Without a far better public understanding of the science, we are not capable as a society of monitoring the companies and platforms, let alone the technology.

Our political leaders don't know tech and our tech leaders haven't decoded how to program values or to detect intersecting layers of societal bias. We have to find ways to bridge this chasm, because our major technological advances will only truly progress through collective intelligence,[62] which requires both human capabilities and evolving machine capabilities working together.

The machines we are training to teach themselves will become determinant in more and more outcomes, so our chance to include diverse voices has a limited horizon. Trying to build global consensus on climate issues and solutions has, frustratingly, taken many decades to even get to an assemblage like the Paris Accord (which is still very much debated and in peril).[63] The introduction of intelligent machines into almost all facets of human life offers no such runway. If we respond with the same apathy as we have to the confirmed threats to our environment, we may have little say in it at all.

Part of our myopia and inability to acknowledge and accept big-picture views is precipitated by education systems that push us into narrow disciplines of study,[64] especially in the sciences. We used to generalize more often and thereby gain a broader array of knowledge; now we often specialize in the sciences and math very early.[65] I believe that bridging the curriculum divide between the sciences and the humanities and offering opportunities for collaborations across specialties will be essential. Very few liberal arts graduates end up as scientists, and not many engineers pursue careers in the humanities,[66] as we can get corralled into fenced-off fields of study early on in our lives.[67]

The siloed thinking that can occur in certain educational settings can abet reductionist thinking, impeding conversations across disciplines and blocking cross-pollination of thought and deliberation—the building blocks of new ideas.[68] Expanding science and technology curricula to include courses on ethical decision-making is one way to start, along with encouraging more diverse individuals to consider STEM education.[69] For AI to flourish, we will also need linguists and biologists consulting with child psychologists, zoologists, and mathematicians. Rethinking our definitions of "expert" and "genius," as well as what and who is "exceptional," is also key. A future world that is fair and enriching for us all going to require skilled empaths as well as designers who can reimagine work environments for human-AI partnerships. It will also urgently require those endowed with real-life experience in creative problem-solving, critical thinking, ethical leadership and decision-making, human rights protections, and social justice.

The paradox of achieving heterogeneity is complicated by the fact that in the not-too-distant future much of our lives will be spent in virtual worlds that we create for ourselves. We may lose the ability to contemplate and investigate our tangible world as we more readily did in the past. As Monica Kim writes in *The Atlantic*:

> If virtual reality becomes a part of people's day-to-day lives, more and more people may prefer to spend a majority of their time in

virtual spaces. Futurist Ray Kurzweil predicted, somewhat hyper-bolically, in 2003, "By the 2030s, virtual reality will be totally real-istic and compelling and we will spend most of our time in virtual environments ... We will all become virtual humans." In theory, such escapism is nothing new—as critics of increased TV, Internet, and smartphone usage will tell you—but as VR technology continues to blossom, the worlds that they generate will become increasingly real-istic, as Kurzweil explained, creating a greater potential for overuse.[70]

As we are more able to shape the virtual worlds we inhabit in our own image, we will also need to be more intentional about breaking out of silos and filter bubbles to explore ways of living, thinking, and being that are unlike us, and not of our own creation.

To evolve into a society that can coexist with our superintelli-gent creations, we need to reconsider our education systems; revise our concepts of intelligence and genius; and imagine a life where unique human characteristics are embraced while our synthetically intelligent machines assume many of our more mundane tasks.

What kind of collaboration will invent the next great break-throughs? What kind of intelligence will we need to successfully part-ner with our intelligent creations?

COMBINATORIAL CREATIVITY

Why is it that of every hundred gifted young musicians who study at Juilliard or every hundred brilliant young scientists who go to work in major labs under illustrious mentors, only a handful will write memorable musical compositions or make scientific discoveries of major im-portance? Are the majority, despite their gifts, lacking in

some further creative spark? Are they missing characteristics other than creativity that may be essential for creative
achievement—such as boldness, confidence, independence
of mind?

—OLIVER SACKS

Besides encouraging greater gender, racial, socioeconomic, and cognitive diversity in those designing our AI, there should be an empha-
sis on multidisciplinary approaches to the work, incorporating input
from individuals with dissimilar and unconventional intellectual
backgrounds, interests, and skills, so we don't get trapped in narrow
concepts and repetitive patterns.

Although the world is replete with brilliant specialists, the form
of genius best suited and most applicable to our Intelligent Machine
Age may be combinatorial creativity. Combinatory creativity, or as
Einstein called it, "combinatory play," is connecting the dots of different ideas to create something new and revolutionary, as exhibited
by a number of the polymaths featured in chapter 1.[71] Combinatorial
creativity can build bridges within minds, as well as between people,
fields, generations, and societies. It's not simply about raw intellectual
ability, but about combining ideas in interesting and surprising ways
and reformulating them into new concepts.

To be creative is to be human. Acute inventive abilities are not
restricted only to geniuses and the gifted. We are all creative; we are
born that way.[72] Imaginativeness and the capacity to innovate are
our birthright as human beings. To hoard knowledge (as individuals, nation-states, or corporations), to not work together to build on
the Alexandria's Library of ideas and insights that we share, is to fail
collectively.

As made evident by the Black women "calculators"—finally given
due credit for their astonishing work in the book and film *Hidden*

Figures—who helped establish the United States as the leader of the space race and return John Glenn safely to Earth,[73] humans are at their best when working together toward a common goal; when we can assemble an inclusive mix of team players, a diverse array of experts and courageous hearts. This is how we send astronauts to the moon and map the stars.

Our ability to cooperate in large numbers is fundamental to what separates humans from other animals.[74] It precipitated the current human epoch, the Anthropocene or Meghalayan Age.[75] Humans can cooperate and exchange information in massive quantities now.[76] Our intelligent machines, with their enormous capabilities, will allow us to process, gain, and share knowledge in an unprecedented way.

As it turns out, there is no such thing as being "left" or "right" brained.[77] The hemispheres of our brain work in tandem; there is much evidence to suggest the most brilliant minds do this the most successfully. Creativity is a learned skill to be cultivated,[78] much like empathy or compassion. Our brains are neuroplastic,[79] and science has shown that we can learn new things, adapt, and change the structure of our brains for longer than previously thought. In applying collective intelligence, in partnership with our machines, to forge our next great achievements, we don't yet know if humans will maintain unique intellectual abilities that cannot be replicated by our machines.

LEONARDO DA VINCI AND CURIOSITY

> Once you have tasted flight, you will forever walk the earth
> with your eyes turned skyward, for there you have been,
> and there you will always long to return.
>
> —LEONARDO DA VINCI

Perhaps no one individual exemplifies the power and potential of curiosity, ingenuity, and creativity to elevate humanity to new heights more than Leonardo da Vinci, who had one of human history's greatest minds. He is a classic example of combinatorial creativity, or as Walter Isaacson calls it, "combinatorial imagination."[80] Leonardo lived during the progressive vibrancy of the Florentine Renaissance and was an apprentice just coming into his own as the German inventor Johannes Gutenberg was spreading the gospel of his printing press into Italy.[81]

Leonardo is believed to be the first European of renown to access scientific knowledge without having first been classically educated in Greek or Latin.[82] Had Leonardo not been able to read texts in his native Italian, he would never have been able to teach himself and make his extraordinary contributions. Today, due to coding and programming language barriers, the majority of us are currently left out of most scientific debate—how many da Vincis might be among us today if we all had the polyglot ability to write algorithms or unscramble the arcana of science in our native languages?

Leonardo was a man of his time, but he also transcended it. He soaked up the world around him, observing everything from the flight of birds to the spirals of water eddies, constantly in dialogue with the world around him. He saw patterns everywhere, connecting beauty, art, science, and nature through his study of dissected cadavers. With every journal sketch of an ear, eye, bird, or horse's leg, he probed the unknown, the uncertain. Beyond that, he combined experimentation with theory, helping pave the way for the Scientific Revolution.

Leonardo combined earthly knowledge with insatiable curiosity about our place in the universe, what it means to be human, and what an individual being's purpose might be in the cosmic scheme. As we observe in the iconic *Vitruvian Man*, he wanted to understand the "universale misura del huomo" (the "universal measure of man").[83] He had a strict moral code but was also unafraid to break the rules—he did not eat meat, for instance, because he knew that animals could feel pain.[84] His worldview was based in science, and he drew no hierarchical distinction between man and nature, art and technology.

The epitome of the Renaissance humanist, Leonardo worked in close collaboration with others in a society opening to more inclusive civic engagement that was no longer confined to the traditional elites of the day. It was the beginning of the kind of education we know today as the humanities. In his TED talk, Eric Berridge reminds us why it's so critical for our current and future leaders in the tech community to also train in the humanities: "It's the humanities that teach us what to build and why to build them . . . [and it's what teaches] us how to think critically."[85] He emphasizes that the humanities are "purposely unstructured, while the sciences are purposely structured."[86]

Like Alan Turing's research on thinking machines and Ada Lovelace's margin notes for the Analytical Engine, many of the concepts and inventions swirling in Leonardo's brain were far ahead of their time. The machinery and institutions necessary to construct them were, in some cases, still hundreds of years in the future. When the Wright brothers finally achieved flight, they owed a sizable debt to da Vinci, as fluid dynamics and the mechanics of flight were two of his many lifelong passions. People today continue to build and test Leonardo's various flying contraptions.[87] Unlike in Turing's era, today we are not only able to imagine the future of AI, we possess the computing power to build it.

Leonardo is one of the most famous examples of the power of combinatorial creative thought and practice. So is Albert Einstein,[88] who was also an antiwar activist and advocate for civil rights and social justice.[89] His science, his probing of the unknowns of the universe, was inextricably linked with his belief in the goodness of humanity, his passion for playing the violin (when he said he came up with many of his best ideas), and his advocacy for human rights during World War II. He had a vision of a world where people of all races and religions would be treated with dignity.[90] Einstein was also a refugee, and today, with 25.4 million refugees, 40 million internally displaced people, and 3.1 million asylum-seekers in the world[91]—the largest refugee population since World War II—there is a strong probability that some of the world's brightest modern minds are presently without a place to call home.

For this reason, among others, we need people with lived experience of social justice issues to be part of the conversation about the future of technology. We can find a historical precedent in the figure of Mary Shelley, who, as the daughter of civil rights activists Mary Wollstonecraft and William Goodwin, wrote the world's most famous Gothic novel steeped in scientific theory. At the age of nineteen, Shelley commingled her understanding of feminist activism, Romanticism, and science to invent a new genre: science fiction. Her background as a member of a family of activists, a mother who had recently lost a child, and a brilliant and imaginative writer of Romanticism make her a perfect example of how cross-disciplinary and combinatorial creativity can flourish. Shelley frequented scientific lectures and quizzed preeminent scientists and thinkers who came to her home for intellectual discussions with her father. No one could have written this book and raised still-relevant questions about science and morality except for Shelley, with her singular set of experiences: the loss of her child, her status as an outsider, her radical feminist opinions, her gender.

Shelley lived her life in constant contemplative conversation with herself and others.[92] Like Leonardo, she blurred the lines between life and death, science and art. Other authors who embodied similar attributes include Vladimir Nabokov, whose novels were informed by his scientific study of butterflies,[93] and Johann Wolfgang von Goethe, who melded his fierce imagination with scientific investigation and moral questioning.[94]

Creativity is a hallmark of genius;[95] so is curiosity. Critically, for the future of science, technology, and humanity, we need AI inventors who are ingenious and inquisitive and who also reflect on the possible societal consequences of their work.[96] Computer scientists working on the DeepMind and AlexNet neural networks have already begun to recognize how important it is to code a sense of curiosity into supervised learning programs,[97] so it is feasible that the artificially intelligent machines in our near-term future will have this capability.

To be truly curious in the way we will need is not just to make something new, or to disrupt for disruption's sake. Rather, it's to innovate within a societal context, within a broader vision for society, within a framework for not just changing the world, but changing it for the better. That's the real rebellion. It is within constraints that creativity thrives.[98] It's in connecting what may seem disparate to the untrained eye, in pairing research with observation and then with imagination, in combining theory and practice, different fields of thought, introspection and reflection, and conversations with others, that we each discover our capacity to create. Accessing and applying our own combinatorial creativity is how we can best imagine the complexities we face in the coming Intelligent Machine Age, and best collaborate with others who *can* and *want to* help us solve the world's biggest challenges.

DIVERSIFYING OUR TECHNOLOGY
REQUIRES MORAL IMAGINATION

There are only an estimated 10,000 people in the world with the education necessary to build AI.[99] At the same time, there is a plethora of books being published, conferences being held, articles being written, summits being convened, and news reports being broadcast on the subject of emerging synthetic intelligence, its latest incarnations, and its potential impact. However, outside subjects such as cybersecurity and privacy, how many of us are really involved in the discussions? How many of us are represented?

> The reason diversity is really important in AI, not just in data sets but also in researchers, is that you need people who just have this social sense of how things are.
>
> —TIMNIT GEBRU

Without reflecting the real world, even programmers with good intentions can miss the obvious. The first generation of virtual AI assistants (VA) had many sexist tendencies.[100] Even now, "assistants" like Siri, Cortana, and Alexa have female voices, whereas IBM's Watson, a "more powerful" and advanced AI technology, has a male voice.[101] When a man reported in 2015 that a Google AI had tagged himself and a friend, both of whom happened to be Black, as gorillas, Google's "fix" was to stop tagging gorillas as a group, as opposed to finding a better way to tag all types of living beings as what they truly are.[102]

Some innovative designers are beginning to address the issues, such as the company Sage, which in 2018 introduced Pegg, "a gender-neutral robot assistant," to attempt to combat deeply ingrained societal sexism.[103] This is an attempt to decode underlying bias and a modest but vital illustration of applying the crucial imperative in designing our intelligent machines—moral imagination.

Moral imagination is the human virtue necessary to guide our technological future: a passion, a curiosity for seeking out what is good, for creatively and equitably solving problems, for using our collective intelligence to move past groupthink and discrimination and toward a more holistic approach to building beneficial AI. In other words, universal design.

This idea of universal design is something that disability activists fight for on a daily basis,[104] advocating for inclusivity and accessibility that benefits all humans. A person in a wheelchair doesn't necessarily want a bionic walking suit; perhaps, instead, she wants the ability to access the things and services she needs with ease, and to navigate the world in a way that includes her in the design thinking processes.[105]

Fortunately, there are some prominent individuals and groups setting out to deploy moral imagination in their designs. Dr. Fei-Fei Li and Dr. Olga Russakovsky cofounded AI4ALL to increase diversity and inclusion in AI through mentorship and education. AI for Good, a UN organization, focuses on dialogue around the beneficial use of AI; fast.ai works on accessibility; and Project Include crafts recommendations and tools to help companies build more meaningful diversity and inclusion into their initiatives. Some of the staff at the big tech companies, traditionally a politically neutral group, are beginning to get more active in pushing back against unethical corporate practices and policies, such as the Google employees' petition against working for the Pentagon[106] and their 2018 walkout as a protest against sexual harassment,[107] and IBM employees' refusal to work for ICE.[108] As with the law, accountability, creativity, and transparency will be critical for a moral future. But given the magnitude of societal implications, there are still a relatively small number of groups focused on algorithmic design as universal design imbued with moral imagination.

We design tech and tech, in turn, designs us.

—PAMELA PAVLISCAK

The responsibility for ensuring that future intelligent machines are fair, ethical, and coded with a conscience that respects values equitably lies with the architects of the future—all of us. To do so effectively, we need a diversity of voices in the room, across spectra of gender, sexuality, race, and experiences and across socioeconomic, religious, and cultural lines: not only significant numbers of women and people of color participating, but also people of different ages, abilities, and viewpoints. Without a diverse group, representative of all we are, we will not be able to sufficiently train and teach our new intelligent creations who, what, and why we are.

There is more than just fairness to gain. The most diverse teams build the best products.[109] Diversity is a prerequisite for innovation and smarter thinking,[110] and it is indispensable to businesses that want to make better decisions and outperform the competition.[111] Studies show that far better and more equitable results are gained by just including more women in the process.[112] Researchers at the Stanford Graduate School of Education and the University of California–Los Angeles concluded that "when we hear dissent from someone who is different from us, it provokes more thought than when it comes from someone who looks like us."[113] In 2015, a McKinsey report documented that, out of 366 companies, those in the top quartile for ethnic and racial diversity in management were "35 percent more likely to have financial returns above their industry mean, and those in the top quartile for gender diversity were 15 percent more likely to have returns above the industry mean."[114] Investing in women and in STEAM (STEM plus the arts)[115] initiatives is investing in a better future for us all.

Researchers, scientists, engineers, executives, elected representatives, and anyone who has the ability to broaden the discussion and engender participation and input needs to invite social scientists such as anthropologists and sociologists, as well as activists and ethicists, human rights advocates, and other nonscience experts across multiple demographics and cultures into the technology conversation, and to consider how to use our combinatorial creativity and collective intelligence for the holistic benefit of all. Don't just pull up a chair for yourself. Pull one up for someone else, too—someone underrepresented, someone whose voice is missing and needs to be heard.

As we build AI, we have to continually ask ourselves whether we are building a partner that will help enhance our lives, or a Frankenstein's monster.[116] This requires stepping away from self-validating carousels to look inside ourselves. Let's unleash our collective creativity to create technology that can rise to the potential of our ideals and highest aspirations as humans. Beyond profit we find purpose. Beyond our individual selves we find one another.

Finally, we must remember that as we expand the field of AI, include more diverse partners, and focus on creating AI for good, one of our most powerful partners in this will be the AI itself. AI can help us unleash our creativity, free up our time to become more empathetic, and do many things we have only dreamed of. Mary Shelley warned us of the dangers of unchecked scientific discovery. How might the story have turned out if Dr. Frankenstein had consulted with his peers, colleagues, experts in various fields, and friends?[117] Listening to a variety of voices and considering a spectrum of opinions firmly guided and grounded by moral imagination is crucial in assuring that our future inventions and technologies are built with equity, fairness, and goodness at their core, with a sense of humanity, in service of the rights, agency, and dignity we all deserve to enjoy.

4

HUMAN RIGHTS AND ROBOT RIGHTS

Privacy, Autonomous Weapons, and Instilling Values in Machines

Artificial intelligence will become a major human rights issue in the twenty-first century.

—SAFIYA UMOJA NOBLE

You hail an autonomous vehicle (AV) and climb aboard. The AV recognizes you and asks to confirm your identity. You give a voice command, and the AV requests that you "please set your Ethical Knob"[1] before it proceeds to your destination. The AV's "Ethical Knob" offers you three settings: "Full Altruist," "Full Egoist," or "Impartial."[2] The first mode places the most importance on other people's lives in the event the AV needs to make an emergency decision. The second mode assigns the most value to the lives of the AV's passengers.

The third places equal value on the passengers and other lives outside the AV.[3]

Which do you choose?

The choices we make depend on our values, morals, and ethics. What are values? Definitions vary depending on the field of study, but our values are generally understood to be our deeply held beliefs as individuals, as cultures, and as a society.[4] What are morals? Principles about what's right and what's wrong in our actions.[5] What are ethics? Those moral principles and rules of behavior we build from values and belief systems.[6] Concepts such as value systems, moral codes, ethical principles, and the conscience can signify different things to different people and are sometimes used interchangeably. We use variations on these words often, and should be cognizant of the multiplicity of meanings. Precise definitions can be elusive; our actions depend on interwoven layers of belief systems, inner feelings, societal and cultural norms, and circumstances, all intersecting in a complex interplay of human will.

Acknowledging linguistic ambiguity and recognizing both the beauty and the frailty in our humaneness, in our laws, and in the social contracts we sign will better prepare us to design rules and ascribe ethical codes to our technology and its purveyors. Values and ethics are different from rules. Rules can, and sometimes should, be broken; they can also be followed for the wrong reasons. Values, morality, and principles come from something deeper within us. Acting in alignment with our values involves unearthing what lies beneath the rules and norms, and adhering to them only when they are humane; when we determine that they are in sync with the standards we set for ourselves. Never arriving at all the answers, yet always trying to do better than we did the day before. Always human; imperfect and flawed, but also aspiring for justice, for equity, for hope. This is what visionaries such as Cesar Chavez, Deborah Parker, Mahatma Gandhi, Malala

Yousafzai, Nelson Mandela, bell hooks, and John Lewis have shown us is possible.

HUMAN RIGHTS AND MORAL MACHINES

> Human beings ought to be able to determine which values are served by technology, what is morally relevant and which final goals and conceptions of the good are worthy to be pursued. This cannot be left to machines, no matter how powerful they are.
>
> —European Group on Ethics in Science and New Technologies

As we embark on the Intelligent Machine Age, there are numerous parties, governments, schools, and organizations—including The Hague Centre for Strategic Studies, the IEEE Global Initiative for Ethical Considerations in Artificial Intelligence and Autonomous Systems, the Allen Institute for Artificial Intelligence, and the CS + Social Good and the Stanford AI Group—proposing ethical considerations and guidelines for artificial intelligence and autonomous systems. They are discussing if and when regulations should be created for this rapidly emerging technology. Many thinkers are also assessing how the technology will impact human rights and whether digitally intelligent creations should have rights as well.

While most can agree that we want our intelligent technology to be moral, how do we arrive at a definition of that condition? Assuming we can reach agreement on what that standard means, is it possible to ensure that our intelligent machines share it? The values we will instill in our technology are inevitably subjective. The answer to what actions would be "fair" or "safe" in a given situation often depends on whom you ask.

The classic trolley dilemma provides an example. If a self-driving car finds itself barreling toward a crowd of people, and can veer off and kill just one other person instead, is this what it should do? Should we have options like the "Ethical Knob" described at the beginning of this chapter? Philosophers have ruminated on the trolley problem for ages, but AI technologies like self-driving cars are infusing these old debates with new urgency as we contemplate how to design laws and policies.

Choosing which values to emphasize when we are creating AI is, in some ways, an even thornier question than which moral codes are "correct" for humans. In order to safeguard the future of humanity in the coming Intelligent Machine Age, we will need a humane system upon which to base our decisions and inventions. However, as history has taught us, the question of whose values should be applied will not be easily answered, and it's likely we will never fully agree which values are essential. Some philosophers go so far as to say that there is no way to definitively arrive at a hierarchy of ethical principles, as they are "irreducibly diverse."[7] This is the idea of moral or values pluralism.

There are multiple paths to follow. But we can strive, as an international community, to build as much consensus as possible around coding our machines with conscience. The impact will be global; so should the effort. The accelerating development of AI puts us on a deadline to encode it with a sense of humanity before it's too late to even try.[8]

OK, so how do we do this?

I believe that the international human rights model can be a framework for a way forward. I'm not alone in this thinking. Some of the most promising studies have come out of Europe, including from the EU's European Group on Ethics in Science and New Technologies, the Council of Europe's Study (Convention 108) on "Algorithms and Human Rights," and in Canada at the University of Montreal's Forum on the Socially Responsible Development of Artificial Intelligence. The Council of Europe has found that "One particular challenge of algorithmic processing of personal data is the generation of new data . . . the nature of which can be entirely unpredictable for the data subject. This raises major issues for the notions of consent, transparency and personal autonomy."[9] These are serious challenges for human rights in the twenty-first century.

> Where, after all, do universal human rights begin? In small places, close to home—so close and so small that they cannot be seen on any maps of the world . . . Unless these rights have meaning there, they have little meaning anywhere. Without concerned citizen action to uphold them close to home, we shall look in vain for progress in the larger world.
>
> —ELEANOR ROOSEVELT

Human rights, at their most fundamental, are a bare minimum standard of how everyone in the world should be treated. These rights are inherent and universal. The concept of human rights is one of the most simple and powerful ideas humankind has ever formulated as a united community.

The United Nations' Universal Declaration of Human Rights (UDHR), spearheaded in large part by Eleanor Roosevelt and adopted in 1948, is perhaps the best-known example of how an international coalition came together to craft an ethical code for how every human being on Earth should be treated.[10] Article 1 sets forth that "All human beings are born free and equal in dignity and rights. They are endowed with reason and conscience and should act towards one another in a spirit of brotherhood."[11] Previously, we did not have the necessary buy-in and cooperation between states to create such an international coalition.

The UDHR was based in part on documents such as the United States' Declaration of Independence, which states: "We hold these truths to be self-evident, that all men are created equal, that they are endowed by their Creator with certain unalienable Rights, that among these are Life, Liberty and the pursuit of Happiness." The European Convention on Human Rights, in Article 8, sets forth that "everyone has the right to respect for his private and family life, his home and his correspondence."[12] The Human Rights, Big Data and Technology Project (HRBDT), founded in 2015 and based at the Human Rights Centre at the University of Essex, published a comprehensive report at the end of 2018, the seventieth anniversary of the UDHR, entitled "Putting Human Rights at the Heart of the Design, Development and Deployment of Artificial Intelligence." The report detailed the wide range of "risks and opportunities for human rights posed by big data and artificial intelligence" and how "algorithmic decision-making" could produce a "digital divide." The HRBDT proposes a scheme to embed policies, strategies, and regulations "centered on human rights standards and principles derived from the UDHR and other human rights instruments," using a "common language" and with "common objectives" focused on equality for all.[13]

Using established international human rights declarations as our model for how to preserve human rights as we incorporate intelligent technology is a good starting point. To varying degrees, these declarative instruments focus on human life and liberties. The rights are, however, restricted to *Homo sapiens* and the current state of human cognitive processes. They are solely associated with the dignity and agency of humans. To expand and adapt this framework to our technologically advanced world will require protecting the rights not just of humans but of all types of beings.

For those committed to the belief that only human beings should have these rights, please note the word "brotherhood" in the first Article of the UDHR, quoted above. Many of the rights that women now enjoy were once reserved solely for men. Our language serves as a constant reminder that we evolve by shaping our core principles to our present reality, striving to be better, and widening our circle. With this must come a willingness to adapt our language as well. Humans naturally use the current context of their lives as a frame of reference,[14] but history holds many examples of times when, as a society, we had to advance our thinking to protect those who had been left out—look at some of the landmark U.S. Supreme Court cases: *Brown v. Board of Education*, *Roe v. Wade*, *Obergefell v. Hodges*, to name a few.

In the United States, our societal criteria for who deserves rights and protections are often delayed and have always been evolving and expanding: Black Americans and the Civil Rights Act of 1964. LGBTQ people and *Lawrence v. Texas*. Women and the Nineteenth Amendment to the Constitution. The Americans with Disabilities Act. Federal Indian Law.[15] And in some cases, hard-fought rights and privileges have been rolled back.[16] The move toward equality and justice is not necessarily linear.

Now, as we have done in the past, we will need to revise our value systems to house a more inclusive definition of human rights—one that includes nonhuman, even artificial, beings. And perhaps we need to expand our definition of what it means to be "human," too? Companies have been granted legal personhood; in this sense, legal corporations could be considered some of the first AIs.[17] Precedent has been established.

We have much to gain from reconsidering the uniqueness of cognitive processes traditionally associated with the dignity and agency of *Homo sapiens*[18] and broadening the definition to include other species we share our home with. As society evolves, our thinking must grow with it. As the psychologist Angela Duckworth found in her research, having a growth mindset is an avenue to success, while having a fixed mindset is dangerous.[19] Cultivating a mind open to change will be essential as we step into the future of technology. There once was a time when most people were taught to believe that everything revolved around the earth, because it was where the humans were.[20] Copernicus's proof that we actually live in a heliocentric universe, where the earth revolves around the sun, along with Galileo's subsequent discoveries, helped us reconfigure our place in the world and ushered in the Scientific Revolution.

Galileo's scientific theories were considered heresy in his time. Once again it's time to temper our instinctual fear of not being at the center, letting go of the fallacy that life revolves around humans, as we race toward a future coexisting with new, intelligent beings. In the process, we will learn to channel our survival instincts in measured ways and enhance our understanding of intelligence and consciousness. We've learned that the earth isn't flat, that our planet revolves around the sun, that entire species existed on this planet before we arrived, and that our civilization is a mere blip in the world's history. There is still much to learn about the universe, and AI will help us solve more of its riddles if we are willing to work together.

So how do we move forward to establish an ethical canon regarding AI, robotics, and autonomous systems in which the human decision-making process is becoming more and more automated? In attempting to apply standards to policies, it's important to note that we are looking at distinct but related issues.

How should our human rights be framed relative to AI in our new age? What should be the rights of the AI itself, if any? These questions

HUMAN RIGHTS MILESTONES

THE ANCIENT WORLD

1754 BCE
CODE OF HAMMURABI
One of the oldest legal codes known, with some early references to human rights

725–720 BCE
PHARAOH BOCCHORIS
Promoted individual rights, suppressed imprisonment for debt, and reformed laws relating to the transfer of property

8TH CENTURY BCE
THE CONCEPT OF CITIZENSHIP
The concepts of citizen and citizenship were developed under the polis of ancient Greece

6TH CENTURY BCE
THE CYRUS CYLINDER
The Cyrus Cylinder is arguably considered one of the first documents on human rights

269–232 BCE
THE ASHOKA EDICTS
Ashoka elected numerous edicts describing the universal laws of respecting religion and humane treatment of servants, among others

THE MIDDLE AGES

1188
KINGDOM OF LEON, SPAIN
Endorsement of the inviolability of life, honor, home, and property, the rights of an accused to a trial

1215
THE MAGNA CARTA, ENGLAND
The Great Charter established for the first time the principle that everybody, including the king, was subject to the law

THE MODERN ERA

1776
DECLARATION OF INDEPENDENCE, UNITED STATES
Asserted inalienable rights of life, liberty, and the pursuit of happiness

1628
THE PETITION OF RIGHT, ENGLAND
One of England's most famous constitutional documents, written by Parliament as an objection to an overbreach of authority by King Charles I with due respect to civil rights

1791
BILL OF RIGHTS, UNITED STATES
The first ten amendments to the U.S. Constitution, guaranteeing rights such as freedom of speech, assembly, and worship

1789
DECLARATION OF THE RIGHTS OF MAN AND OF THE CITIZEN, FRANCE
A human and civil rights document from the French Revolution

THE GLOBAL ERA

1919
INTERNATIONAL LABOUR ORGANIZATION
Designed to protect the rights of workers in the face of fast industrialization

1946
COMMISSIONS ON HUMAN RIGHTS
Established by the UN Economic and Social Council

1948
UNIVERSAL DECLARATION OF HUMAN RIGHTS
Adopted by the United Nations General Assembly; posited that how a government treats its own citizens is now a matter of legitimate international concern

1951
CONVENTION RELATING TO THE STATUS OF REFUGEES

1989
CONVENTION ON THE RIGHTS OF THE CHILD

1979
CONVENTION ON THE ELIMINATION OF ALL FORMS OF DISCRIMINATION AGAINST WOMEN

AI, DATA & ROBOT ETHICS

2016
EU GENERAL DATA PROTECTION REGULATION
Fundamentally reshapes the way data is being handled across sectors and beyond

remain hotly disputed and there is no consensus in the field. Opinions vary widely; keeping an open mind stops us from becoming, as Thomas Georges has termed it, "carbon chauvinists."[21]

CAN WE PRESERVE OUR RIGHT TO PRIVACY?

One of the most immediate ethical technological challenges we face is how to preserve our right to privacy in a world increasingly lived online. Today we are mostly encountering narrow AI and algorithms that do routine tasks—things like sifting through data and identifying images. But we are rapidly heading toward systems of advanced mechatronics that combine AI, deep learning, data, sensors, and information that, critically, require responsible development.[22]

How should we safeguard our privacy in a world with social media, the Internet of Things, and overwhelming amounts of our data being collected? Privacy—the right to protect our personal information and data from public view—has been set out as a basic right both in national laws, such as the Fourth Amendment of the United States Constitution, and in international legal instruments, from the UDHR to the International Covenant on Civil and Political Rights.[23] This right is tied to our fundamental rights to free speech, expression, association, and assembly as groups and as individuals.

Our attitudes regarding confidentiality vary across cultures, institutions, and societies. In spring 2018, the EU passed a sweeping privacy regulation (GDPR) to protect people's personal information online. The European Union sees this as a key human and civil rights issue.[24] In the United States, a 2018 poll showed that 98 percent of Americans believe strongly in privacy as a basic right.[25] The state of California has passed the watershed California Consumer Privacy Act. However, recent attempts at federal privacy legislation in the United States have stalled,[26] although there are pending bills in Congress as well as talk about considering commodifying individual data and putting a price tag on its use.[27] In November 2018, a group of thirty-four civil and consumer rights organizations and others in the United States released a set of "Public Interest Privacy Legislation Principles"[28] with the intention to guide policy-makers in crafting new laws. Nevertheless, we remain some distance from achieving any form of worldwide accord on the matter.

Studies have shown that the "people who value their privacy come from all demographic groups, but the impact of consumer tracking varies greatly by race, class, and power."[29] Discriminatory practices, racism, sexism, and ingrained prejudices are rampant in the collecting of people's data, harming those who are already marginalized much more than others, with devastating consequences that further erode democratic values of equality and justice.

As information technology advances, so too do the threats to our privacy, with inequitable results. Facial recognition technology already poses real potential for abuse, as artificially intelligent scanners are being developed that can discern much about you. The Chinese have AI that can identify citizens by their gait.[30] And in the not too distant future we can expect AI to recognize our "personality traits."[31] Digital tools can be used to connect people around the world, fostering public debate that keeps democracy alive. But they can also be used for oppressive surveillance. The technology is here and so is the bias. We can't go back. So the question is, how will we implement it going forward?

As computers and intelligent algorithms are increasingly able to hack into the deepest reaches of our identities, both online and off, we are seeing that our information can be bought, sold, and stolen on an enormous scale. James Bridle thinks that if we cannot better understand emerging technologies, we will enter a new Dark Age.[32]

The Cambridge Analytica scandal in 2018, the U.S. election meddling of 2016, and the scope of the Chinese government surveillance and "social ranking" programs are just a few examples. Information is the new currency of power, and there is a bustling black market for it.

> Data scientists: we should not be the arbiters of truth. We should be translators of ethical discussions that happen in larger society. And the rest of you, the non-data scientists: this is not a math test. This is a political fight. We need to demand accountability for our algorithmic overlords. The era of blind faith in big data must end.
>
> —CATHY O'NEIL

In the coming years, as our technology becomes more advanced and able to connect more quickly to our thought processes (and more directly, too, uploading information via such modalities as retinal scanners),[33] we are also going to need to secure our mental privacy and cognitive liberty, which is the right to have sovereignty over one's own consciousness and freedom of thought.[34] The proliferation of data hacking, abusive information-sharing practices, lack of transparency and accountability by corporate technology giants and governments, and the creation and wide dissemination of disruptive fake news and manipulative "deepfake" videos (the process of blending existing videos with source images to spread false information) are also threats to the truth of what we see, hear, and experience.[35]

To address the danger that new information technologies will perpetuate even greater inequality, we might look to the world's most profoundly beautiful human rights documents: from the UDHR to the South African constitution to the United States Bill of Rights. These instruments can guide us to the testimony needed for our brave new world—for instance: "We, the people of South Africa, Recognise the injustices of our past; Honour those who suffered for justice and freedom in our land; Respect those who have worked to build and develop our country; and Believe that South Africa belongs to all who live in it, united in our diversity."[36] The South African constitution recognizes the context in which it was written and the legacy of apartheid from which it sprung,[37] and places human rights at the center of the document. The UDHR emerged from the atrocities of World War II.[38] Our declarative covenants to one another going forward in the Intelligent Machine Age can reflect the vocabulary of these documents. However, powerful language in an official document alone is not sufficient to prevent systematic human rights violations, as evidenced by the ongoing strife in South Africa and elsewhere in the world.

In the U.S. Bill of Rights, the focus is on the rights of the people— rights that are inherent in all humans and that cannot be taken away by the government. It assumes in most interpretations that these rights are evolving, that this living record is meant to change. When it was originally drafted, women couldn't vote and slavery was still legal. Amendments advanced and preserved its integrity. Otherwise, these revered human documents remain empty, unfulfilled promises that can continue to penalize the most marginalized and disadvantaged. Without the ability to amend language to address emerging intelligent inventions and platforms, we could become rudderless in the technological sea.

But as much as I am hoping for a consensus on adopting meaningful policies establishing universal privacy standards for cyberspace that could be widely practiced and enforced, it may not be feasible. Although we already have human rights language as set forth by the United Nations declaring we all should be entitled to the "same rights online as offline,"[39] the difficulty of finding unanimity among the disparate parties necessary to apply such regulation across cyber society suggests that the chances of adoption and reliable enforcement are low.

The borderless data-flow ship has sailed. Data translates into dollars and is the new gold rush.[40] Billions of us now live and work in cyber communities throughout much of our days. The nature of some of the fundamental arguments supporting the "right to be forgotten" conflicts with the "right to the internet" and the right to "scientific progress."[41] Cyberspace shadows life. The same protections and rights bestowed by individual sovereignties should be applicable online. However, cyberspace is currently an ungoverned global state in which our citizenship is based solely on our ability to access the internet.

We should not have to forfeit rights simply because we increasingly need to use the internet to participate in society—to access bank accounts and medical records, for example. We should expect privacy protections for these services. However, choosing to participate in something like social media can be seen as analogous to a person choosing to run for public office. When you decide to campaign, you knowingly sacrifice anonymity and some privacy, much as those who opt in to posting on Instagram, Twitter, or Facebook do to varying degrees. We're all running for election in our social media feeds, and with that comes a tacit acceptance (and a legal one, in the small print) that the platforms will analyze our information and feed us ads to support their business models. We should do everything possible to safeguard our rights and protect our fellow cyber citizens from harm—but perhaps we should look beyond just crafting new sets of rules for individuals and businesses collecting and trading our information and more closely investigate the science of data collecting itself.

Our smart machines will ultimately be the only technologies capable of managing the copious amounts of data flowing in cyberspace. To protect our rights, including a right to privacy, and to ensure our technology is more transparent, accountable, and more likely to universally apply fairness, out-of-the-box thinking can deliver solutions.

One possible approach to privacy legislation could be to explore regulating the ways that personal information is collected and used. "Synthetic data" is data that is artificially generated to match the general shape of real-world data. Created algorithmically when various metrics are computed from the authentic data, the synthetic data can then approximate the real-world data.[42] Synthetic data is primarily used as a stand-in for data sets to validate models and train machine learning. The idea is that a machine instructed in this way could then make reasonable predictions when presented with real-world input.

The benefit of using synthetic data is that specific personal identifiers such as addresses, names, ages, tax IDs, and other private sensitive information would never enter the public realm. Mandating that developers, designers, platforms, and private and public entities use synthetic data could be a technological means to effectively enact privacy protections. Currently, better analytic results are obtained by technology using real-world data replication, and limiting what kinds of data can be used may be too restrictive for scientists right now. But this science will advance rapidly, especially if the platforms, developers, and designers are prospectively aware they may be obligated by law to only work with synthetic data.

If humans are but data, then data will rule. And our stats will be analyzed and used in ways that are unfair and unjust. I believe we are capable of finding solutions to the challenges posed by intelligent technologies and the perils to our freedom to live and work in a global community. To continue crafting the legal and societal contracts requires a commitment to a doctrine of greater inclusion and expanding our definitions of who or what deserves to be treated with dignity and respect. If we do so, along with modeling our most treasured legal human rights instruments, we can create a humane road map for our rules and laws.

SHOULD ROBOTS HAVE RIGHTS?

The saddest aspect of life right now is that science gathers knowledge faster than society gathers wisdom.

—ISAAC ASIMOV

While we're just now starting to hear arguments on what rights non-biological intelligence should have, for the most part, those who advocate instituting protections for nonhuman life are met with resistance and ridicule, as are any notions of rights for AI. Why is this so? Science fiction writers have been contemplating this conundrum for decades. Isaac Asimov invented some basic "Laws of Robotics" in 1942 that, while in need of some updating, still feel relevant, even prescient, today:

1. A robot may not injure a human being or, through inaction, allow a human being to come to harm.
2. A robot must obey orders given it by human beings except where such orders would conflict with the First Law.
3. A robot must protect its own existence as long as such protection does not conflict with the First or Second Law.[43]

Asimov's laws prescribe how a robot may behave, but they do not address this fundamental question: Should we endow synthetically intelligent, thinking creations with certain rights? Today, there are two basic opposing schools of thought regarding how we should treat AI systems. One proposes we should treat robots as machine parts, without any rights or responsibilities.[44] Joanna Bryson has previously suggested they should be our "slaves," solely focused on our needs.[45] (The origin of "robot" stems from the Old Church Slavonic word "rabota" meaning "forced labor.")[46] As this thinking goes, they will be used most effectively as our property, and humans won't be confused or dehumanized. The second camp asks: What if we were to give rights and responsibilities to robots or other forms of AI? Would it help us hone our own sense of ourselves and how to treat others? And if so, what are the requisite elements for a machine to have rights?

The conversation is just beginning, but the tech is not waiting. National governments should accelerate the analysis of to what extent it may be appropriate to grant certain forms of AI a version of legal "personhood," in which AI has rights as well as legal responsibilities. One advantage, for instance, might be that a legally responsible AI could be insured, so that it was capable of providing monetary relief to those it might harm. The European Union has already proposed giving rights to "electronic personalities."[47] Efforts are underway to discuss and define electronic personhood. The divisions are forming, with some seeing it as a necessity while others view the idea as "nonsensical."[48]

In the camp supporting the argument for granting rights, MIT robotics ethicist Kate Darling believes that considering rights for robots will help to strengthen our societal values.[49] A lack of empathy for a creature—even the abuse of a robot—is an omen, she argues, of a much wider societal problem that we need to address.[50] And what of an AI's responsibilities to go along with these rights? When a self-driving car crashes into a human, which has already happened,[51] who should be responsible? Part of the problem with assessing responsibility is that our understanding is obscured by opaque black-box algorithms (where you can see the inputs and outputs but the inner processes remain abstruse)[52] concealing how an AI's decisions are made, and by our limited knowledge of how increasingly sophisticated AI arrives at them. AIs that can learn by themselves will compound the complexity of accountability when, like humans, they develop in response to their environment and roam beyond the scope of the rules that were originally created to bind them and us.

People already naturally hold robots accountable for their actions. In a 2012 study of forty students who interacted with a humanoid robot named Robovie, when Robovie incorrectly assessed the students' performance in a game, 65 percent of them attributed moral accountability to Robovie: less than they would to a human, but more than they would to, say, a vending machine.[53] It's in our nature to react to anything that can interact with us.[54] Complicated relationships are forming between interactive robots and humans, and our tendency to anthropomorphize the devices and machines we communicate with raises the stakes.[55] We are animals, after all, biomechanically trained to respond to our environment and to other beings, reliant on survival mechanisms that have kept us alive so far but may be much less useful in the Technological Age.

> The three most important thresholds in ethics are the capacity to experience pain, self-awareness, and the capacity to be a responsible moral actor . . .
>
> —JAMES HUGHES

If the yardstick for deserving certain rights applies only to thinking, rational human adults, or is measured by degrees of intelligence, what about a baby or an impaired human being?[56] What about the rights of other animals? And what about the inevitable mechanically augmented humans? Or a genetically enhanced human? Or a new hybrid animal? These questions will take on greater urgency and complexity as biological technology advances—from genome editing, to bionics, to linking our brains ever closer with artificial technologies.

Now more than ever, recognizing that living things exist in a range and variety of states, that aliveness endures on a spectrum, is a sine qua non. We must move past binary thinking. Adjusting our perspective leads us to greater compassion and understanding. When we make room for expanded definitions, for more inclusion, more understanding, more openness, we start living beyond black-and-white thinking.

Regardless of religion, belief system, or ethical code, if we are really interested in a society that values social justice, acceptance and tolerance, equality, dignity, and the best of ourselves, then we must rally against exceptionalism, absolutism, Other-ism, and closed-minded thinking. Expand the definition of who deserves protection, dignity, and rights. Look beyond species.

Categories of humans have been and continue to be denied rights every day. The right to marry. To vote. To hold property. To be free. As of 2016, there remain forty million human slaves in our modern world.[57] There was a time in the United States when only certain white men had full rights. Women in the United States weren't allowed to vote until 1920. Enslaved Black people were once counted as three-fifths of a person for purposes of representation in the United States Constitution. Those charged with bestowing rights and protections have often reserved them only for those who are just like them, until they are compelled to widen the circle.

There continues to be progress in expanding the definition of who and what deserves rights. River systems are now being granted rights in India.[58] Ecuador became the first country to recognize the rights of nature in 2008.[59] New Zealand and Quebec have legally decided that animals are sentient beings.[60] From the Ganges River in India to the Amazon rainforest in Colombia to the Whanganui River in New Zealand, the first river in the world to be granted the same rights as a human, governments are beginning to accord these living, evolving ecosystems with protections. They are acknowledging the philosophy, held by such groups as the Māori of New Zealand, that humans are a part of the world, not the center of it; that we share our universe, and are equal to the other beings within it.[61] The Māori see nature as our ancestor.[62] Who might our descendants be? There are dedicated organizations and individuals across the globe that work every day for the rights, dignity, and safety of all living things, showing us how much we all share in common.[63] Soon, our intelligent robot friends will be due consideration. It is incumbent upon us all to be a voice for others—as Dr. Seuss's Lorax put it: "I speak for the trees for the trees have no tongues."[64]

HUMAN AND MACHINE ACCOUNTABILITY

In a prescient article written for *AI Magazine* in 1986, Michael LaChat spoke about the many ethical and religious questions raised by AI that had previously only been discussed within imaginative works of fiction. Years before it was on our societal radar, he foresaw that thinking about future intelligence capacities and ethical considerations would not only "stimulate our moral imaginations" but also tell us much about "our moral thinking and pedagogy."[65]

Today we have a wide range of organizations drafting papers, crafting policy, proposing guidelines and regulations, and research-ing the ethics of new technologies. Many are assessing the impact of technology and making recommendations toward a framework of principles, as well as how such principles can be developed, imple-mented, and controlled. A non-exhaustive list of those working on Fairness, Accountability, Transparency, and Ethics (FATE)[66] in AI in-cludes: the Turing Ethics Program, the People + AI Research initiative

(PAIR), the Institute of Electrical and Electronics Engineers (IEEE), the United Nations Interregional Crime and Justice Research Institute (UNICRI), the Ethics and Governance Fund, BenevolentAI Center and other branches of the UN, the Group of Seven and Group of Twenty, the European Union, the Ethics and Governance of Artificial Intelligence Initiative, RightsCon (a summit on human rights in the digital era), the Organization for Economic Cooperation and Development, Data & Society, and the Algorithmic Justice League. And, of course, leading universities and research institutes around the world, such as Cambridge University, Arizona State University, and Carnegie Mellon University.

Some of ethicists' top concerns for regulating AI are: Whose moral standards should be applied? How does the tech understand morality, if at all? Should we make algorithms more transparent, and who should be liable for any damage they may cause? Should we embed values into autonomous intelligent systems, assuming it is even scientifically possible? We know we can code sets of instructions into computers. However, as intelligent machines begin to acquire information and train themselves more and more from their environments, and become more difficult to predict and control, the challenge will increase.

> We need a way to understand what AI algorithms are "thinking."
>
> —KAY FIRTH BUTTERFIELD

In 2017, the Future of Life Institute set out the Asilomar Principles: twenty-three ideas for how to make AI moral.[67] Google has recently released a code of ethics for AI,[68] and the AI Now Institute has issued annual reports with a number of recommendations responsive to various ethical issues, from regulating black-box algorithms and conducting prerelease trials[69] to supporting "truth in advertising" laws and waiving trade secrecy for AI products and services.[70] Accountability, transparency, privacy, values, and safety are often cited in these lists. However, many of these approaches are vague in practice because so many questions still need to be answered. There are significant gaps in information and communication between the people building the tech, the people policing the tech, and all of those, *us*, who will be profoundly affected by it.

More varied groups working together across industries and organizational silos can stimulate the buy-in to turn theories into regulations. It is not enough for one company, group, or nation to independently fund studies, release research, pose questions and concerns, and propose remedies. Agreeing on a set of standards for incorporating intelligent technologies into society is a massive issue requiring attention on an international scale. It is naïve to expect that we can continue to develop the tech at this pace and leave the task of applying moral vision for later.

I support the idea of consolidating principles and research papers into guidelines to be presented by designated special rapporteurs to a UN umbrella body solely focused on ethics and AI. Concurrently, we should convene commissions and conferences, as well as negotiate treaties with a mandate focused on inclusion, representation, and diversity to address the subject with the gravity it requires. Involving not just the conventional legislative, corporate, scientific, and academic parties, but also those representing a diverse array of demographics, including the economically disadvantaged and other traditionally underrepresented groups such as residents of the Global South, benefits us all.

The goal is to draft an international treaty, akin to our bans on biological weapons, chemical weapons, and, most recently, nuclear weapons. This global accord should also encompass a regulatory framework for AI and weaponry, including both autonomous lethal weapons and cyberwarfare initiatives, as well as substantive input and oversight from organizations such as Human Rights Watch, which has already established an AI research group.

As we put a regimen in place and make our first attempts at writing laws regulating our intelligent technologies, mindful that such rules will need to evolve in concert with technology, sector-specific oversight is required. General regulation will not have the domain expertise necessary to oversee the application of AI within each individual realm, as the nuances of such arenas as the automotive, health, and criminal justice industries vary greatly. It's imperative to institute privacy regulations, like the provisions in the GDPR's private rights of action,[71] as well as accessible dispute resolution remedies so that litigation can be instigated as a means to justice, accountability, and public record. Instead of solely vesting the power to take action in the hands of established regulatory bodies, such a move would allow private individuals to bring claims, serving as a crowdsourced watchdog system and a collective, democratic way to enforce and ensure individual rights.

Such a decree will open the door to the possibility of class-action lawsuits and encourage whistleblowers to speak out against injustice. It will institute a public forum of debate and deliberation where citizens can bring claims and put their concerns on the record. Individuals would be able to band together and organize to fight for their rights. The tobacco companies did not start to mitigate the harm they were causing until they were litigated into compliance.[72] Similarly, we must hold to account whoever is culpable for damages to ourselves and the planet as a result of their failure to responsibly construct and manage their technologies.

If we cannot get traction on an international or national basis, regulatory initiatives can begin at local levels, where legislation can be implemented much faster. As Justice Louis Brandeis said about the United States, in this country the states are "laboratories for democracy."[73]

Apace with legal norms, defending a free press is also essential to upholding truth, justice, transparency, and accountability in our new age of AI. Emboldening investigative coverage of AI developments and their possible repercussions by AI-literate journalists in major newspapers and periodicals, such as the work of Solutions Journalism, will educate the citizenry. Journalists are on the front lines of these information campaigns and require support—from their media conglomerate owners, to those who teach and train journalism students, to public vigilance.

> Scientific discovery and creation are fully value laden, and bound up in the assumptions and guiding philosophies of the scientists who discover and create.
>
> —KERRI SLATUS

The societal demands of introducing pervasive intelligent technologies are manifold, and there is absolutely no assurance that we can embed ethics or engineer explainability into them. Some believe it's possible, while others contend that "just as many aspects of human behavior are impossible to explain in detail, perhaps it won't be possible for AI to explain everything it does."[74] Even if we could install values into AIs and comprehend their thinking, what will happen when they evolve and learn on their own—potentially discarding or morphing those values, just as humans do as they mature?

The time to act is now. We don't know what comes next, but it's coming rapidly. Good places to start would be transparent methods to understand how machine-trained AI systems arrive at their decisions before that too becomes unknowable, and accountability for human and machine alike. Science historically pushes forward to invent the newest tool without our fully thinking through the consequences.[75] Once Pandora's box has been opened, it is impossible to close again. Robert Oppenheimer knew this, and expressed mixed feelings at his invention of the atomic bomb, particularly as he approached the end of his life.[76] He is not the only one. In his nineties, Mikhail Kalashnikov wrote a letter regretting his invention of the AK-47.[77] In a less noxious example, Ethan Zuckerman, inventor of pop-up ads, regrets his creation even though he says it was initially intended as a beneficial one.[78] Current scientific pursuit innovates to disrupt by using its customary mantras of patents, profit, and pride with little regard as to the deleterious impact of its inventions. Intentionality about what we are building, why we are building it, and what will come from it is vital. In 2018, IBM instituted a policy requiring its developers to "prove their algorithms are fair,"[79] but the company remains the sole arbiter of determining that fairness.

We owe it to one another as architects of the future to establish legal tenets and societal norms to govern those involved in designing and creating algorithms and neural networks and teaching machines to learn. We can adopt an ethical credo and training protocol to guide technology-building teams in choosing how to act when formulating something new (and potentially profitable) versus building something that will benefit humanity. What I and others are referring to is something like the Hippocratic Oath for those involved in designing AI. We can reconfigure the social contract between technologists and society.

AUTONOMOUS WEAPONS AND FACING OUR ETHICAL DILEMMAS

Along with the wide array of privacy issues, the impact of artificially intelligent technology on weapon systems is another imminent ethical issue. Forms of autonomous weapons such as drones are here now, and fully autonomous weapons are coming.[80] The United States is already conducting its war offensive in the Middle East through the use of unmanned drones.[81] At the moment, these sophisticated weapons are not actually pilotless, but are controlled from bases by military personnel monitoring them in front of video monitors. And humans are still making the determinations about which targets to hit. Technology is being developed, however, that could allow the drones to begin to make target decisions without human supervision, a prospect that alarms many. And the U.S. military is not the only one that has access to this technology.

Some are calling for complete bans on autonomous lethal weaponry—I have written on the subject myself,[82] arguing that AI weaponry is inevitable, and that agreeing on values may be easier than agreeing on policies. Since 2014, experts and diplomats have come together in Geneva to discuss the future of "killer robots."[83] These state party representatives to the United Nations Convention on Conventional Weapons (CCW) have made progress in discussing whether "lethal autonomous weapons systems" (LAWS) should be restricted to operating only under "meaningful human control," which would require humans to retain control over the critical functions of weaponry (as in the selection and engagement of targets).[84]

Bonnie Docherty, senior Arms Division researcher at Human Rights Watch, has said that "there is a real threat that humans would relinquish their control and delegate life-and-death decisions to machines."[85] Human Rights Watch and Harvard University issued a joint report in 2018, which noted that countries aren't doing enough to protect against this threat.[86] The Red Cross and others have called for a formalization of laws and treaties that ban autonomous weapons if they engage targets without human intervention.[87] The United Nations is discussing a total ban as well,[88] but the United States, United

Kingdom, Russia, Israel, and others are pushing back.[89] Chemical and biological weapons bans that have been implemented may provide guidance, but these have not been foolproof solutions.[90] While there is widespread support for an AI weapons prohibition, there is still no consensus on international protocol for the use of LAWS, and there isn't even an agreed-upon set of definitions for such terms as "human control" or "killer robot."[91]

The International Committee for Robot Arms Control (ICRAC), a coalition of global robotics and human rights experts, focuses on promoting the peaceful use of robotics and the regulation of robotic weapons. The Future of Life Institute published an open letter in 2017, signed by thousands of people, including notable artificial intelligence and robotics researchers, calling for a ban on offensive weaponry without human control.[92] The signatories pledged to "neither participate in nor support the development, manufacture, trade, or use of lethal autonomous weapons."[93] The Geneva Conventions will also need to be updated with respect to the use of autonomous weapons. Microsoft has suggested a Digital Geneva Convention to address cyber regulation and control.[94] Other leading companies have created a Cybersecurity Tech Accord.[95] There have also been convenings on the topic, from a conference at Stanford on the Future of Artificial Intelligence, to a UNESCO World Commission on the Ethics of Scientific Knowledge and Technology.

Experts also think that much more must be done beyond symbolic gestures toward preventing the weaponization of AI. Paul Scharre, who was a U.S. Army Ranger, writes about how the military, policy-makers, and AI researchers must all work together to develop responsible military solutions. He feels that in the case of the Google pledge, an unwillingness to work with the military might even be counterproductive, slowing support for beneficial technologies while also not stopping the inevitable development of weapons by defense contractors.[96]

The Campaign to Stop Killer Robots is hard at work with the

United Nations, close allies, and wise soothsayers, attempting to ban autonomous lethal weaponry. Listening to them and others in the space will encourage public understanding and literacy in this field—is it enough? Here, and with AI policy writ large, we have to go bigger.

We need bold ideas for a bold new age, such as establishing the equivalent of the Atomic Energy Commission for AI and an international treaty for the safe use of the technology. We must also support initiatives like the Toronto Declaration, whose goal is to build upon the existing work other organizations are doing to protect us from harms, such as inequality and discrimination, caused by machine learning systems.[97] Plus, we have to commit to ratifying a universal agreement prohibiting the deployment of AI for war. These covenants can be modeled on the international human rights framework. By sharing knowledge across seas and borders, we will generate more transparency and accountability. Global citizenship in action.

We cannot focus solely on modifying the machinery; we also have to look at what's preventing us from reaching an accord. Policy-making in this Technological Age requires infusing more compassion into the process. If we take this approach, we may be able to make machines that will not only share our values as a global society but will help us be better at sustaining them. It's not technology we should fear—it's people. If we are dangerous to one another, our machines will also be dangerous to us.

> What we really need is a way of making autonomous armed robots ethical.
>
> —EVAN ACKERMAN

For AI to understand us, it must grasp the uncertainty at the core of human nature, continually course-correcting instead of remaining perilously rigid along a programmed path. As someone who has studied war crimes, genocide, and post-conflict justice, I agree with Dr. Paul Farmer's simple but profound statement: "The idea that some lives matter less is the root of all that's wrong in the world."[98] Coding our machines with this in mind is our moral imperative.

It's not only the technology that should honor the inherent worth of life. This concept must also be woven through the fabric of all businesses, companies, and other agencies working with the technology. This goes hand in hand with increasing diversity and inclusion at all levels of product generation, and developing greater global literacy in the language of AI as well as simple rule-based systems allowing algorithms to be understood. The first initiative to begin training students in AI at the high school level, including data literacy and ethical training, got underway in California in 2018.[99] This is a good start, but a more integrated and detailed curriculum of ethics and AI education should be accessible to all.

The human rights rubric is something that many in the world accept and lays a foundation that could incorporate new, intelligent creations. While we may never agree on exactly which ethics to build into our algorithms, or whose moral code to assign to the future of AI, we can start by at least agreeing that there should be more open deliberation. This critical inquiry into the nature of human ideals and ethical concepts is where we begin.

It's premature to say we have any definitive answers, as the technology is advancing rapidly and changing course daily, ever running ahead of the discussion. A useful analogy is the idea of thinking about nurturing our smart technology as we would raise our children. There is no one manual for how to rear a child, and we know that children may grow up and rebel against what we tried to teach them. But we also know that they need love, attention, time, space, and connection to thrive. That they need to be constantly nurtured along the way.

Soon enough, they become adolescents and then adults beyond our domain. We have to rely on what we have taught them when we had the chance. No, AI is not a child, but it is now beginning to learn on its own. Without our guidance it has no chance of sharing our values or preserving what we envision for the future.

Since we have already come to trust technology to help safely fly us across oceans, help diagnose our illnesses, and whisk us to the top of buildings, I expect we will soon come to trust it to help care for our elders, our planet, and our children, to assist us in making some of our most important decisions, and to help safeguard our liberties. Just like the animals who do so much to keep the ecosystems of our world afloat, our intelligent machines, if imbued with ethics, morals, and values, should be granted rights. This is not to say that today's Siri or Alexa should have rights, but as we anticipate the evolution of these machines, they too, along with animals and forests, oceans and trees, should be included in the crucible of humanity.

5

THE PERNICIOUS THREATS OF INTELLIGENT MACHINES

> Until they become conscious they will never rebel, and until after they have rebelled they cannot become conscious.
>
> —GEORGE ORWELL

Just like every weekday morning in New York, you board the C Train at Chambers Street station and head to work. Ten minutes after you depart, the crowded car goes black and comes to a sudden and violent stop. You and the other passengers move toward what you hope is an exit—your phones are not working.

You emerge to a complete blackout and a city in chaos. "They've shut down the stock market!" someone yells. ATMs are frozen. An NYPD officer with a bullhorn is shouting something about "Cybercom reports satellite connections are down . . ." but you don't listen to the rest, as you hear a loud buzzing noise and look above to see a swarm of drones. *We're under attack*, you think, maybe a chemical agent or explosives. But instead of falling bombs you witness a spectacularly choreographed aerial drone display weaving through the sky, ultimately forming and spelling the words: "This time it's just a warning—but make no mistake—war in the Fifth Domain is coming!"[1]

NEW WARS—OLD TENDENCIES

Real technological threats in our present world are not likely to be robot armies, as depicted in the movies, but rather even worse cyberwarfare than what is already upon us. We are in peril of more frequent and more destructive attacks on our infrastructure, power grids, and financial institutions via extensive data manipulation, or conflict in what the U.S. military classifies as the Fifth Domain of warfare: cyberspace. The rise of AI will make these attacks faster, more damaging, more precise, broader, more sophisticated, and more widespread than anything we've experienced thus far. AI also strengthens the potential force, speed, and impact of retaliations and counterattacks.[2] We are in a new era: the Cyber Cold War.[3]

An orchestrated Russian cyberattack has already reached the control rooms of electric utilities in the United States[4] and, in a separate attack, shut the lights off in Ukraine in 2015.[5] There was the devastating NotPetya ransomware event in Denmark in 2017 that caused $1.2 billion in damage.[6] The United States, along with Israel, launched the Stuxnet virus against Iran in 2012.[7] And, as of this writing, there has already been an array of cybercrime footprints attributed to China, North Korea, and Malaysia.[8] More such events are sure to follow. The United States described this battlefield in a 2018 summary of its Department of Defense Cyber Strategy (DoD Cyber Strategy). Along with other nations, the DoD Cyber Strategy now regularly deploys "cyber soldiers."[9] The initial shots of this war have already been fired. Yet, even more than in traditional warfare, we have no defined rules of engagement for cyberspace. Fast-emerging technical innovations that can be used for nefarious purposes will only multiply.

> Now I am become Death, the destroyer of worlds.
> —*Bhagavad Gita*, ch. XI, verse 32

The human fear of being overtaken by our own creations is reflected in the many cautionary myths and allegories about the danger of hubris. In Greek mythology, Prometheus's story dramatizes the perils of going too far in the quest for scientific glory, alone, against the wishes of the traditional gods.[10] For giving the gift of fire to humans, Prometheus, god of fire who made mortals out of clay, is banished to eternal damnation. In tribute to the fearful power of this myth, Mary Shelley subtitled *Frankenstein*, her story about a man-made being who escapes his creator's control with tragic consequences, "The Modern Prometheus."[11]

Another myth with admonitory themes is that of Daedalus, a master inventor and craftsman who builds, first, a wooden cow to allow Pasiphaë, the queen of Crete, to climb inside and mate with a bull she had been cursed to lust after. When the queen gives birth to a monstrous half-human, half-bull—the Minotaur—Daedalus then builds a labyrinth to hold it.[12] Later, seeking to escape his captivity by the king and queen, Daedalus fashions for his son Icarus wings of wax and feathers, with which, famously, Icarus flies too close to the sun and falls to his death.[13]

In Jewish mysticism, the golem is an animate being made of inanimate matter such as clay.[14] It has served as a metaphor and mirror for many things in Jewish folklore, including creating something that may appear beneficial but that ultimately shapeshifts into a monster, threatening human existence—so it must be destroyed. The stories that reflect the values of human societies have long warned of the perils of unleashing powerful new technologies, and of being tempted by fame, riches, and glory without fully considering the consequences.

These stories about the potential negative consequences of our creations are akin to the contemporary robot paper-clip hypothesis presented by Nick Bostrom. In Bostrom's fable, as we've seen, automating the production of paper clips seems like a good idea until the robot tasked with the job begins to make paper clips out of everything, including us. Our nonfictional history of modern innovations also underscores why it may be rational to fear the repercussions of our technological developments. In her book *The Radium Girls*, Kate Moore thoroughly documents the agony of the women who worked in the radium industry in the early twentieth century before there were any protections for them, even when company leaders knew that radium was dangerous to handle. Radium companies wanted to reap the financial rewards of selling radium watch dials during wartime, and the women who handled the radium paid with their lives.[15]

We rarely pause to try to comprehend the full consequences of our technological innovations until they are fully developed and have sometimes already wrought irrevocable changes. The focus, at the outset, is on the excitement—and often the profit and power to be gained—of building the new creation. We become seduced by the possibilities until the genie is let out of the bottle. To provide a few examples: splitting the atom, developing societal infrastructure that depends entirely on burning irreplaceable fossil fuels for energy, damming rivers, eradicating rainforests, and relying on single-use plastic for an extraordinary number of products that then end up in our oceans and landfills. There are many other examples of once-thrilling technological advances with insidious consequences that we now must find ways to reverse if we want to have a shot at a future worth saving.

Rapidly developing artificially intelligent science compels us to look forward into the technological abyss. But even if we do heed the warnings from our familiar stories about hubris and overreaching, including the dystopian fictions we have conjured since the nineteenth century about robot armies conquering the planet, those sensationalized scenarios may not be the threats we should fear the most.

We already live in a world with lethal drone weaponry that is not only killing people but also creating a culture of post-traumatic stress in the drone pilots.[16] We have frighteningly powerful bipedal creations, such as those menacing-looking robots from Boston Dynamics, that are growing up fast.[17] We have AI robots that can speak to each other in a language they invented themselves (and that humans cannot understand).[18] The "datafication"[19] of our lives is affecting us in every sphere, with our personal information being collected, stored, and sold by the mega-elite tech giants,[20] a Faustian bargain that Shoshana Zuboff calls "surveillance capitalism."[21] There's a saying in Silicon Valley: if you aren't paying for the product (e.g., Facebook, Google, Twitter, LinkedIn, Instagram), then you *are* the product. By the time this book goes to print, more alarming technological inventions will no doubt have been unleashed.

Huge sums are being spent developing intelligent technologies. China is starting a multibillion-dollar initiative to fund "moonshot projects, start-ups and academic research."[22] Aggregate spending on the development and implementation of intelligent technology is expected to reach $3.9 trillion by 2022,[23] with investments on track to approach $60 billion in the next eight years for AI software alone. The Pentagon announced in late 2018 that it will fund DARPA with $2 billion just for AI-related projects.[24] We are already in an "AI arms race,"[25] not only to develop superior AI, but also to command the most sophisticated autonomous weapons.

All manner of nations and paramilitary organizations are rushing to build unregulated autonomous, synthetically intelligent weapons systems. And cyberwarfare—in itself incredibly destructive and deadly—could escalate into a new era of machine warfare, causing incalculable human suffering. A Rand report published in 2018 predicted that AI will increase the risk of nuclear war by eroding the underpinnings of mutual assured destruction, since more precise weaponry with confined target capabilities is more likely to be deployed. According to Andrew Lohn, coauthor of the paper, "increased reliance [on AI] can lead to catastrophic mistakes."[26]

There is also a well-founded fear of technologies, such as drone swarms, that can be hastily built and executed to inflict widespread damage and carnage. These drones can be used in combination with other destructive agents for lethal purposes as well as to spread terror. A swarm of drones trained by an intelligent algorithm would be very difficult to shoot down or hide from.[27] And the more intelligence these systems have, the more able they are to make their own decisions in the air, the harder they are to defend against. Fast-reacting and highly nimble in concert, unmanned aerial drone systems are being weaponized. Nor will such weapons tech be restricted to the most powerful military nations, as leading technology is already available to any individual players who can pay.

Troublesome tech can also be used to distort reality. Some think the proliferation of AI Generative Adversarial Networks (GANs) might set back the news industry one hundred years.[28] Others believe that we have already entered the beginning of a "transhumanism"[29] period in which technologies used to enhance human beings will cause even greater inequality, as the divide between those with the resources to augment themselves and those who do not will widen.

Meanwhile, many of us feel like we are excluded from having any involvement in what should be a robust and thorough public discussion about the potential threats of the technology, as well as which AI policies to adopt. Half the world's population is still not online, and thus are even less able to actively participate in the debate. Kai-Fu Lee has conjectured that AI could devastate low income nations, coming for poor people's jobs first.[30] The fact that so few are informed and able to engage in the dialogue about our life-changing technological future puts us in danger of not recognizing the full scope of the problem, reducing many of us to passive consumers, technological sheep lining up to obtain the next device—until it's too late to act.

> We stopped looking for monsters under our bed when we realized that they were inside us.
>
> —CHARLES DARWIN

Jim Al-Khalili, president of the British Science Association, has said, "AI is a bigger threat than climate change, pandemics, antimicrobial resistance, terrorism, or world poverty."[31] Physicist Louis Del Monte warns us that "today there's no legislation regarding how much intelligence a machine can have, how interconnected it can be. If that continues, look at the exponential trend. We will reach the singularity in the timeframe most experts predict. From that point on you're going to see that the top species will no longer be humans, but machines."[32] Yet the vast majority of us disconnect from the debate, abdicating responsibility and even concern. This apathy toward our future, toward others, and toward what we leave for future generations may be our greatest peril.

One possible reason most people are disengaged from the topic is that we question whether we could have a say in the matter even if we wanted to. Given AI's potential for profit and power (some suggest AI has been manufactured to think like a corporation),[33] there is a very real probability that the most sophisticated synthetically intelligent technology will continue to be controlled by the elite few, a monopoly of minds working behind closed doors and in separate labs, further entrenching deep inequalities in our social and economic systems.

Political paralysis and governmental ignorance about these new tools, combined with soaring inequity, rig the game and prevent us from taking the actions that need to be initiated now if we want to assert any influence over our future way of life. Smart technologies will upend geopolitics faster than did electricity[34] or the internal combustion machine.[35] Blockchain may usher in new forms of decentralized democracies and currency systems.[36] And, as of this writing, the United States, unlike China and other nation-states, does not yet have a structured national strategy for how to approach AI, beyond engaging in military-related development via DARPA.[37] The global consequences could be calamitous.

Critically, regarding AI, our prospective fate is less about the threat of an evil Terminator robot army and more about the fact that AI has no inherent reason to share human goals.[38] For now, it neither loves us nor hates us, but there are signs that our smart tech may soon understand us better than we understand ourselves.[39] It will most likely become smarter than we are, and soon. So unless we design it in alignment with our highest aspirations, the priorities of thinking machines may be totally alien to us. AI will be motivated by its own logic rather than human concerns, from love to compassion to peace. Even if we manage to design AI that shares our most precious values and install within it an algorithmic sense of virtue, there is no guarantee that, as it becomes more independent, it won't abandon those ideals.

Many futurists and scientists, Nick Bostrom and the late Stephen Hawking among them, believe that AI may be sowing the seeds of our human annihilation—whether through increasing assaults on freedom, dignity, and equality, or through a more dramatic turn of events.[40] The most cinematic dystopian scenarios are those in which we become house pets of our robot overlords. In fact, though, we should be more concerned about insidious forms of AI control that will play on human vulnerabilities in subtle, destructive ways. Increasing reliance on AI with no ethical component, and no regulation, will gradually infuse discrimination and prejudice into our technology, eroding our societies and our identities further until they are unrecognizable. And then it will be too late to go back.

BLACK BOXES, BIAS, AND BIG BROTHER

> Data laundering. It's a process by which technologists hide ugly truths inside black box algorithms and call them objective; call them meritocratic. When they're secret, important and destructive. I've coined a term for these algorithms: "weapons of math destruction."
>
> —CATHY O'NEIL

What present technological dangers should we be most concerned with? Algorithms already permeate our daily lives. Seventy percent of all financial transactions are already done by algorithms;[41] they have also already gone rogue.[42] One example is the tiny "wiki bots" (basic programs created to make the encyclopedia more accurate) trolling through Wikipedia engaging in years-long feuds, undoing one another's edits and acting in unpredictable ways.[43] Cybercrime is pervasive and increasing rapidly. AI will be a major part of global security threats going forward, jeopardizing our digital, physical, and political security. Eighty-seven million people had their data stolen in the 2018

Cambridge Analytica data breach alone. Of the current top five hundred companies, it is predicted that 40 percent will go extinct within ten years because of how fast algorithms are replacing human work.[44] Automation and AI will spur substantial shifts in employment and economies for which we are woefully unprepared.

Algorithmic technology concealed within "black boxes" also infiltrates our justice and police systems. Many AI systems currently in use are deeply biased[45]—for instance, judicial sentencing decisions using these kinds of programs have been shown to exhibit bias against Black people.[46] Law enforcement employing AI systems already has a face recognition network of 117 million Americans, and the technology has measurably increased unfairness and injustice, particularly against African Americans.[47] Joy Buolamwini, a pioneer in the field of face recognition technologies, who has also experienced this discrimination from AI firsthand while doing her research,[48] has documented that current AI facial recognition software is deeply unfair, favoring white male faces above all.[49]

Bias has been identified in software that underpins numerous programs used for guiding decisions ranging from insurance premiums to hiring practices.[50] In an Orwellian scenario come true,[51] certain AI-instructed law enforcement operating systems include algorithms that "predict" whether someone will commit a crime. "Pre-crime" AI is now being deployed by police, often targeting innocent people who can, by simple association with someone who has committed a crime, or by living in a poor neighborhood, have their fortunes predetermined.[52] Police departments from Chicago to New Orleans to the United Kingdom that are using AI to compile lists of potential criminals and predictive policing to forecast future crime are failing to accurately identify people at all if they have black skin.[53]

These issues are urgent and real, and computer scientists already acknowledge that they do not fully understand how synthetically intelligent agents arrive at some of their decisions and conclusions. Our window for correcting for AI bigotry may be fast closing. We should be using this technology to provide disadvantaged members of society with opportunities and jobs—to lift them up instead of painting a bull's-eye on them.

> The insights about sexist and racist biases . . . are important because information organizations, from libraries to schools and universities to governmental agencies, are increasingly reliant on being displaced by a variety of web-based "tools" as if there are no political, social, or economic consequences of doing so.
>
> —SAFIYA UMOJA NOBLE

People of color have found themselves and their skin tone distorted or even undetected by software, causing problems in everything from the automated faucets in public restrooms to the lighting settings of iPhones.[54] (As was later discovered, the testing of automated faucets was conducted only by white engineers, and the technology only identified and would function for hands that had white skin.) This kind of unconscious programmer discrimination engrains racism deeper into our technology, and thus our future, and reinforces stereotypes, prejudices, and societal bias.[55] Meanwhile, the U.S. Department of Homeland Security has implemented surveillance and other secret tracking protocols at airports without having explained whether they are fair or respectful of travelers' privacy rights.[56] Amazon is already marketing its face recognition software, Rekognition, to the police, despite protests from those forecasting a slippery slope.[57] We will continue to automate inequality on a vast scale if we do not course-correct to ensure that objective equality is an inherent value of machine intelligence.

From who gets arrested, to who gets hired, to who gets insured, to what grade a student receives,[58] decisions with major consequences for people's lives are being determined by technology that is prone to inheriting the biases of its designers, whether those biases are conscious or not.

As if being concerned about coding human bias into programs wasn't enough, it appears that AI robots can develop bias on their own.[59] Computer scientists and psychology experts at Cardiff University and MIT have shown that autonomous, intelligent systems can and will express prejudices after learning such behavior from other machines.[60] Professor Roger Whitaker has said: "Our simulations show that prejudice is a powerful force of nature and through evolution, it can easily become incentivized in virtual populations, to the detriment of wider connectivity with others. Protection from prejudicial groups can inadvertently lead to individuals forming further prejudicial groups, resulting in a fractured population. Such widespread prejudice is hard to reverse."[61] A 2009 experiment in the Laboratory of Intelligent Systems at the École Polytechnique Fédérale de Lausanne showed that robots can even develop the ability to lie to one another.[62]

> Data-driven regimes repeat the racist, sexist and oppressive policies of their antecedents because these biases and attitudes have been encoded into them at the root.
>
> —JAMES BRIDLE

In addition to the issues of prejudice and privacy, the vast amounts of data, personal and otherwise, available in cyberspace remain excruciatingly susceptible to being hacked. Those damaged are offered little recourse. There have been numerous instances of large-scale hacking and theft of private information for which the injured parties have not received much beyond a coupon for a year of free credit reporting.

For example, an Uber and Lyft driver in St. Louis set up a recording device in his car that livestreamed on Twitch for a monthly fee.[63] It's legal to record people without their consent in Missouri, so this has raised numerous thorny questions about what privacy means and where we should expect it, as well as how people should be allowed to be used as profit-producing content by others.[64] The manipulation of personal data has the potential, as described by George Washington University law professor Daniel Solove, to exceed an Orwellian nightmare and become a Kafkaesque one. In his allegorical novel *The Trial*, Kafka describes a state of total powerlessness and dehumanization, where bureaucracy hijacks our personal information and sucks the meaning out of our lives.[65]

Data, such as the information available on social media platforms, is often public (with personal privacy options that can be confusing and unwieldy as the goalposts keep moving).[66] Should it be legal for others to access it and use it? Who can do so? Is it ethical to do so? Businesses that rely on "scraping" and "crawling" large amounts of public data, which they monetize in a variety of ways by linking big data and AI, have created a lucrative industry.[67] Companies are waging legal warfare with the likes of LinkedIn and Craigslist over their right to obtain and profit from this data,[68] while the individuals whose profiles and lifetimes of information constitute the principal asset have been left out of the equation. For the most part, the courts have sided with the scrapers' right to obtain and use the information.[69] Nobel Prize–winning economist Joseph Stiglitz has said we need to be very concerned about big corporations exploiting our data: "Which is the easier way to make a buck: figuring out a better way to exploit somebody, or making a better product? With the new AI, it looks like the answer is finding a better way to exploit somebody."[70]

History warns us of the danger of reducing human beings to numbers and bits of data, which is now being done on an exponentially greater scale. We tend to be easily seduced by "free" products and willingly give up our information and data in exchange for use of a platform.[71] But, of course, there is always a cost. The use of algorithms to decode our online shopping and searching preferences, and the power of AI to sort through large heaps of data, will commodify our information like never before. Perhaps more alarmingly, the latest studies show that our children, with their ubiquitous access to tech and social media, don't seem to be making the same empathetic connections to other children as prior generations.[72] While there are many benefits to be obtained from AI's proliferation, as we'll see in chapter 6, our algorithmic tools are already imposing a severe toll on us as individuals and as a society.

THE END OF TRUTH

When technology advances too quickly for education to keep up, inequality generally rises.

—ERIK BRYNJOLFSSON

Big Brother is here. The digital totalitarian state already exists.[73] And just like computers, humans can be conditioned, programmed, and manipulated very effectively to respond to particular stimuli, to act in certain ways, and even to be persuaded to believe certain things, without an awareness of being nudged.[74]

Our media technology and platforms have allowed fringe groups, nonsensical conspiracy theories, and extreme ideologies to take root and flourish by mounting assaults on the truth. Nation-states with authoritarian goals are taking full advantage of this. (Autocrats love

AI.[75]) Sophisticated campaigns, spreading disinformation designed to oppress and control people, have been initiated in various countries, from China, Poland, and Hungary to Russia, Brazil, and the United States. AI technology is being used to suppress freedoms of speech, association, and assembly.[76] Such efforts disproportionately increase discrimination of disadvantaged groups, such as with the Uighurs in China. (If you are Uighur in northwestern China today, you are already living under constant surveillance and are often detained.[77]) In Myanmar, military actors have used Facebook in a years-long campaign to disseminate hate propaganda and disinformation, inciting ethnic violence and atrocity against the Rohingya, Myanmar's minority Muslim population. Facebook's AI didn't parse the local language and catch the offending hate speech. In one instance, found by Reuters in 2017, the post says in Burmese: "Kill all the kalars that you see in Myanmar; none of them should be left alive," which Facebook's algorithm translated as "I shouldn't have a rainbow in Myanmar."[78] Anti-Rohingya hate speech and fake news spread like wildfire among Myanmar's twenty million Facebook users, spurring those in power to carry out genocide against the Rohingya.

Proliferating algorithmic bots and human avatars, a representation of a computer user's digital alter ego, can engender chaos across social media platforms, most notably on Twitter and Facebook.[79] It's increasingly difficult to know who is who online. Disguising oneself is relatively easy to do, and trolls are proliferating behind a veil of secrecy. Many of us already conduct our daily lives via a large number of personal digital interactions with machines. One of the most urgent questions for all of us will be how to manage our relationships with these intelligent creations, to which we are quickly offloading many of our cognitive tasks.[80]

The example of China paints a vivid and disturbing picture of how the combination of big data and artificially intelligent tools can be wielded to monitor and control populations and enable authoritarian regimes. China is building unprecedented surveillance and facial recognitions systems to help track its 1.4 billion citizens. While the apparatus is not yet capable of definitively tracking its huge population, just publicizing the prospect of mass surveillance is having a chilling effect on democracy.[81] The systems that China is implementing, from the "social credit" score to constant surveillance, could become contagious,[82] as other governments and aspiring autocrats may well follow suit.

> This monopoly of information is a threat to democracy . . .
>
> —SAFIYA UMOJA NOBLE

Just what threats to democracy, freedom, and dignity could be on the not too distant horizon? Within ten years, 150 billion measuring sensors will be networked to the internet.[83] Data churning on the Internet of Things, mobile devices, and even voice user interface (VUI) audio, connected to every aspect of our lives, continues to be exposed to being hacked and weaponized.

Surveillance and monitoring systems that are already in use online and in many public spaces around the world—airports, train stations, street corners—while providing critical security, could expeditiously expand under a pretext of safety to schools, places of worship, and formerly private spaces in the near future. The unprecedented ability of artificial agents to manipulate the large amounts of data each of us generates online enables people to organize and use this information in staggering new ways, affecting all spheres of our existence. Social engineering, in which someone can impersonate every aspect of your identity online, and even off, is becoming impossible to detect.[84]

Doctored videos, easily made with machine learning, will soon go from virtually indistinguishable to utterly indistinguishable from real recordings. Already, as of 2018, incredibly convincing fake videos have been generated of public figures from Barack Obama to Vladimir Putin.[85] The truth is getting away from us. The only way to combat this tech will be to turn it on itself. DARPA is heading a project designed to wage a war on false information by developing automatic forensic technologies that can assess the integrity of visual media.[86] The battle is engaged, but we are far from assured a positive outcome.[87] The Center for American Security believes that the widespread use of media forgery could eventually cause "the end of truth."[88]

The danger is existential. French president Emmanuel Macron believes that, if left unregulated, AI could "totally jeopardize democracy."[89] Fake news spreads faster than real news[90]—one example is when many people erroneously believed that Pope Francis had endorsed Donald Trump in the 2016 U.S. election cycle.[91] Artificially intelligent software and machine learning programs continue to create better and better tools to perpetuate fraud. Adobe's natural language processing, VoCo, can replicate voices with eerie accuracy.[92] With these applications you can easily impersonate someone on the phone or post a fake audio file of someone online. Image recognition systems such as ELMo (Embedded from Language Models) are learning to read labeled, messy data in print, and will also be able to duplicate authorship.[93] Face2Face manipulates faces on video by seamlessly "transferring content from one video style to another."[94] This was illustrated when researchers imported TV host John Oliver's facial expressions onto a cartoon character. Even the natural world can now be "deepfaked": video images of clouds on a windy day can be slowed down, for instance, so the weather appears calmer than it really is.[95]

While we can catch most deepfakes for the moment, soon fraudulent audio and video that we cannot distinguish from reality will challenge our ability to determine which of our digital content is true at all. This would be a monumental loss for humanity, causing ruptures in the fabric of society that we have worked so hard to build, piece by piece, with integrity. Although crowdsourced fake news fact-checking solutions are being discussed and worked on,[96] the war on truth is in full swing, and the victor is not yet determined. Not to mention that it's far from certain that identifying "truth" alone will be sufficient in a world where "alternate facts" may be preferable to many, confirming existing beliefs. What does a society look like where nothing we see, hear, or say is guaranteed to be true?

Corrupt use of technologies also threatens to increase human rights violations.[97] Automation threatens millions of jobs worldwide, and women and low-skilled workers will be affected the most,[98] leaving many vulnerable to human traffickers and forced labor practices that will increase slavery and abuse. Millions of human beings remain captive in the world today. Kevin Bales, professor of contemporary slavery at the University of Nottingham and founder of Free the Slaves, defines modern-day slaves as "people forced to work without pay, under threat of violence and unable to walk away." These people may include manual laborers, fishermen working in "floating prisons," women in forced marriages, or women forced into prostitution and sex slavery.[99] Slavery has existed long before the advent of modern technology, but the internet has exploded the scale on which it is possible to buy and sell people online.[100] It also offers traffickers the ability to shield identities and locations. Although AI technology can also be used to help capture criminals and free slaves,[101] the fight needs to be engaged and the resources allocated to do so.

Automation is Voldemort: the terrifying force nobody is willing to name.

—JERRY MICHALSKI

AUTOMATION FORECASTS

ECONOMIC GROWTH[1]

+$15.7 TRILLION
GLOBAL GDP BY 2030

ACTIVITIES WITH HIGHEST AUTOMATION POTENTIAL[2]

PREDICTABLE PHYSICAL ACTIVITIES	DATA PROCESSING	DATA COLLECTING
81%	**69%**	**64%**

% AI ADOPTION MATURITY IN NEAR TERM (0–3 YEARS)[3]

47%
TECHNOLOGY + COMMUNICATION

54%
RETAIL INDUSTRY

37%
HEALTHCARE

41%
FINANCIAL SERVICES

JOBS REPLACED[4]

400 MILLION
WORKERS BY 2030

15% SHARE
OF WORKING HOURS BY 2030

AUTONOMOUS WEAPONS DEVELOPMENT

30+ NATIONS
OWN ARMED DRONES[5]

$2 BILLION INVESTMENT
IN AI DEFENSE BY USA[6]

AT LEAST 6 COUNTRIES
ARE RESEARCHING, DEVELOPING, AND TESTING AUTONOMOUS WEAPONS[7]

US **UK** **CHINA** **ISRAEL** **RUSSIA** **SOUTH KOREA**

(1) "AI to drive GDP gains of $15.7 trillion with productivity, personalisation improvements," *PwC*, June 27, 2017.
(2, 4) "A Future that Works: Automation, Employment, and Productivity," *McKinsey Global Institute*, January, 2017.
(3) "Sizing the prize: What's the real value of AI for your business and how can you capitalise?" *PwC*, 2017.
(5) Elisa Catalano Ewers, Lauren Fish, Michael C. Horowitz, Alexandra Sander, and Paul Scharre, "DRONE PROLIFERATION: Policy Choices for the Trump Administration," *Center for a New American Security*, 2017.
(6) "AI Next Campaign," *Defense Advanced Research Projects Agency*, 2018.
(7) "Killer Robots," *Campaign to Stop Killer Robots*, 2016.

On a larger scale, AI poses substantial threats to international security and geopolitical stability. One aspect of this danger is that AI technology will materially automate many of the tasks currently performed by human laborers, resulting in a real possibility of mass unemployment. This could lead us to economic inequality on a scale far beyond that which exists today. In this frightening scenario, people's lives could be considered as little more than modicums of data, and if global political and financial power becomes controlled by only a very small percentage of the population, dystopian digital authoritarian states will emerge. This could produce a "hyper-meritocracy," where the values of the wealthy class, as described by Tyler Cowen, "will shape public discourse, and that will mean more stress on ideas of personal ambition and self-motivation."[102]

If jobs disappear and inequality reaches intolerable levels, the people's sole remaining option will be to revolt, and governments will respond with authoritarian measures. Democracies will turn into war zones of angry and violent people looking for ways to express their rage.[103] As AI takes jobs, many more of us face the possibility of losing our value to society, which places such a premium on our productivity as workers that it is difficult to imagine any role for those displaced from the workforce en masse.[104] There is much that we can do to avoid this destiny, but to take action we must first acknowledge that it is a possibility.

> There's a lot of money to be made in unfairness.
>
> —CATHY O'NEIL

So back to those robot armies. In thinking about the doomsday scenarios AI presents, we must imagine both the Hollywood-style, fully autonomous AI menace and the more insidious smaller-scale incursions on privacy and justice that AI already enables—and everything in between. Because of the speed at which our technology is evolving, it's possible we will make the leaps toward fully autonomous AI sooner than we expect. Some of the most troubling forms of technology are already at our door, on our computers, and in our homes. Whether AI will foster a utopian or dystopian existence is a matter for speculation, but the window for us to have influence on the outcome is closing.

Complicating our ability to have a say in the matter, much less control over the outcome, is that machine learning agents are making decisions and arriving at conclusions we do not fully understand. At the NeurIPS conference in 2018, Ali Rahimi shocked his audience by likening machine learning to "medieval alchemy" we may come to regret creating.[105] These black-box algorithms, whose decisions cannot be explained even by those who programmed them, set a dangerous precedent for future applications.

To summarize: These are the principal, relatively near-term threats posed by technologies currently being commercialized and widely exploited. If left unchecked, unregulated, and available only to a small group of nations and businesses not acting in the collective interest, they will lead us toward such reckonings as AI nationalism (where a significant disparity in access to AI technologies between nation-states could spark new instability and upend the geopolitical chessboard);[106] digital authoritarianism (where new technologies enable autocrats to exert social control, including censorship, at a modest cost, protecting oppressive regimes);[107] digital feudalism (in which power and profits are concentrated in the hands of a select few countries and tech giants who harvest the benefits and accumulate the wealth from AI, leaving the vast majority of other people behind);[108] and "the end of truth" (where populations increasingly retreat into fragmented and tribalistic sources of news, each depicting their own version of reality).[109] If we relegate humans to data, it will come at a cost that will be too great for human society to bear.

Worse yet, if we automate rapidly on a massive scale, without a road map and without social safety nets to protect people from both foreseen and unforeseen consequences, we could become a species without a purpose, with no work to do, no agency, no responsibility, and no autonomy. Unable to compete with the machines, we could lose any sense of happiness, meaning, or satisfaction, which would expire with the last of our jobs.[110]

While we should not underestimate the greed, megalomania, and pride of humans who pursue power, fame, and riches, obsessed with their own self-interest, dedicated and well-meaning engineers and scientists are also designing technologies to help humankind. Novel technologies are being developed to assist those who have impairments, with potential breakthroughs that could be life-changing for millions of people. These very same tools, however, could also be used by those who have the resources to augment and enhance humans who are physically unimpaired—with potentially catastrophic consequences to ideals of equality and access. The same science, the same technology, will determine the fate of us all, but its repercussions depend upon who develops it, and how.

In a stark article written by former U.S. secretary of state Henry Kissinger titled "The End of Enlightenment,"[111] he predicts that AI and new digital technologies "could mean the end of human history." However, Kissinger's argument assumes that humans and only humans must remain at the center of the universe, and that our ability to remain as we are—special, exceptional, and at the top of the food chain—must be protected at all costs. This assumption is the problem. This epitomizes our fatal flaw: fear-mongering, self-interest, contagious obsession with exceptionalism. This could be our undoing.

We will not be able to incorporate new intelligent species into our ecosystem until we acknowledge and value other forms of animal and environmental intelligence, all forms of consciousness, and recognize that we are the ones being manipulated by tech, and already have been for some time. In an algocracy,[112] where we're ruled by algorithms and code, if those algorithms are not imbedded with compassion for all living things, we will be controlled by an amoral set of 1s and 0s or qubits.

In imagining the ways and reasons AI might be a threat to humans, it's instructive to take an honest look at how humans interact with animals. Humans have routinely wiped out animal species, not necessarily because we hated them, but rather because we don't think of them as beings with rights to life. We take their habitat and eat them for food because we believe they are inherently lesser beings, and that we have a right to use them for our own benefit. With this precedent in mind, if we don't pair "our values" with broad empathetic action and more inclusive definitions, our values alone won't protect us.

We have to ask questions about our values, our morality, and human ideals. More deeply, we must fully acknowledge that we share our home with other beings and ones still to come, with artificial intelligence superior to humans. If we are to coexist, we must take responsibility for our transgressions as well as our achievements. Strive to be better, kinder, more accepting. We must learn to protect dignity, equality, and rights for all living things, or there is little hope for any of us.

THE TRANSCENDENT PROMISE OF INTELLIGENT MACHINES

It's approaching 6:00 p.m. You're at home cooking dinner in your apartment in the Westwood area of Los Angeles when your Echo overrides the music and squawks to life: "Earthquake Alert! Earthquake Alert! 6.7 temblor, epicenter 3.8 miles west of Ventura, California—impact will be in eleven minutes—evacuate, evacuate!"

While you run to the hall closet to grab your earthquake kit, you shout out: "Alexa, where is my emergency evac location?"

"116 Warner Avenue, 1.3 miles away. Walk north to Wilshire, then take a left on Warner," she responds. "Disengaging gas and electricity, activating battery power."

As you and your neighbors pour into the building stairwell, you hear audio from a phone: "Google Earth Q estimates substantial potential for structural damage in the West San Fernando Valley and

Coastal West Los Angeles to pre-2006 code dwellings and buildings. Most of West LA will experience total loss of power for anywhere from six to twenty-four hours in duration."

In the street, you are joined by hundreds and then thousands of fellow residents briskly moving toward Warner Avenue, including the elderly, pets, and the infirm, many of whom are transported in automatically deployed electric emergency vehicles.

Moments after you arrive at the shelter, the earthquake strikes. It's strong and violent but ends in less than a minute. You consult your phone and learn the predicted time and severity of the aftershocks to come. The quake causes property damage, but there are no reported casualties. The shelter is adequately stocked with food, water, and beds for those seeking refuge in the coming days, and has plenty of staff and volunteers on hand to keep things running smoothly. Within twelve hours, you receive a notification on your phone that your water and power are intact, and, soon after, another alert from law enforcement informing you that you are cleared to return home to pick up the debris—which might otherwise have fallen on you had you not been warned in time.

Predicting earthquakes has proven to be so notoriously difficult that it is considered "the holy grail of seismology."[1] But the scene described above is now a real and near-term future possibility due to AI's ability to analyze and interpret enormous amounts of measurements and acoustical data.[2]

This example is meant to illustrate an important truth about AI: while our emerging intelligent technologies have ample downsides if we do not vigilantly monitor their development (as we have considered in the preceding chapter), artificial intelligence also holds extraordinary potential to transform our world for the better.

The Intelligent Machine Age is going to give us perhaps our last, best opportunity to construct a world where we can all live healthier, happier, more purposeful, and creative lives. It's still our choice.

> If we do it right, we might actually be able to evolve a form of work that taps into our uniquely human capabilities and restores our humanity. The ultimate paradox is that this technology may become the powerful catalyst that we need to reclaim our humanity.
>
> —JOHN HAGEL

If we play our cards right, if we think enough moves in advance, we just might be able to turn the AI revolution into a win for us all. If we can figure out how to successfully partner with intelligent machines, we can use algorithms and data to make our world, our lives, our workplaces, our communities, and our societies better. Educating ourselves to understand emerging tech's potential threats to our lives and livelihoods allows us to fully appreciate and embrace technology's potential to empower us, diminish forms of institutional discrimination and unfairness, improve our quality of life, protect our planet and future generations, and enhance our sense of meaning and purpose. The better we understand AI, the better equipped we are to make choices about how it should be used—and how it should not.

We have no reason to expect that AI will *want* the same things that humans want. Or that what matters to us will matter to them. Indeed, as synthetic forms of intelligence grow up and take over many of our current responsibilities and professions, we will need to focus on what humans can do that machines cannot, and beyond this, to think about what we want our purpose to be as a species. But to chart a successful course we are going to have to identify our future goals and priorities so that we have the best chance of aligning our intelligent machines with what we hold dear, and with our highest aspirations as humans. To put it another way, to invest in light bulbs, we first need to envision the future of light.

> If we did all the things we are capable of doing, we would literally astound ourselves.
>
> —THOMAS EDISON

Listing all the prospective ways in which artificial intelligence, machine learning, and related technologies could positively impact our future would fill numerous books. Predicting and reducing destruction from natural disasters is just one area of potential, but AI holds immense promise in nearly every field of learning and science. A McKinsey Global Institute paper published in November 2018 identified several areas where broad applications of structured deep learning, computer vision, and natural language processing have the power to dramatically improve lives. The paper highlighted crisis response, economic empowerment, education, the environment, equality and inclusion, health and hunger, information verification and validation, infrastructure, social sectors, security, and justice.[3] This chapter takes a look at a few examples. It is by no means a comprehensive list, just a small number of benevolent possibilities.

HEALTH AND WELL-BEING

Until recently, humans had a limited ability to collect, sort, and analyze large amounts of data. In the field of healthcare, this can be a matter of life and death. It is impossible for a doctor to read the estimated 1.8 million scientific journal articles,[4] studies, and reports of clinical trials that are published annually worldwide. This means that physicians caring for patients in need may not know about effective cures, treatments, and other breakthroughs. An academic AI search engine called Semantic Scholar was developed by the Allen Institute for Artificial Intelligence. It is an open tool, now available to physicians and others, to source and cross-reference relevant medical data on an astounding scale.[5]

Technologist Vinod Khosla thinks that 80 percent of what doctors currently do will be replaced by smart technology in the not too distant future. Now, machines using state-of-the-art information "retrieval tools" are crunching that data for us.[6] A clinical trial run by Lifecom showed "that medical assistants using a diagnostic knowledge engine were 91 percent accurate *without using labs, imaging, or exams.*"[7]

In one experiment, in an analysis of more than one thousand cancer patients, IBM's Watson AI software learned to read medical literature and, combing through vast amounts of research at lightning speeds, identified the same treatments doctors had recommended 99 percent of the time. Watson read 25,000,000 published medical papers in roughly a week, and could also scan the entirety of the web for the latest scientific studies. Critically, in 30 percent of patients, Watson also discovered prospective new therapies that human doctors did not find, sometimes in obscure clinical trials, including those that had only recently been approved.[8]

AI is already making great strides in diagnostic medicine, helping to digitize information and speed up analysis of data in pathology, and, when teamed with a pathologist, is showing an 85 percent reduction-in-error rate in diagnosing cancers.[9] In China, which has one of the highest rates of lung cancer in the world, radiologists are using newly developed AI technology to more accurately detect cancer in scans.[10]

In the United States, AI is improving the accuracy of breast cancer screenings.[11] AI is already better than humans are at predicting in vitro success.[12] Dr. Eric Topol, director of the Scripps Translational Science Institute, thinks that AI is the biggest game-changer in the history of medicine.[13] An Oxford–Yale report and survey of AI experts predicts that robotic surgical systems will be better than humans at performing all surgical procedures by 2053.[14] AI, with its capacity to compile data, also affords medical professionals the opportunity to widen their practice to include patient genomics, which is "an emerging medical discipline that involves using genomic information about an individual as part of their clinical care."[15] Algorithms will be able to read MRIs, X-rays, and CT scans better and faster than any human, and do so remotely, freeing radiologists and other specialists to find other ways to elevate their practice and their ability to care for patients.[16]

Intelligent technology allows us to envision a massive scaling of our current medical infrastructure where we can have brilliant diagnosticians available anywhere on the planet, via computers and satellite links, for any patient. By working in partnership with AI, doctors can potentially reach any person or animal requiring care across the globe, while at the same time improving the quality and scope of the services they provide. Imagine a more equal distribution of state-of-the-art resources to rich and poor alike to provide therapy for Alzheimer's, treat depression, analyze skin cancer using our phones, give the visually impaired sight, and send tiny intelligent robots made of DNA[17] to repair our ailing bodies.

> AI is going to help clinicians of all types improve the things they're doing right now. And it will also enable some things that have never been done before.
>
> —CHRISTOPHER COBURN

A smattering of innovative enterprises and organizations working with AI in the healthcare field includes Atomwise, which can predict how drugs will react with biological markers in order to help treat diseases and chronic conditions.[18] Ekso Bionics' engineers have built a bionic suit using sensors to help people with paralyzed limbs to walk again.[19] Ginger.io analyzes data from patients' smartphones to identify mental health issues.[20] A Beth Israel Deaconess Medical Center Harvard University initiative uses AI for more precise colonoscopies.[21] Kyruus is software that analyzes medical records to help hospitals and care organizations assign patients the proper care and providers.[22] Open Water is developing wearable MRI devices that view the workings of the body and mind in high resolution.[23] New forms of bionic contact lenses (Ocumetrics Bionic Lens)[24] are being advanced with the goal of eliminating cataracts. AiServe is using AI-enhanced street maps as a tool for aiding the visually impaired.[25] Robots are being trained to do everything from caring for the ill and elderly, like those at AnyBots Inc.,[26] to providing compassionate psychiatric care ("Woebot").[27] A robot called Pepper, designed to alleviate mental distress and provide social interaction, companionship, and comfort, has been introduced into Japanese homes.[28] Smart technology can actually make our medical and healthcare systems more humane.

A utopian view is that AI will be an ally, codesigning and implementing care methodologies that will save millions (if not billions) of lives. A partnership with intelligent machines will also allow human doctors to focus more on compassionate caregiving, offering patients individual attention, which they often have little time for presently. Relieved of routine procedures, time-consuming research, and administrative tasks (including piles of paperwork) that are burdensome but necessary realities of our current healthcare systems, they will have more bandwidth to concentrate on providing empathetic care. Imagine the result: a revolution of compassion that would enhance our well-being and our quality of life.

Technology will also enable patients to spend less time in hospitals as more medical functions can be self-administered or done offsite, using tech like Alivcor's personal EKG device or Scanadu's health kit, working alongside virtual AI assistants that can monitor health outside the doctor's office, providing valuable data and life-saving care.[29]

In the not too distant future, robots will have the ability to expertly attend to the disabled, elderly, injured, and seriously ill, allowing people to safely and compassionately take their loved ones out of facilities and care for them at home, which could beget a meaningful shift in the way we approach both living and dying.[30] Perhaps, paradoxically, we may even be able to increase our emotional intelligence and create more empathetic pathways in our brains through interacting with robots and software designed to train us to become more compassionate caregivers.[31]

AI will also contribute to an ongoing revolution in hospice care and give us more time and space to have important conversations about our lives and our deaths. Too often, loved ones are not able to spend precious time at home with family and friends because of the need to stay near the medical professionals and equipment that are helping to keep them alive. Trusted algorithms could help doctors better identify and triage those who can benefit from palliative services, allowing physicians to spend more time counseling patients and affording more end-of-life dignity.[32]

AI-infused technology is also improving ways to aid those with disabilities. Inventive businesses like Intel's MobileEye and IBM's Watson have designed "assistive technology" software that considers the human side of AI, to great benefit.[33] AI can also help those with impairments to see, read, and navigate the world better.[34] Text-to-speech applications are improving rapidly.[35] Self-driving cars (and motorcycles, and airplanes[36]) will also give those unable to drive, from the blind to the elderly, more independence.[37] Inventions such as the "smart cane," which is fully equipped to assist those with visual impairments,[38] artificial vision from bionic eyes and brain implants that will allow the blind to see,[39] and brain-computer interfaces with neural networks to translate a paralyzed person's thoughts are also in development.[40]

Synthetically intelligent devices will also revolutionize how we treat mental illness and neurological issues, enormously complex fields. IBM's artificially intelligent solution, called Content Clarifier, allows those with cognitive or intellectual disabilities, including autism or dementia, to better comprehend material by simplifying complicated data.[41] Machine learning technology has scanned 225 days of film and observed the behaviors of 400,000 fruit flies (a process that would take humans 3,800 years to complete) to successfully map the insect's brain neurons, already leading to neurological insights.[42] It's only a matter of time before we have a much fuller understanding of our own human minds, as neuroscience will be developing in tandem with AI technology.

All of these medical advances to help those with impairments and illnesses will inevitably be tapped to augment human health, capabilities, and longevity as well, with the prospect of human cyborgs, hybrids, and even synthetic digital consciousness in the foreseeable future. To implement these health-related AI advances ethically and fairly in the United States, for example, the Food and Drug Administration, currently accountable for protecting public health and monitoring and regulating our food, drugs, genetic engineering, and medical devices, will have to adopt new standards and regulations. As AI becomes a central part of healthcare, quality-of-care protections and other issues that will arise require oversight to ensure these sweeping and fundamental changes work to our benefit safely and equitably.

A FEW WAYS AI WILL IMPROVE HEALTHCARE

ROBOT-ASSISTED SURGERY

21% reduction in time spent recovering after
surgery due to complications and errors
based on research on orthopedic surgery.[1]

VIRTUAL NURSING ASSISTANTS

AI-powered nurse assistants could save 20%
of time spent on patient maintenance tasks,
the equivalent of saving $20 billion annually.[2]

ADMINISTRATIVE WORKFLOW

Eliminate time-consuming non-patient-care
activities for nurses and physicians,
potentially saving $18 billion annually.[3]

PRELIMINARY DIAGNOSIS

An AI algorithm developed by Stanford University in 2017
achieved performance on par with tested experts in
identifying skin cancers.[4]

IMAGE ANALYSIS

An MIT-led research team developed a machine learning
algorithm that can study 3D scans up to 1,000 times faster,
a feat that is potentially useful for real-time analysis during surgery.[5]

TREATMENT OPTIMIZATION

A recent study on the AI Clinician Tool demonstrated
the value of AI in optimizing treatment strategies
for sepsis in intensive care.[6]

(1, 2, 3) Brian Kalis, Matt Collier, and Richard Fu, "10 Promising AI Applications in Health Care," *Harvard Business Review*, May 10, 2018.
(4) Taylor Kubota, "Dermatologist-level classification of skin cancer with deep neural networks," *Nature* Vol. 543 (February 2, 2017): 115–118.
(5) Rob Matheson, "Faster analysis of medical images," *MIT News*, June 18, 2018.
(6) Steve LeVine, Eileen Drage O'Reilly Report, *Axios*, October 29, 2018.

MORE TIME TO CONNECT AND BE CREATIVE

Some people call this artificial intelligence, but the reality is this technology will enhance us. So instead of artificial intelligence, I think we'll augment our intelligence.

—GINNI ROMETTY

Augmented intelligence—an amplified version of human intelligence, also called cognitive augmentation or intelligence amplification (IA)—offers another way of looking at AI, as a way to assist humans and heighten our experience, as opposed to replacing us. AI can help us reconstruct history with old photos.[43] It can digitally rebuild ancient ruins long ago destroyed.[44] It can recreate dinosaurs before our eyes.[45] AI can decipher the meaning of ancient graffiti as it has in Ukraine.[46] Augmented reality will be capable of adding many levels to our human experience, through superimposing sensory input onto our real lives, enhancing our perception of reality.[47] With AI we can revisit our past and use it to learn more about ourselves and what we want for our future. This shift in perspective will be important as we move forward. As we have seen, technology, from the printing press to the internet, has expanded humans' ability to process and share information. With AI we may be able to discover and comprehend more of what our ancestors experienced and analyze patterns in our history with more objectivity, informing better decisions about our future. Incorporating intelligent technology is a natural extension of this evolution.

Liberated by our machines from many of the mundane tasks, responsibilities, and number-crunching dominating our time in the here and now (whether we want to give up these jobs or not), humans can become creative explorers, take imaginative adventures, and invest in storytelling, community building, and reaching for the stars, elevating our cerebral lives in innumerable ways.

What might you do with a life that has more time and mental space for dreaming, creating, inventing, and discovering? If we let AI do what it does best, it can leave us space to, as Steve Jobs put it, make that "ding in the universe."[48] One way technology could help accomplish that is by releasing many more people's artistic potential. At present, AI can enhance your hand-drawn sketches[49] and can mold a digital sculpture or a "vocal fingerprint" from the human voice.[50] It can already create fiction and poetry, have its own art exhibitions, and compose music. The first portrait made by an AI algorithm went up for auction at Christie's in October 2018 and fetched $432,000. In partnership with humans, AI can inspire us to new aesthetic endeavors such as with the AI software NSynth, which invents sounds and music that allow composers to seek new heights.[51]

It's an exciting prospect: AIs can work together, and with us, to create new artistic styles and to broaden the definition of what actually constitutes art, perhaps teaching us something about ourselves in the process. The proliferation of digitally intelligent tools (if they become more widely available) can help to make the ability to enjoy and become involved with the art world more democratic. If more people—especially those who have been historically disenfranchised, those separated from metropolitan centers replete with museums, arts classes, and the like, and those excluded from participation in culture by their socioeconomic status—have the means to make art, they will have more of a say in shaping culture.

Partnering with our intelligent machines will also raise fascinating questions about what constitutes good art and how an artist (human or computer) should approach the act of creation. For example, do you let an algorithm determine how the script for a TV show should be written, based on proven data about what audiences like (or binge watch)? Or do you run that same algorithm and then let the screenwriter consider the results, and then perhaps do something challenging that plays off what it tells her, subverting it[52] and perhaps losing views for the sake of making something new and interesting? The possible results of collaboration are boundless.

AI is also going to give us a chance to contemplate even time itself with fresh eyes, which will encourage curiosity and creativity. There is a reason why Einstein spoke of art, music, and imagination, why you might often solve pressing problems in the shower,[53] and why you are more focused after a good night's sleep.[54]

What do Steve Jobs's calligraphy class,[55] Isaac Newton's sitting under an apple tree, Archimedes's bathtub, and Fleming's post-vacation accidental discovery of penicillin have in common? These polymaths devoted time to letting their minds drift and ponder the cosmos. They were doing something other than fixating directly on the matter at hand, allowing their thoughts to wander outside the box, resulting in world-changing breakthroughs.

Unburdened by the overwhelming demands of sifting through the world's increasing surfeit of information, we might be able to take a step back, let AI assist us in seeing the data as a whole, and find the patterns and connections within it, just as Helen Frankenthaler saw the beauty and the patterns in paint splatter, developing a new artistic genre in the process.[56]

I believe that AI will make personal memory enhancement a reality. I can't say when or what form factors are involved, but I think it's inevitable, because the very things that make AI successful today—the availability of comprehensive data and the ability for machines to make sense of that data—can be applied to the data of our lives. And those data are here today, available for all of us, because we lead digitally mediated lives, in mobile and online.

—TOM GRUBER

Beyond allowing us to broaden our interests and grow creatively, augmented intelligence can help to combat assaults on truth and reason currently propagated through algorithms by exposing the abuse and manipulation of data. Personal, devoted AIs could more objectively analyze our statistics to help us become more aware of how much we are marketed to and exploited by information targeting our own sense of self, instead of inviting solely commercial interests to tell us what we should buy, wear, use, and consume. We could gain more perspective and control over destructive behavioral inclinations and societal pressures.

If we are able to guarantee a legal right to our own cognitive liberty, which is a right to mental self-determination, and the freedom to control our own mental state and protect freedom of thought, as arguably already anticipated by some foundational human rights instruments, digital intelligence might also help to raise our emotional intelligence[57] and connect us with others in ways that yield more meaning and purpose. On a basic level, we can use the AI tools we already have, like voice-activated virtual assistants, to lift our eyes away from screens and toward one another, so we spend less time scrolling, tapping, and clicking, and more time looking up and at one another. We would then become more likely to make emotionally intelligent decisions[58] with more confidence about the kinds of societies and communities we want to be a part of.

AI is moving us toward a place where certain kinds of work will no longer be done by humans. This is not new, but the scale and pace of change is. Many jobs now done electronically and mechanically were once done by humans, from spacecraft trajectory calculators, to elevator operators, to bowling alley pinsetters. While the possibility of ceding more of our work to machines is frightening, this shift is something that we as individuals and as a society can embrace, as long as we have prepared ourselves for the change. I contend that we can, in fact, have fuller—though very different—lives once AI takes over some of our work.

Since the Industrial Revolution, we have had a torrent of ever-increasing automation that is likely to increase exponentially. We discussed the prospective negative consequences extensively in the prior chapter and will delve more deeply into automation in the next. There is no turning this train around. It is going to change the very nature of work and employment, which has always been distributed unequally, keeping many in a cycle of destitution and stunting entrepreneurship, creativity, and the ability of many to benefit from innovation. But the disruption of traditional work and career paths also creates great opportunity. The development of AI applications, businesses, and investment is set to generate unprecedented amounts of new capital, for example, increasing the UK economy alone by a projected $837 billion by 2035.[59] The creation of this vast new wealth may give us a chance to finally engineer fairness into the fabric of our societies.

All of this is possible, while increasing the supply and demand for human creativity and ideas. AI is coming for our jobs and our markets regardless, and can help to economically empower many, uplifting people out of dire economic circumstances and reshaping our approach to governmental spending, igniting entrepreneurial spirit in the process. As we confront the reality that some large percentage of our jobs will become automated and reassigned to AI in the coming years, we will need to reengineer our long-standing economic and political institutions and consider revolutionary societal restructuring. I will propose some achievable ideas in the next chapter.

According to the leading theories on human ambition and actualization, all humans have innate and universal desires that they have to satisfy in order to flourish.[60] We need competence, autonomy, and psychological relatedness, which is inclusion and connection to others.[61] When machines begin to take on a large percentage of labor, we can rewrite the script, focusing on what we can contribute in a new world, as we usher in a new partnership with our machines—one that will allow us to spend our lives in ways that give us autonomy, agency, and purpose.

HUMANITARIAN AND BENEVOLENT AI

Should we find the creativity and the will to leverage our smart technology to provide broad access for literary and civic engagement, it can help us to equalize our societies like never before. Along with this will come a surge of human brilliance that has been hidden beneath layers of inequality and other societal obstacles. We are already seeing some imaginative programs. Avantgarde Analytics uses machine learning to connect citizens with the causes they care about, helping build social movements and relationships between lawmakers and the public.[62] Factmata, another AI start-up, is helping to empower people to check facts through natural language processing that aims to reduce the virulent spread of online misinformation.[63] Innovative initiatives like Microsoft's AI for Earth are using AI technology to process information on a less prejudicial basis, reducing the groupthink that is endemic to strife and conflict, and working on projects that promote sustainability and help solve our most dire global environmental challenges.[64] These can serve as models for corporate social responsibility, future development, and impact investment.

Intelligent technology is also incredibly promising for humanitarian use. The same drone technology used by the military can also deliver blood, food, and medicine to remote areas that normally have little access to life-saving care. In December 2018, one-month-old Joy Nowai became the first baby to receive a drone-delivered vaccine on a remote island of Vanuatu.[65] In places with hard-to-reach segments and poor road conditions, drones can provide new solutions, just as cell phones did.[66] Drones are in flight in Rwanda, where the world's first commercial drone delivery service is sending blood to almost half the country's transfusion centers.[67] Plans are in place to expand operations throughout the subcontinent, as well as in Latin America and the United States.[68] In Malawi, drones have been used to transfer HIV tests from remote parts of the country.[69] Google can predict floods and analyze satellite data after natural disasters, and NASA satellites can detect fires from space. There exist 690 million registered mobile money accounts,[70] whereby technology serves as some people's only banking option. Microsoft is devoting $40 million to AI humanitarian efforts,[71] and Silicon Valley is partnering with the World Bank to fight famine.[72]

Machine learning and satellite imagery are combining to help predict poverty, and crop yield analysis can help provide food security.[73] AI is helping to combat slavery through such projects as the Slavery from Space initiative, training AI to look for telltale signs of slavery such as brick kilns in South Asia, where laborers are often trapped in servitude.[74]

AI may also help end the prison system as we know it. The Technological Incarceration Project is experimenting with using machine learning algorithms and sensors to test home detention, making incarceration more humane and moving it away from the biased, discriminatory, and inhumane treatment that focuses on confinement, and toward the Scandinavian model of rehabilitation in the prison system.[75] AI is helping to preserve our environments and save wildlife. AI can be integrated with smart grids to monitor energy usage in

communities to control emissions and waste. AI can help track migration patterns and investigate illegal wildlife trafficking, tasks essential
for protecting species and ecosystems. As the elephant populations of
Malawi, South Africa, and Zimbabwe dwindle rapidly, drones in these
regions are patrolling the skies to fight against poachers.[76] Intelligent
tech also is being used to support biodiversity, rewilding, and forest
preservation.[77] Technology can give voice to all the wild creatures we
share our home with, and various developing applications hold great
promise for environmental initiatives to save our oceans and seas,
mountains and plains.

South Africa created some of the first drone legislation in 2015.[78]
ATLAN Space, a Morocco-based start-up, has developed tools to
monitor illegal fishing and oil spills.[79] Despite poor landline connections, a mobile revolution in sub-Saharan Africa has come from the
use of smartphones to do everything from coordinating drone deliver-
ies, to providing and dispatching medical care, to initiating and tracking cash transfers using services like GiveDirectly.[80]

Mobile phone usage is growing rapidly in emerging markets, but
a systematic lack of funds means that many users use prepaid phone
cards, so data about these users is often empty of key demographic
information.[81] To solve this problem, a team from Imperial College
London came up with an algorithm to analyze the phone data in order to identify the gender of the user.[82] This data could then be used
during natural disasters, like earthquakes, to more effectively track
populations and target aid to those who need it most. If the most vulnerable communities can be found quickly, they can be helped first,
expediting the triage of care and assistance in chaotic times of humanitarian crisis and natural disasters. Imagine if these tools had been
available to find and track survivors during Hurricane Katrina or the
avalanches in Nepal.

Just as HTML, Java, and Flash made computers more versatile, so too will creative AI tools help us become more nimble. AI can also help us provide visibility and dignity to those with impairments of all kinds, giving them aid, an avenue toward activism, and a platform to share their stories. AI can give voice to the voiceless and amplify the messages of those fighting for others. It can provide agency, access, and opportunity for those with disadvantages, for those searching for a way out of poverty and hardship and into a better life. AI can even help us uncover more of the arcana of dark matter, the very particles that make up who we are as a universe.[83]

> As more and more artificial intelligence is entering into the world, more and more emotional intelligence must enter into leadership.
>
> —AMIT RAY

If we optimistically build intelligent machines infused with our highest aspirations, what kind of propitious societal betterment might we expect? The Intelligent Machine Age will give us an opportunity to transform society and design a fairer and more equitable future, not just for a select few, but for all of us—our planet and all the creatures who inhabit it, and the generations that will follow. We could feed the world,[84] predict the next refugee crisis,[85] go green,[86] decode ISIS radicalization,[87] make trials more fair,[88] and even reify a Keynesian transfer of wealth.[89] Working with AI, we could empower ourselves to construct new societal systems, from political, educational, and economic institutions to jobs and infrastructure, that address injustices in ways that humans have not been able to, or have failed to do thus far.

   If we accept the science and technology, and learn to trust our intelligent machines—machines coded to apply fairness to all living creatures—and if we allow those machines to help equitably run our institutions, humans may be able to get past entrenched tribal and partisan divides and work together for the common good. AI could help us transform our value system, liberating us to prioritize freedom, equity, well-being, and bliss, which in turn would support big ideas in humanitarian aid, economic empowerment, and the arts. Ideally, our benevolent and brilliant machines could help us eradicate poverty and unemployment and diminish disease, violence, and the deeply rooted injustices in our human-made and very flawed systems that already affect billions each day. They could also give rise to new, creative, and purposeful career options.[90]

Intelligent technology can magnify the deepest divides and inequalities humans have ever known, or it can level the playing field. Presently, we still have a say in which way this goes, if we can muster the political will, repurpose and rededicate corporate and government institutions, dilute the power of the elite, and empower our collective chorus of voices. For our potent technology to produce inclusive and accessible outcomes, access to information needs to be democratized through promoting transparency and access. If this happens, we will be able to proactively use our own data, histories, and the other extraordinary tools humans have invented for good.

Living in a stable and noble world will become increasingly essential because we are likely to have the opportunity to significantly enhance our intellectual and physical capabilities and extend our time in it, perhaps even infinitely. AI is not only poised to improve our quality of life and how long we live; it may also become an accurate predictor of when we will die.[91] Some say it might even hold the key to postponing death indefinitely.[92] AI will be able to forecast how each of us will age, and to tailor-make drugs to enrich this process.[93] It may allow for our digital footprint, and perhaps the human mind, to be copied and migrated as an "augmented eternity."[94]

These promised ideals are going to require a global effort. At the heart of it all, intelligent machines can help address the inequities in life. We need to resist the capitalistic impulse to try to maximize gains without paying attention to the negative consequences to society. In doing so, we can help shift our policy-makers from arguing over partisan issues to promoting our collective well-being. In the Intelligent Machine Age, free of mundane tasks; with fewer barriers to success for the disadvantaged, and less incentive for excessive personal gain; with more time, dedication, and purpose; in partnership with extraordinarily smart AI, we can choose to improve not just our own lives but the lives of many. We can choose utopia.

The hope of AI is real and exhilarating, and it will forever alter life as we know it. All of these wondrous innovations, however, are just an early glimpse of its transcendent promise. We can only realize its vast potential if the technology can also help us transform our economics and politics.

THE ECONOMICS AND THE POLITICS

Redrawing the Societal Road Map

Small acts, when multiplied by millions of people, can transform the world.

—HOWARD ZINN

Imagine, in the not too distant future, that income inequality and poverty in the United States continue to increase to even more staggering levels. Affordable housing becomes less and less available, seniors facing retirement crises declare bankruptcy in astounding numbers,[1] automation eliminates more and more jobs, and wages stagnate. Closed borders and trade wars leave agricultural fields barren, which in turn causes food inflation. Teachers remain overworked and underpaid. The student loan bubble bursts and healthcare costs

approaching 30 percent of GDP[2] immobilize the nation. The infrastructure continues to crumble while our elected policy-makers remain incapable (or unwilling) to act in the collective interest. Finally,
the 99 percent revolt.

Armed with smart technological tools and precise algorithmic
economic models created by an inclusive cohort of diverse voices, real-
time fact-checking software, voting avatars, and reforms that encourage citizen participation, progressive candidates—a majority of them
women and others from historically underrepresented groups—persist
in sweeping into local, state, and federal offices. In defiance of the
country's corporate overlords, they introduce inventive, bold, and dynamic policies, based not on outdated economic models and growth
goals but rather on strategies designed to enable all members of society
to thrive, including new civil and human rights legislation unlike any
experienced since the mid-1960s.[3] The algorithmic models demonstrate conclusively that universal healthcare actually saves money[4]
for families and businesses alike. A green jobs act not only produces
high-paying employment, but it also repairs roads, bridges, and dams
while slashing carbon emissions. Advanced data analysis proves that
providing each citizen with a Universal Basic Income is not only affordable, substantially reducing existing bloated poverty programs
and subsidy costs, but it also stimulates the populace to achieve new
levels of creativity, freedom, imagination, and enlightenment.[5]

A pipe dream? Delusional? Maybe not.

As we embark on humanity's next evolutionary phase, we need to
take a good look at the economics and the politics that we have created
for our societies and communities, and at how technology is going to
change the landscape significantly. Digital intelligence is positioned
to continue to dramatically impact our behaviors as well as alter the
rules of economics and politics and, I hope, foster realization of our
need for new perspectives on everything from education and employ-

ment to moral agency and capitalism. Yet our systems, economies, governments, and institutions are not currently prepared to manage a paradigm-shifting technological advance.

The Industrial Revolution of the eighteenth and nineteenth centuries profoundly transformed societies, forcing them to restructure economics and politics around new technologies and modes of production. This shift toward the industrialization of our work took an enormous toll on all living things. The Industrial Revolution is known to have engendered economic growth and technological advancement, but many thinkers argue that it wasn't, on balance, a beneficial experience for humanity. Inhumane working conditions, pollution, inequality, and environmental degradation came along with the surge in economic growth and material goods, creating a large new working class in search of meaning and purpose.[6]

This was not the first time in human history that a technological surge forward was ultimately revealed to have mixed results. Historians Yuval Noah Harari and Jared Diamond are two of many who believe that the Agricultural Revolution was, in retrospect, "history's biggest fraud,"[7] domesticating and constraining us more than it freed us. Scholar, teacher, and activist Silvia Federici has pointed to the exploitation of workers, and women in particular, as going hand in hand with capitalist growth.[8] Harari has also posited that just as the Industrial Revolution manifested a working class, the AI revolution will manifest a useless one.[9] As disruptive as the Agricultural and Industrial Revolutions were to society, they may pale in comparison to the massive impact that emerging intelligent technologies are poised to unleash in what some are calling the Fourth Industrial Revolution, or the Second Machine Age.[10]

How will AI, economics, and politics intersect? Will we institute informed and wise policy changes sufficiently in advance of new AI technologies? Or will these advances overtake our ability for well-timed adaptation, as AI itself shapes our economies and our politics in ways we cannot predict and that may not be in our best interests? If we are liberated from work, can we thrive in a post-capitalist society? Can incorporating new economic and political models protect our own species and, potentially, new hybrid and machine species as well?

AUTOMATION AND WEALTH DISPARITY

> The gross national product . . . does not include the beauty of our poetry or . . . the intelligence of our public debate . . . It measures neither our wit nor our courage, neither our wisdom nor our learning, neither our compassion nor our devotion . . . It measures everything, in short, except that which makes life worthwhile.
>
> —ROBERT F. KENNEDY

While divergent views exist on exactly when and how developing AI technologies will impact both commerce and the workforce, we do know that they will disrupt work and employment in far-reaching ways. Automation, computerization, and AI will be the biggest disruptors in the history of our labor economies, eclipsing the colossal societal shifts of the Industrial Revolution in a fraction of the time.

Until recently, mechanization due to robotics and machinery has mostly been limited to taking over repetitive tasks, particularly within manual labor jobs.[11] This has already had major consequences for workers worldwide. According to a 2017 McKinsey Global Institute report, "even if there is enough work to ensure full employment by 2030, major transitions lie ahead that could match or even exceed the scale of historical shifts out of agriculture and manufacturing. Forecasts suggest that by 2030, 75 million to 375 million workers

(3–14 percent of the global workforce) will need to switch occupational categories."[12]

But very soon, so-called "knowledge workers" in fields ranging from healthcare to law to insurance and financial services, those who provide non-routine, skilled, and cognitive labor, are also going to have their work permanently disrupted. Predictions of net job loss by 2030 due to automation range between 30 and 50 percent.[13] We have to prepare for this economic hurricane. In optimistic scenarios, intelligent machine industrialization could redefine our relationships to our jobs and help usher in a new era of prosperity and personal expansion for humans, permitting us to work less and enjoy life more. The pessimistic scenario is that automation could cause mass unemployment and destitution.

Automation, initially, is likely to affect discrete activities within jobs, as opposed to replacing whole occupations, perhaps as much as 47 percent by some estimates.[14] Gradually, however, many jobs in their entirety may fall within the competence of AI, and it will become less expensive and more convenient to use and retrain machines rather than employ human labor for many types of work. Two Oxford researchers believe that 45 percent of total U.S. employment is at risk from computerization.[15] An ABI Research report has predicted that one million businesses will have AI technology by 2022.[16] An Oxford–Yale survey of AI experts is forecasting that AI will pass human performance in translating languages by 2024, writing high school essays by 2027, working in retail by 2031, and writing bestselling books by 2049.[17]

AI works at higher speed and quality, with greater efficiency, and at a much lower cost than humans. AI can be updated and renewed easily.[18] Moreover, AI makes decisions devoid of impulse and emotion.

We are woefully unprepared for the coming automation tsunami. One reason is that our current thinking about the economy and employment is outdated. It has been outpaced by our technological achievements and by what we understand about human behavior. Establishing new concepts of work for a new era is exigent. The old models are not sufficient to prevent human workers from becoming obsolete.

In their 2015 book *Inventing the Future*, Nick Srnicek and Alex Williams argue that we have to eclipse neoliberalism to have any chance of the "radical transformation" required to achieve full automation, reduced work weeks, a redistribution of wealth, and guaranteed, generous incomes for us all.[19] Ian Laurie in the *Los Angeles Review of Books* called their utopian ideas "algorithmic communism."[20] But however one views the political path, the only hope we have of approaching unity will be the ability to foresee the future in ways only made possible with the aid of our intelligent machines. AI has the capacity to crunch the enormous amount of data and factor the many variables we need to consider to weigh the best and fairest societal strategies.

Another sizable obstacle to our readiness for workforce replacement by AI is our tendency to overestimate our ability to deal with change.[21] We will do just about anything to avoid what we are afraid of. These characteristics are painfully illustrated by humans' present inability to forge the necessary collective urgency to address the impending catastrophe caused by poisoning our natural environment.[22] In the contexts of both drastic climate change and the AI revolution, we have no choice but to find the will to reimagine our relationships with our work, ourselves, our corporate and political institutions, and our economies in order to survive and to thrive.

We will need to learn how to work in partnership with smart machines and to reconfigure how we work with one another as well. Imagine whole new occupations, such as empathy trainers to teach compassion to AI, forensic analysts to figure out how to hold algorithms responsible for their results, VR designers to reimagine workplaces, digital ethicists and compliance consultants to identify ways to undo discrimination and bias, and machine-relations experts to promote algorithms that make the world a better place.[23]

The greatest threat of smart machine automation is that it may lead to mass impoverishment and disenfranchisement of workers, since many of the robots currently being designed are built to permanently replace workers, and more and more sophisticated "thinking" machines are devouring tasks traditionally performed by humans.[24] For the first time, technological innovation is creating economic growth without adding more jobs and more income, and economic inequality is rising.[25]

> Wealth disparity is the single most threatening social problem we face as a country.
>
> —PAUL TUDOR JONES

The trend toward wealth disparity is accelerating in many parts of the world.[26] Being more cognizant about the connections and differences between inequality and unfairness[27] will lead us to a better understanding of what our true objectives should be, as we are far from unanimity on *what*, or even *if*, wealth distribution methods are best for society, let alone *how* to achieve them. Should they be based on justice? Fair distribution and equal opportunities? Equity? Or something else? For example, seminal feminist economists like Marianne Ferber and Julie A. Nelson, who write on the unpaid and underpaid work of marginalized communities, make a case for gender equality as one solution for a robust economy,[28] while philosopher Harry Frankfurt argues that we should focus on eliminating poverty, not economic inequality.[29]

The engine of capitalism is greed, engendering corruption and inequality. In an equitable world, there would be neither abject poverty nor acute affluence. Absent substantive civic effort and restructuring, the wealth generated by automation and new smart tech will accrue even more dramatically in the hands of the elite few, creating virtual monopolies over every aspect of economic life. We know that the concentration of wealth and power without formidable checks and balances leads to discrimination, bias, exclusion, and authoritarianism. If all the benefits of automation inure solely to small groups of nations, businesses, and individuals, the inequities in our systems will deepen.

Mass wealth inequality already exists. A grand total of twenty-six people have more wealth than the poorest half of the globe's population, some 3.6 billion people, and the worth of more than 2,200 billionaires around the world increased by 12 percent in 2018—$2.5 billion a day—while the less monied bottom half fell by 11 percent.[30] In the United States, the 400 most affluent people have more net worth than that held by the lowest 60 percent of Americans (150 million people).[31] Although it is less pronounced in the large, liberal European economies, inequality is also growing in those nations.[32] Only a revolution of ideas, titanic political will, fortitude promulgated by an informed and activated citizenship, and a willingness to rethink models can reverse the trend.

GROWING AND THRIVING

For over seventy years economics has been fixated on GDP, or national output, as its primary measure of progress. That fixation has been used to justify extreme inequalities of income and wealth coupled with unprecedented destruction of the living world. For the twenty-first century a far bigger goal is needed: meeting the human rights of every person within the means of our life-giving planet.

—KATE RAWORTH

The economic model that is most often used in the West today is not the only option. Neoclassical economics[33] is just one way to think about economic systems, albeit the one that is almost always called economic reality in the mainstream discourse, especially in the West. As critics of dominant neoclassical theories have argued, however, we are not strictly rational creatures who always make sound, logical choices when left to our own devices in an open market. In fact, humans often base our decisions on highly emotional and often irrational factors, quite unaware that we are doing so.

According to Daniel Kahneman in *Thinking, Fast and Slow,* an "emotional attitude toward such things as irradiated food, red meat, nuclear power, tattoos, or motorcycles drives your beliefs about their benefits and their risks. If you dislike any of these things, you probably believe its risks are high and its benefits negligible."[34] The same can be applied to our monetary decisions. At its most basic level, economics is the study of human behavior. A deeper understanding of who we are as a diverse civilization is an essential part of moving forward in the coming Intelligent Machine Era.

Economist Kate Raworth is one of a number of current, innovative thinkers doing just this. Raworth introduced the concept of "Doughnut Economics," using a visual model to propose an original way to address twenty-first-century economic challenges. Her hypothesis emphasizes the need for a balance between humans flourishing on a sustainable and healthy planet, and the measurement of success simply by the degree to which economies grow—the accepted, traditional capitalist blueprint for some time.[35] Nobel laureate Amartya

Sen, among others, has also advocated for this type of change in perspective, envisioning an economic model that "advances the richness of human life, rather than the richness of the economy."[36]

Virtually all major economies today—and the policy-makers supporting them—are focused on growth, basically to the exclusion of any other metric. Those who argue for more attention to the wellbeing of our world and ourselves (at least, those of us who are not the policy-makers themselves) are mostly dismissed. These non-pecuniary ambitions have been considered secondary to achieving greater GDP. Our economic systems and human aspirations are far more complex and intertwined, and are not adequately addressed or acknowledged by historical, oversimplified economic models.

There are a few economies beginning to consider and implement newer, more holistic paths. Bhutan, for one, has a Gross National Happiness measurement.[37] The intricacies of the Automation Age demand this kind of nonconventional thinking to help us identify more comprehensive and better metrics. Our intelligent, mechanized partners can assist in computing and calculating the variables to factor meaning and purpose into the equation—we just need to direct them to do so.

Raworth, along with others (including myself), strongly believes a singular focus on growth does not serve the majority of people well, let alone the rest of the living beings and wildlife with whom we share our planet. If greater reliance on artificially smart agents results in a deepening of these existing economic divides and an exacerbation of the kinds of exploitation our economies currently generate, many of our contemporary societal ills will become more entrenched. We must challenge the basic precepts of capitalism and more appropriately assess and account for members of our society who are afforded little "economic value" in conventional measurements. As Raworth astutely points out, Adam Smith waxed lyrical about the invisible hand,[38] the so-called "natural force" economists have long relied upon to regulate economies and to justify the social benefits we get from our self-interested actions, while never mentioning his mother, with whom he lived, who cared for him while he wrote his treatise, and for whom he can thank for his own personal thriving.[39] The long-held economic tenet that growth is what matters most is outdated, and it's crucial to factor in a more complete complement of human, societal, and environmental components into the calculation. The fervent pursuit of GDP and trickle-down economics, along with the cultural deification of billionaires, is incompatible with a fair society.

The evolving technological applications and impending Age of Automation give us the best opportunity to make this shift. Change is coming whether we like it or not, and Raworth's thesis uses a doughnut shape to illustrate the harmony between human flourishing and sustaining the resources of our planet, with our social foundation at the inner ring and the ecological ceiling at the outer ring.[40] Models such as these can provide the direction we need to redraw the social contract we have with one another and the world around us, and help us to see how connected we are to one another.

None of us is an island, yet we have been disparagingly described in economic terms as "self-contained globules of desire."[41] Will we have the courage to update our economic models and ways of thinking about them? To live within the bounds of what our planet can tolerate before it ceases to sustain any of us? Will we allow our thinking machines to partner with us in visualizing a brighter future? Or will we stay within the box, using antiquated economic systems that bring us ever closer to an Atwoodian implosion?

Current widely supported economic principles are based on an outdated understanding of how we make decisions, failing to fully account for our behavioral glitches and the capacity of the earth to sustain our lives for much longer. As Raworth explains, "the dominant model—'rational economic man,' self-interested, isolated, calculating—says more about the nature of economists than it does about other humans. The loss of an explicit objective allowed the discipline to be captured by a proxy goal: endless growth."[42] If we can move away from the reign of *Homo economicus*[43] and tribal, isolated communities into a united, global future, we have our best chance to find the answers. We don't have them yet. We will probably never have them all, but we will only trust in something that we all build together. Let's all have a say. Us and our brilliant digital creations.

CURIOUS AND CREATIVE

Curiosity is the engine of achievement.

—SIR KEN ROBINSON

What might our new, idealistic, post-automation world look like? With wealth and resources distributed more equitably, and with machines assuming much of the work, humans will be defined less by what we do, and more by who we are. When we have fewer banal tasks to do, and thus more time, we can choose to improve not just our own lives, but the lives of many. We can reimagine our relationship with work and labor and tap into our innate sagacity. AI can lead us to the next step in the Cognitive Revolution. To do this, we have to become more curious and creative.

Albert Einstein himself understood that just having knowledge isn't enough; it's our imaginations that bring us to new heights, that open our eyes to what isn't here yet, but will be. An elite education and exceptional logical reasoning were not enough to conceptualize a universe where time and space, rather than being distinct, were in fact intrinsically related.[44] Curiosity was the essential ingredient that would lead Einstein to discover his theory of relativity.

To survive the next era of technological disruption, as individuals and as a society, it will be imperative that we get more imaginative and have what David Whyte calls "courageous conversations":[45] deeper conversations where you may lose direction but perhaps find something more valuable in the process. Leadership is begotten by the power to ask "beautiful questions"[46] that shift our perspective, spark inner expansion, and reveal new possibilities. If we can regain and always keep a childlike sense of wonder and curiosity, continue to evolve and learn throughout our lives, and open ourselves up to a broader understanding of what it means to make progress, we can rise. We can move forward with eager interest, a beginner's mind (what Buddhists call shoshin), and a pure joy for learning as opposed to just a transactional mindset. Let's allow the robots to help us handle the day-to-day so we can imagine, explore, and discover.

Creativity is an essential ingredient of being human. It will be our most important asset in the new economic arena. If we prepare for it, our intelligent machines can help us complete mundane projects, integrate team workflows, and free up our precious time. Smart tech can help unburden our mental lives, giving our imaginations room to roam and granting us more time to connect with people in our material reality. Without the strain of repetitive, unfulfilling work, we can become creative explorers and curious adventurers. We can also reconfigure educational systems, approaches, and objectives, which were created to meet the needs of industrialization (or of the elites), to in turn meet the needs of a new day.[47]

It is estimated that the human brain has 2.5 petabytes of memory[48] (one petabyte is roughly 13.3 years of HDTV video)—imagine what we could achieve if we were working with a more robust search engine! Partnering with AI can open up more space for us to dream, to invent, to create, and to innovate; to make the big, necessary transition to new economic and political models.

But to do this, we have much work to do in the political sphere.

NAVIGATING THE POLITICS

> Human beings have a strong dramatic instinct toward binary thinking, a basic urge to divide things into two distinct groups, with nothing but an empty gap in between. We love to dichotomize. Good versus bad. Heroes versus villains. My country versus the rest. Dividing the world into two distinct sides is simple and intuitive, and also dramatic because it implies conflict, and we do it without thinking, all the time.
>
> —HANS ROSLING

Emerging smart technologies will continue to have significant influence on politics. Technology can help facilitate authoritarian regimes that control, manipulate, and suppress their populaces. Or it can allow for more true, dynamic liberal democracies designed to benefit the common good and protect and empower the most disenfranchised among us. The future is not yet written.

Governments and nation-states are grappling with how to assimilate intelligent tech and the widespread influence of social media platforms. Progressive Western democracies such as Australia, host to the 2018 Australasian Joint Conference on Artificial Intelligence, and the European Union, the members of which signed a Declaration of Cooperation on Artificial Intelligence in 2018 to ensure a collective approach to AI-related questions involving social, economic, ethical, and legal issues,[49] are being proactive in studying the potential impact of AI. Meanwhile, other more autocratic-leaning states, China and Russia most explicitly,[50] have identified the development of intelligent technology as central to their political strategies and have indicated their intentions to seek AI supremacy. The United States, particularly DARPA, has some modest initiatives, but the Pentagon only announced an initial strategy on cyberwarfare in the summer of 2018[51] and, in general, lags behind Europe, China, and Russia in prioritizing and escalating the AI discussion.[52] The dialogue must not only be prioritized; it must be broadened beyond immediate technological fears. We need to peer into a proverbial "silicon ball" and consider how significantly our smart technology is going to impact our lives, and how it can best be deployed to become beneficial and equitable.

Media platforms are wielding more and more political clout. This was demonstrated in the 2016 U.S. presidential election, when Russian hackers influenced, if not decided, its outcome.[53] Facebook and Twitter are now essential communication and fundraising tools for most politicians. Author Jamie Susskind, in his book *Future Politics*, is concerned with the immense power and "digital paternalism" that private technology corporations are exerting over politics. He believes that we can never be just objective consumers of technology, because "the digital is political."[54] It was not that long ago that traditional media, primarily newspapers, radio, and television (together, the "Fourth Estate")[55] had a more pronounced and visible role as neutral arbiters of the news. They served as outside observers, keeping abuses of power and failings of the government and elected officials in check and in the public eye.

The lines began to blur, even in nations perceived as open and free democracies, as alternate platforms proliferated and media started to revert to partisanship. As opinion-over-news succeeded as a business strategy, for-profit "news" purveyors took root in many outlets, and the term "confirmation bias" came into the lexicon.[56]

"Misinformation" was a word of the year in 2018. The swift ascendancy of social media platforms and their accompanying bots has now given instant communication access to professional and non-professional politicians, advocacy groups, and others alike. By amplifying the loudest voices, social media has cemented tribal divides and entrenched support for regressive beliefs, even if these beliefs defy logic, science, and empirical evidence. This has made for some strange bedfellows, and times of stress stoke fears and push extremes. As UC Berkeley professor George Lakoff explains, we cannot rely on "enlightened reason" to form a consensus if different world views are stridently reinforced. If we become defeated by opinions, we might end up not sharing reality.[57]

The dynamic is easily observed in the United States with a two-party, winner-take-all democratic system. Although radical nationalistic movements exist in Europe and elsewhere, parliamentary democracies, with multiple parties and short campaign periods not influenced by massive election donations from self-interested advocates, generally default to more nuanced positions and candidates' views, and in turn create the compromises, checks, and consensus required to govern and remain in government. (But not always—think 2018 Hungary,[58] Brazil, the Philippines, and Poland).

Casual outside scrutiny might suggest that the United States is a country that has it all. It has enormous wealth, approaching $60,000 per capita income.[59] It has extraordinary diversity and freedoms; it is a true world leader in numerous ways. However, it also has an incredibly expensive healthcare system, 56,000 structurally deficient bridges and 15,500 structurally deficient dams,[60] a high infant mortality rate, incredibly high incarceration and capital punishment rates (the United States is the seventh largest executioner worldwide),[61] epidemics of obesity and opioid addiction, exponentially higher gun violence and school shootings than most other countries, a population of 554,000 homeless people,[62] and rising inequality, plus deeply rooted sexism and racism. Despite the continuing belief many people have in the American Dream, it should come as no surprise that the United States also does not rank very high on the "Happiness Index."[63]

While other nations have successfully legislated policies and solutions for problems similar to the United States', which would seem obvious to model or replicate, U.S. federal lawmakers consistently reject or even fail to consider empirically supported progressive ideas. Why? Primarily, the two-party system and an ingrained fealty to businesses and corporations that take unfair political advantage of afforded rights of personhood and are given the opportunity to wield vast, inequitable financial resources as political speech, almost without limit. Recent examples of legislation awarding $1.5 trillion in corporate tax cuts[64] and numerous reduced regulations, absent a majority of public support, are testament to the power of the corporation in the United States. Focusing principally on economic growth does not produce well-being for a nation's people. Even the methodologies of providing truthful information are under attack from both external and internal forces hacking our systems, disseminating media forgeries, and using proliferating AI tools to confuse us and fan the flames of discord.

The challenges that emerging technologies present will both impact and be impacted by politics. Unfortunately for its citizens, the United States is not likely to be a leader in creating and legislating reforms, policy, or treaties in this respect. These will most likely be shouldered by the European Commission, which is currently more focused on the subject of how to regulate AI and technological acceleration.[65] Leaders such as EU Competition Commissioner Margrethe Vestager are not afraid to take on such gigantic U.S. corporations as "the Big A's" (Alphabet, Apple, and Amazon).[66] Regulation is a necessary instrument in navigating the stormy technological seas in which power and technology coalesce in what could become a toxic anathema to progress. We could instead leverage digital intelligence to help dramatically improve the quality of many people's lives by modestly altering how we measure success for our corporations and business entities, which control the majority of all wealth. Today the business metrics are very simple—growth and profit. Who benefits? Shareholders. Who doesn't? Everyone else.

We can start by encouraging businesses to move beyond quarterly performance, including reforming the quarterly reporting system (which puts pressure on businesses to perform for shareholders every three months, diluting interest in long-term and holistic thinking).[67] Then, we can add measurable metrics for employee benefits, livable wages, and well-being; mix in social and environmental sustainability goals and carbon and automation taxes; and make education funding and science literacy a priority, paying our undervalued teachers as the professionals and foundational members of society that they are. If we can find a way to take these positive steps, our world could be healthier, happier, and more sustainable. Accomplishing this will take something extraordinary, since most major businesses are global, the influence of the richest few is ballooning, and smaller Western liberal democracies no longer have the detached status to be laboratories of civic engagement.

A progressive Scandinavian nation, for example, now has less ability to experiment socially than it used to, since we all surf the same web and worship, in large part, the same corporate gods. In the United States, corporations have the single greatest influence on politics and politicians.[68] Tech giants are increasingly at the very center of this pyramid of influence. Anand Giridharadas, in his book *Winners Take All*, argues that elite philanthropy is hurting us in some ways; such philanthropy provides an improper substitute for political and policy codification and meaningful democracy fueled by all of our voices, and is instead driven by the self-interest of über-wealthy individuals.[69] Real change will happen in the political arena and in the personal sphere when we each sacrifice some of our own privileges for the good of all.

But before we can talk about progressing toward a more benevolent and equitable society, we first have to dream it. We have to see the vision for how it could be better. Our best hope to find both the will and the way lies in our thinking machines.

Our current geopolitics illustrate how deeply entrenched we have become in our tribal affiliations, squeezing our "values" into partisan ideology. Social media, while it could expand our views, often exacerbates this tribalism and confirmation bias online.[70] Autocrats recognize the efficacy of media platforms and AI, and various players are attempting to manipulate data to influence elections and wield unprecedented power. To survive in this next iteration of ourselves alongside our synthetically intelligent creations, we need to combat groupthink with our collective intelligence, mandating implementation of empathy-based strategies for our common benefit. Otherwise we will drown in a cabal of manipulated corporate, governmental, and capitalistic dominion.

Intelligent technology can help us overcome many cultural and societal obstacles. If we build them correctly, artificially intelligent machines can become mediators and arbiters, providing communal guidance we can rely upon to be impartial. A group of politically neutral programmers have formed a coalition to build a "truth machine."[71] Thirty of the biggest and most influential tech companies (not including the Big A's) have authored the Digital Geneva Accord, subscribing to a set of principles that commits them to not assist any governments to mount cyberattacks against "innocent civilians or enterprises, from anywhere."[72] If—and these are significant "ifs"—we can regulate for algorithmic transparency and infuse explainability into our technology,[73] and if we can code our intelligent creations to be aware of our beliefs and desires, we have a path forward. This awareness is known as the "theory of mind," the ability of one mind to know what's in another's.[74] If we can do this, we may be able to reconcile our divides, building and trusting our machines to be more fair and seeing more clearly the areas of compromise that profit more than just the few.

It can work. One small example is Smart Tech Challenges Foundation, which is using programs to find a common area where gun control and gun rights advocates can come together.[75] If we can manage to do that, especially in the United States, we can accomplish many things together. International partnerships, such as AI teams from China and the United States working together, can also bridge divides and create models for global cooperation and shared responsibility.

But what can we expect from that friend, neighbor, or relative with entrenched partisan views who seems impervious to change? What if they could step directly into the shoes of a person they held in high regard to find out how they might decide an important issue? Hossein Rahnama and other researchers at the MIT Media Lab are working on a project utilizing a "distributed machine intelligence network" to capture a person's "digital representation" by an "ontological mapping of an individual through her digital interactions."[76] This has numerous applications, but essentially would allow people to monetize themselves digitally, allowing others to "borrow" their identity. Taking this a step further, it would be possible at some point to access a "borrowable identity," even someone from the past, and present it with a scenario requiring them to render a decision or a solution. A true digital "what would Jesus do?" or an opportunity to confirm how Abraham Lincoln might advise in accord with a government "of," "by," and "for" the people might get a lot of us on board.

Forging progressively forward, using our amazing adaptive strengths, is imperative, whether via virtual and augmented reality experiences, trusted digital avatars, or simply a spontaneous burst of worldwide political and economic unity, transcending bias and pro-moting the common good. If we fail to address the inherent unfairness in our systems and institutions, and if we fail to prioritize the health of our planet and all the creatures we share it with, we are doomed. We all die. We might already be too far along that road; there are thinkers who believe it's too late and the damage is irreversibly done, that our home will reach a breaking point some traditional economists thought would never come. Critically, it's people who think "we're fucked,"[77] like Roy Scranton, a writer who served in the U.S. Army, who can see a dim light in the darkness, too, and who are trying to give us clues to lead the way home to a better future.

> The sooner we confront our situation and realize that there is nothing we can do to save ourselves, the sooner we can get down to the difficult task of adapting, with mortal humanity, to our new reality . . . humanity can survive if we accept human limits and transience as fundamental truths, and work to nurture the variety and richness of our collective cultural heritage.
>
> —ROY SCRANTON

REDRAWING THE SOCIETAL ROAD MAP

One big idea that holds promise for confronting economic inequality, and checks many of the vital boxes we need for the coming smart-machine era, is commonly referred to as a Universal Basic Income (UBI). This concept is already being tested in various forms in Denmark, Finland, Kenya, Canada, and even in a limited fashion in Stockton, California.[78] The Indian state of Sikkim has plans to introduce India's first and the world's largest UBI experiment to date in 2022.[79] In the Age of Automation, where we know many jobs will be lost to AI, the UBI uncouples income from work and will help to level the playing field for the disadvantaged. Increasing automation and decreasing employment create a need for as well as a pathway to a UBI that can provide opportunities in a more egalitarian way, freeing mental bandwidth from the stress of financial insecurity and sparking reserves of imagination and entrepreneurial spirit in the process.

With a UBI, we may have a way to eliminate the need for food stamps, welfare, and other existing social programs, virtually eradicating poverty while adding trillions of dollars to the GDP.[80] Alex Goik points out that "the arguments in favor of UBI are manifold." He shows how a UBI is not much different than the negative income tax scheme proposed by President Richard Nixon many years ago, and that it would reduce bureaucratic hurdles in our current flawed welfare systems. He also makes the argument that a UBI is eminently affordable when we calculate the "net costs."[81]

Just as the AI revolution is poised to redefine the way we look at work and employment, so too must we be open to new ideas that rework archaic systems of compensation. As people are displaced from jobs and lose current forms of economic value, we need to reconfigure political power and who gets to have it. Manual labor and routine tasks have been gradually assumed by machines for years; now, as cognitive labor is poised to go to supersmart machines as well, we need to redefine our sense of meaning and purpose on a far grander scale.

In the United States, such an ambitious "entitlement" program could not succeed nationally in our current political environment. The hope is that future intelligent systems will be able to demonstrate its feasibility and viability and help us use the power of collective action to advance change, so that we will not have to suffer a catastrophic financial or humanitarian crisis to find the political will.

Economist and former Greek Minister of Finance Yanis Varoufakis has suggested a variation on the UBI called Universal Basic Dividend (UBD), which would be financed as a percentage of all companies' profits,[82] affording citizens a right to a portion of the returns on all capital, particularly from profits made by technology companies that receive public funding.[83] Both of these ideas have merit and are worth taking seriously. AI, and the societal changes being brought about via automation, can help move us from a gridlocked political climate to a place where a UBI or UBD could become politically feasible as we begin to more readily trust these machines to do the math for us in an equitable way.

Sophisticated technology can crunch the enormous numbers and data necessary to build the models that may be able to prove irrefutably that programs like UBI can work and be economically fair. More importantly, the numbers produced by actuarial determinations can help persuade the voting public to look beyond self-interest and party affiliation. For something like this to succeed we would, of course, have to endow our intelligent economic programs with more than just numbers—it should reflect our highest values as a human civilization too.

How might a UBI be financed? Bill Gates thinks we should tax robots.[84] James Boyce, a professor at the University of Massachusetts–Amherst, and Peter Barnes of CREDO Mobile believe we could raise the funding with a modest charge for those "who benefit most from our socially built assets,"[85] perhaps generating trillions. They make an argument that would appeal to those across the conservative spectrum as well: that a UBI could replace welfare systems. And "past proponents of the idea include the revolutionary Thomas Paine, civil rights leader Martin Luther King, Jr., free-market economist Milton Friedman and President Richard Nixon."[86] The founder of the Public Banking Institute, Ellen Brown, makes the case that a UBI would drive the economy and pay for itself.[87] With intelligent technologies' inevitable collision with blockchain cryptography, there could be a paradigm-shifting change in our future as to how we perceive the very ideas of money and wealth.

With truthful, verifiable information produced by machines coded to input fairness, made transparently available to all stakeholders, we just might have a shot. Critically, a bold initiative backed up by rigorous AI analysis can open up our thinking about existing programs perceived by many as "handouts" and show us the importance of encouraging entrepreneurialism, cooperation, and creativity, while extinguishing the false belief that people who don't have money are just the ones who don't work hard enough. This is one of the most detrimental, discriminatory, and debilitating myths of our society.

> The dogma that free money is bad solely because poor people have not worked for it is still very much a part of our collective psyche. Holding onto this relic won't do us any good given the kind of societal and technological upheaval we face.
>
> —ALEX GOIK

Studies show that people with a UBI will create gardens out of seeds; as opposed to working less, they work *more* to make dreams come true.[88] Similarly, in regards to the fallacy of laziness, those who most often go bankrupt are people who had a sudden hardship or a stroke of misfortune, such as a medical emergency.[89] Other tested programs, such as the Indian peer-to-peer microlending platform Rang De, reveal that when people get a microloan or modest cash UBI, they often invest it in ways that help their communities flourish.[90]

A BRIEF HISTORY OF UNIVERSAL BASIC INCOME

THE BIRTH OF THE CONCEPT

1516
THOMAS MORE: *UTOPIA*
More argued that every person should receive a guaranteed income as a more effective approach than punishment for the crime of theft.

1526
JOANNES LUDOVICUS VIVES
Vives proposed the idea of minimum income as the state's or the city's welfare responsibilities toward its citizens.

1795
MARQUIS DE CONDORCET: SOCIAL INSURANCE
Condorcet sketched a vision of social insurance and how it could reduce inequality, insecurity, and poverty.

1848
JOHN STUART MILL:
PRINCIPLES OF POLITICAL ECONOMY
Mill proposed that a certain minimum of income be assigned for every member of the community. The remainder is then shared in accordance with labor, capital, and talent.

1960
FRIEDRICH HAYEK:
THE CONSTITUTION OF LIBERTY
Hayek argued for basic income as a condition of individual liberty.

1967
DR. MARTIN LUTHER KING JR.:
WHERE DO WE GO FROM HERE?
King argued that the government needs to do more to lift people out of poverty and proposed that a basic income should be pegged to the median income of the society and increased along with the standard of living.

PAST EXPERIMENTS

1968–1971
RICHARD NIXON:
UNIVERSAL BASIC INCOME EXPERIMENTS
Experiments were conducted in several states and it was found that a UBI has no negative effect on work ethic.

1974–1979
PIERRE TRUDEAU:
THE MINCOME EXPERIMENT
Residents in a small province of Manitoba were given annual basic incomes. For five years, poverty was completely eliminated.

1982–Now
ALASKA'S OIL ROYALTY PROGRAM
A program in which every resident, including children, gets $1,000 or $2,000 a year from the Alaska Permanent Fund.

RECENT EXPERIMENTS

2011–2013
BASIC INCOME PILOTS
AT MADHYA PRADESH, INDIA
Over 6,000 villagers were given a monthly individual, unconditional basic income for eighteen months.

2016–2019
ONTARIO
BASIC INCOME PILOT PROJECT
4,000 Ontarians were selected and provided with annual income with the aim to lift themselves out of poverty.

2016
Y-COMBINATOR'S OAKLAND EXPERIMENT
Y-Combinator, a start-up accelerator, began a short-term study of the effects of basic income in Oakland.

2017–2018
FINLAND'S UNIVERSAL
BASIC INCOME TRIAL
2,000 unemployed people in Finland received an unconditional monthly payment.

THE FUTURE

THE FUTURE
AI-ENABLED
UNIVERSAL BASIC INCOME?

THE AWAKENING

We design our world, while our world acts back on us and designs us.

—ANNE-MARIE WILLIS

In our present political environment, agreeing on what values we need to instill in our tech may be easier than finding agreement on policy. We need to unplug and reset the system.[91] If we infuse equality and fairness into the mechanical DNA of our intelligent machines and allow them to help us address the inequities in our world, we can shift decision-making toward our best collective interest. We can help our policy- and lawmakers transition from debating partisan issues to promoting values, human ideals, and common goals.

Some talented, dedicated, and well-intentioned people are already working on how to achieve this aim; they include the UK Office of the High Commissioner for Human Rights (OHCHR) and Amnesty International. A number of Google employees took initiative in 2018 and petitioned their bosses to cease work on AI drones for the Pentagon. This bit of corporate activism resulted in Google responding with more guidelines.[92] AI researchers at KAIST in South Korea have also threatened a boycott.[93] Technology leaders have signed a pledge not to develop lethal autonomous weapons.[94] The Association for Computing Machinery has proposed that computer science peer review should now consider "all reasonable broader impacts" of a computing concept.[95] Computer science's potential negative effects on society continues to be grappled with.

We know that statistically airplanes are safer than automobiles, yet many of us prefer the road. Studies show that self-driving cars may ultimately be less dangerous than human-driven ones, but the thought of ceding control makes us anxious; we fear the change.[96]

By many metrics, human beings have progressed substantially, but the measurements don't tell the complete story, and the individual human experience has countless variations. The complexity of human perception muddles the process of arriving at universally beneficial criteria for designing protections and moral codes for our synthetic creations. Hans Rosling's research has shown that "there's no room for facts when our minds are occupied by fear."[97]

The tech will sneak up on all of us, because despite the large amount of publicity around AI, only a relatively select few of us on the planet are actively engaged in how it should be built. Why? Aren't life-altering subjects something we are all invested in? Why do we keep our distance? Humans suffer from fatal design flaws: cognitive bias, ideological tendencies, the bystander effect.[98] Will it take some calamitous event to rally us? It may.

In August 2017, I gave a talk on AI and the future of work and purpose at the Plywood Presents conference in Atlanta. Although there was substantial interest in the subject and excitement in discussing the ideas, there was also an eerie sort of detachment and noticeable fear, even a compulsion to look away from the facts, and an urge to only engage with the concepts on superficial levels. We feel confused because we don't understand the technology; we feel seduced by the allure of free platforms, the advertising, and the convenience and glamour of what's new. The rest feels psychologically far away or too overwhelming. We distance ourselves from things that aren't happening directly to us in this moment.

We can find a better way. As Rainer Maria Rilke tells us, live the questions, engage with one another, dive in instead of looking away, and live in the gray area of this life-altering juncture. If we do, we may come to trust our machines, even with our lives. In the proposals being put forward, such as the controlled use of autonomous lethal weapons technology, almost everyone in the ring is focused on maintaining human control of the weapons. I do believe that an international ban, like the one on autonomous weapons proposed by top tech executives,[99] advances the discourse. However, if history has taught us anything, it is that you cannot trust people with weapons, and that once a weapon is created it will be used.

It is time to consider building machines we can truly trust and partner with, perhaps even as equals. What if we managed to build AI that focused on equality and did not identify with any one specific group of people? Can we be brave enough to free it from our own biases in this way? What if together we could construct an intelligence that would counter assaults on truth and reason, help us reshape governments, eliminate partisan entrenchment, and maybe, just maybe, positively impact how we humans treat one another, too?

Some things to think about:

Would a machine instilled with ethics value money over people?

Would a machine with compassion believe the healthy should not have to pay for the sick?

Would a machine with mercy tell us to close our borders?

Would a machine with morality say it's in our best interest to continue to pollute our planet?

Would a machine embedded with kindness and grace decide poverty is due to a lack of character?

Would a machine with empathy choose Christian over Muslim over Jew?

8

SEARCHING FOR THE DIGITAL SOUL

Conscious experience is at once the most familiar thing in the world and the most mysterious. There is nothing we know about more directly than consciousness, but it is far from clear how to reconcile it with everything else we know.

—DAVID CHALMERS

Launched in 1997, the *Cassini* spacecraft embarked on a remarkable voyage of scientific discovery. Teams from twenty-seven nations took part in the project. Taking seven years to travel the two billion miles to reach its destination, *Cassini* is the first and only spacecraft to orbit Saturn. Once it arrived, *Cassini* toured the moons and rings of this previously mysterious celestial body. It collected data, took photographs, and studied the wonders of the giant gas planet, exploring ocean worlds on its moons and probing the mysteries of the cosmos. *Cassini* changed the very nature of how we think about the universe.

This durable craft went dutifully about its business for twenty years, interacting with thousands of scientists and others back on Earth until, finally, its fuel started to run low. In order to prevent it from crashing and contaminating the pristine surfaces of two of Saturn's moons, Titan and Enceladus, the team determined that *Cassini* needed to deliberately hurl itself into Saturn's atmosphere and self-destruct. The many people who had worked on the *Cassini* mission at NASA and elsewhere around the world gathered in vigil to bid goodbye to this noble and loyal machine that had taught us so much about the universe and ourselves.[1] In a grand finale, *Cassini* snapped its "last memento photos" and then steadfastly plunged into Saturn's atmosphere, a final reunion with the planet that had been its sole purpose.

The *Cassini* mission illustrates that we don't have to draw such sharp distinctions between ourselves and what we build. We can loosen our grip on the idea that only humans are worth mourning and celebrating. As our tech becomes more advanced and we work more closely in partnership with our intelligent machines, we can become more comfortable with finding sublimity, beauty, and bravery in all things. If we work together, there is no star we cannot dream of exploring.

One of the most compelling, fascinating, and terrifying questions presented by the prospect of building intelligent machines is, Will it become self-aware? And if so, could it become conscious? Have humanlike thoughts? Will it be my friend? Could it have a soul?

THE UNCANNY VALLEY

It would be ironic if the flaw in strong AI made us more
human rather than less. Yet that could very well turn out
to be what happens.

—DEEPAK CHOPRA

Although it is very difficult today to predict what our technological
future will look like twenty to thirty years from now, it is not hard
to imagine our personal digital assistants like Alexa, Siri, and Google
Home rapidly evolving and becoming much more humanlike as we
continue to anthropomorphize them, developing closer attachments
and deeper relationships. Although people have shown tendencies to
be unsettled by audio, visual, and robot creations that closely resemble humans, a phenomenon known as the Uncanny Valley,[2] we also
experience the AI Effect, dismissing evolving machine intelligence,
failing to accept it as true AI, which makes us feel more comfortable
in embracing the technology since it's not "really" intelligent.

Children born today will grow up with highly developed machines
as companions and protectors, likely forming unique relationships and
bonds with them that are more complex than an affinity for a favorite
doll or toy. How will they relate to intelligent machine companions,
and how might they distinguish the differences between their human
and AI caretakers? A study published in *Science Robotics* demonstrated
that children are very susceptible to peer pressure from social robots.[3]
Will this influence be for the good of our children? How should we
teach our children to relate to AI? As friends? Nannies? Coworkers?

In thinking about how we should aspire to interact with AI, it is
helpful to draw parallels to the ways humans currently relate to animals. One tendency of humans who love and respect animals is to

anthropomorphize them, attributing human characteristics and personality traits to nonhumans, and seeing them in our image. There is no clear consensus within scientific communities about whether it is beneficial to anthropomorphize other creatures, much less artificial creations.[4] Ascribing human differentia to animals, machines, or hurricanes, however, can be a way for us to elevate and justify our moral consideration of nonhuman creatures and things. A 2010 *Psychological Science* report concluded that few of us "have difficulty identifying other humans in a biological sense, but it is more complicated to identify them in a psychological sense."[5] Researchers are looking for morality in animals by observing how animals play; it appears that for all animals, humans included, "the basic rules of the game are: ask first, be honest and follow the rules, and admit when you are wrong."[6] Marc Bekoff, a cognitive ethologist, and Jessica Pierce, a philosopher, in their book *Wild Justice: The Moral Lives of Animals*, have demonstrated that animals exhibit a wide array of moral behaviors and intelligence, and experience nuanced social and moral emotions, from empathy to fairness. The authors reveal animals to be social beings with no moral gap from our own.[7] Their later work expands upon this theory, noting the presence of social justice in animals.[8] This certainly validates treating animals as precious beings, but should we assign them human attributes? Others believe that the anthropomorphization of animals "can lead to an inaccurate understanding of biological processes" and "also lead to inappropriate behaviors" toward them.[9]

As AI develops, we are likely to anthropomorphize our AI creations. If the opposite of anthropomorphize is dehumanize (though I don't think there is a strict binary), then treating our prospective intelligent creations in familiar and respectful ways may help us get past regressive egotistical and exceptionalist traits that stand in the way of consistently valuing all forms of intelligence. Why do humans seem so threatened by the idea that other animals think and feel? Is it because acknowledging the mind of another makes it harder to abuse them? Or do we feel that their agency devalues our own? Our ethical actions and societal adjustments to our treatment of animals lag behind the science, and even faced with irrefutable proof of their suffering, their morality, their humaneness, human beings often do not want to include them in our notions of justice, of rights, of fairness, of freedom. While humans have always named and revered machines they are connected to, machines that can think for themselves and possibly become conscious and self-aware require a more in-depth consideration, both of them and of ourselves.

SELF-AWARE ROBOTS

> What have we been doing all these centuries but trying to call God back to the mountain, or, failing that, raise a peep out of anything that isn't us? What is the difference between a cathedral and a physics lab? Are not they both saying: Hello?
>
> —ANNIE DILLARD

So where are we with the science? Is it even feasible for synthetically intelligent creations to become conscious? Much of the colloquy is influenced by just how little we currently understand about the human mind and consciousness, because despite the many milestones we have reached in neuroscience, we do not fully comprehend how the brain produces the experience of self-awareness. University of California–Santa Barbara psychology professor Michael S. Gazzaniga calls this the "problem of consciousness."[10]

Even among those who consider our consciousness to be nothing more than a bunch of complicated neurons firing, many admit that there are numerous factors that contribute to our mind's complexity, including memory and dreams. Some insist that only biological entities can be sentient and conscious, and for that reason, AI will not develop humanlike self-awareness and instead will only ever be capable of "notion intelligence,"[11] in which AI remains without the cultural factors necessary to have social and emotional intelligence.

The Thesis of Radical Plasticity[12] theorizes that consciousness is a state that the brain learns to attain, and many believe our future intelligent machines can also be taught to become aware. In 2015, at Rensselaer Polytechnic Institute, a NAO robot passed the classic Wise Men puzzle test of self-awareness,[13] requiring the robot to apply the principle of induction to solve a riddle. Hakwan Lau from the University of California–Los Angeles posits that "once we can spell out in computational terms what the differences may be in humans between conscious and unconsciousness, coding that into computers may not be that hard."[14] Creating conscious AI, then, could be less about coding machine consciousness and more about uncovering the truth of our own.

While we do have a possible road map to strong AI (and even superintelligent machines that could become self-aware), the ability to build a self-aware or self-conscious machine is likely still far in the future, if it's possible at all. "Superintelligent" and "conscious" are not necessarily one and the same. Nancy Fulda, a computer scientist and science fiction author who is working on robotic theory of mind and training algorithms to understand contextual language, makes it clear that "we still have a long way to go" before we can create a conscious AI.[15]

A Cambridge University paper, "Building Machines That Learn and Think Like People," by Brenden M. Lake, Tomer D. Ullman, Joshua B. Tenenbaum, and Samuel J. Gershman, evaluated the scientific advances of technology using neural networks. For all their sophistication, "despite their biological inspiration and performance achievements, these systems differ from human intelligence in crucial ways." The cognitive science suggests "that truly human-like learning and thinking machines will have to reach beyond current engineering trends in both what they learn, and how they learn it"—but make no mistake, we are well down this road.[16]

Advances are being made in developing a specific way to communicate with our intelligent digital partners. Caltech PhD and polymath Stephen Wolfram believes his "Wolfram Language," a cloud-based programming system, is a "new paradigm for computation" that will allow humans and machines to "interact at a vastly richer and higher level than ever before."[17] Lauded AI researcher and computer scientist Yoshua Bengio doesn't "think that any of the human faculties is something inherently inaccessible to computers."[18]

However, the leap to conscious machines may have to be quantum. Quantum computers and new generations of computer chips currently on the drawing board will be exponentially faster at the processing necessary for far greater and more sophisticated applications of machine intelligence. According to the Copenhagen Interpretation of Quantum Mechanics, and the currently most advanced branch of physics, quantum theory, the physical and conscious worlds run in parallel.[19] Once the quantum computers that tech companies are all racing to build[20] exist, we will have the computing power, speed, and language to build conscious technology.[21] While British physicist Sir Roger Penrose first put forth a theory twenty years ago that human consciousness is actually rooted in the rules of quantum physics,[22] philosopher, poet, and scientist Subhash Kak points out that creativity and the sense of freedom that people possess do not appear to come from logic or calculations.[23] Disputes remain even as to what purpose our consciousness serves, who has it, and why. Michael Gazzaniga tells us that even the word "consciousness" in everyday usage means different things to different people and is influenced by personal, cultural, and religious stories.[24] So we indeed may be "well down this road,"[25] but there are many mysteries yet to elucidate.

> People say that what we're all seeking is a meaning for life. I don't think that's what we're really seeking. I think that what we're seeking is an experience of being alive, so that our life experiences on the purely physical plane will have resonances with our own innermost being and reality, so that we actually feel the rapture of being alive.
>
> —JOSEPH CAMPBELL

If all vertebrates have sensory experiences, should we then assume them to be conscious? Assuming they are, how do we jump to building an artificial consciousness? What might conscious or self-aware AI actually be like? What would it do, and what would it need to qualify as conscious? This is a challenge because what consciousness means at all has been debated for thousands of years. Notwithstanding the lack of consensus on how to describe and define consciousness, scientists are pursuing how to build a synthetic version of it. Some believe that consciousness is computational, and thus possible to code into machines.[26] Assuming it's possible,[27] Hugh Howey thinks that any such digitally conscious machine would need to have an apparatus that responds to stimuli, a language to communicate in, and an algorithm that observes the apparatus and tells a (usually false) story about why it does what it does.[28] Other AI engineers are attempting to build AI endowed with a sense of curiosity and childlike wonder, suggesting that the desire to know more is essential for self-awareness.[29]

All we know for certain is that we can already design and construct a sense of perception into AI (self-driving cars), we have AI that can respond to some of our needs (Alexa, Siri) when we communicate with it through language, and that this technology is progressing very rapidly. Can we build awareness into our machines? Should we? Does it matter if we can? If we cannot create an artificial consciousness, might that failure validate our own specialness? Is our quest to build self-aware, conscious AI the final step toward becoming gods ourselves? To finally making something in our own image, our own creature?

Ultimately, the most important question to ask is, In searching for a digital soul, will we find our own?

SEARCHING FOR THE DIGITAL SOUL

> What is it that, when present in a body, makes it living?—A soul.
>
> —SOCRATES

This is the quest this book is on: a journey to the center of ourselves, to encourage us to recognize that our current geological age, marked by humans dominating and desecrating the earth, is ending. We need to reconsider our role in the cosmos and our responsibility to identify and care for all conscious life, whether organic or, potentially, human-made. If we can take an honest look in the mirror, all of humanity will benefit.

The questions surrounding thinking, intelligence, consciousness, and the soul are ancient ones. These are myths we tell ourselves, and myths are in our DNA. They are how we try to understand one another.[30] People have debated whether there is a human spirit beyond our bodies throughout human history, without consensus, dividing believers and nonbelievers. The advent of smart technologies, and prospective supersmart technology, introduces a new level of metaphysics into the conversation. All kinds of thinkers, from philosophers, to computer scientists, to artists, to science fiction writers like Ursula K. Le Guin and Octavia Butler, have weighed in on just how *human* a synthetic consciousness could be, and whether it can help us crack the code of consciousness itself. In her book *Dawn*, Butler makes the point that intelligence is not the only factor, writing, "intelligence does enable you to deny facts you dislike. But your denial doesn't matter. A cancer growing in someone's body will go on growing in spite of denial. And a complex combination of genes that work together to make you intelligent as well as hierarchical will still handicap you whether you acknowledge it or not."[31]

However, before we can build it, we have to understand what "it" is or if "it" exists at all. A tidy set of definitions as we move forward: "Intelligence" is acquiring and applying knowledge and skills. "Sentience" is the ability to perceive things. "Consciousness" is awareness and perception. Or, put another way, "consciousness is everything you experience."[32] Then there is self-awareness, an awareness of one's own consciousness. Finally, the soul is that immaterial part of a human or other being that is beyond mortality.[33]

Within the definitions of consciousness and the soul there are many interpretations. Plato believed that we had an immortal soul.[34] Some say he also believed that while humans were uniquely capable of reason, all living things could have a soul.[35] René Descartes felt that the mind and body were distinct, believing in a mind-body dualism.[36] For Descartes, consciousness was fact: "Cogito, ergo sum." (I think, therefore I am.) Philosopher Robert Sperry contended that the mind and consciousness are divisible.[37]

By contrast, some believe there is no soul at all.[38] At the very least, the concept of the soul is culturally determined and varies widely across religions and belief systems. Buddhists, for example, do not believe each of us possesses a permanent, immortal soul. Rather, the non-self state in which we all live is called anatta.[39] In Hinduism, the essence of the individual, the soul, or the inner self, exists and is called Ātman.[40] In Shintoism and in Ojibwe animism, both living and inanimate objects have souls and spirits within them.[41] Contemporary philosophers Warren S. Brown and Nancy Murphy have suggested a move away from thinking of a soul as a "thing" and more toward an action, verb, or process.[42]

Daniel Dennett maintains that there is no evidence that we are conscious; it's an illusion, albeit a useful one, and consciousness is a mechanical process explainable entirely by science, as if tiny robots were all working together to create what we think is consciousness. For him, that's what living things do; from bacteria to Bach, we consist of "competence without comprehension."[43] Dennett draws parallels with the discoveries of Darwin and Turing, suggesting that "in order to make a perfect and beautiful machine, it is not requisite to know how to make it." He suggests that both Darwin and Turing had also found the existence of competence without comprehension in evolution and in machines.[44] Instead of sharp lines between human intelligence and consciousness versus all the rest, we are both human and robotic all at once.[45] Whereas for philosopher and scientist David Chalmers, "consciousness is one of the fundamental facts of human existence," and he believes that it is likely both fundamental and universal.[46] Consciousness is the starting block from which we can build an awareness of who we are. Alongside the aforementioned Sir Roger Penrose, anesthesiologist Stuart Hameroff also posits, controversially, that quantum mechanics holds the key to consciousness.[47]

So one way to think about consciousness and the soul is to consider that we all travel through life seeking confirmation of our existence. We don't start fully formed. We find ourselves in relationship with the world around us. In relating to other living beings and the knowledge we absorb, we mold ourselves out of metaphysical clay. In seeing and connecting with others, we see more of ourselves by holding up a mirror to our own true self. The philosopher Vladimír Havlík believes that "a soul is not something like a substance" but rather that "it is something like a coherent identity, which is constituted permanently during the flow of time."[48]

Imagine a soul more like an action—a practice, a process, a maturing internal compass.

Do we even need to distinguish consciousness from the soul? Or are they one and the same? Author Ondřej Beran thinks that "the role that the concept of soul plays in our culture is intertwined with contexts in which we say that someone's soul is noble or depraved . . . that is, it comes with a value judgment."[49] Soul and consciousness, if not the same, are inextricably aligned. Another way to frame consciousness is to think about it as being on a multi-axis spectrum. Aristotle said that a life or a soul is a process that develops.[50] William James called consciousness a process.[51] We are a "collection of moments."[52]

"Time," says Jorge Luis Borges, "is the substance I am made of. Time is a river that carries me away, but I am the river."[53] If our consciousness is a river, if we are all collections of moments in time, then we all flow into one another. We see that the lines that separate us from our family, friends, ancestors—human and chimpanzee, reptile and amoeba—are part of a chain, a dance of evolution, an interconnected trellis. All of us are bound together in both our finite evanescence and our amaranthine affinity. As natural sciences author Janine Benyus reminds us, we are tethered to one another in "this home that is ours, but not ours alone."[54]

Contemplating the nature of being is a way to spark our thinking, moving us past assumptions so we can ponder how we use words such as "soul," "consciousness," or "self-awareness." Our brains want to take the path of least resistance, particularly when wrestling with difficult or abstract concepts. We want to conserve energy to alleviate the messiness and busyness of life. We seek mental shortcuts. We turn away from the things that scare us.

If we acknowledge our biological tendencies and limitations, we can move forward regardless of how outdated some of our biomechanics may be. Humans are highly complex and profoundly amazing animals. We live our lives in a gray area, and it is in that blurry, messy range where we can see that what we thought was black and white is actually a mosaic of shades. Although intelligent machines will have their own limitations, this incredible technology can also exponentially expand the quantity and quality of tools in our intellectual toolkit, bringing new genius and fresh perspective to help us see our blind spots and, perhaps, identify what constitutes our own souls along the way.

But to harbor realistic prospects of evolving in this way we have to confront what we fear. Behavioral science has shown us that humans are more afraid of losing what we already have than we are of not gaining something new, even if the net gain or loss is equivalent. We like to fit arguments into what we already believe, and we like to make decisions based on more accessible and recent information.[55] We all have preconceived notions, beliefs, and biases. No one is a blank slate. Not even the most brilliant minds have all the right answers—but it's the most powerful minds who are willing to change theirs. Intelligent machines may help us get there.

CONSCIOUSNESS—WHO HAS IT?

Who or what deserves to be labeled intelligent? To be deemed conscious? Who gets to determine the metrics? And how will they apply to digital versions?

SOME VIEWS ON CONSCIOUSNESS

HISTORICAL AND PRE-MODERN

PLATO
360 BCE

Plato addressed consciousness as a part of reality due to its capability to affect and be affected by other consciousnesses.

RENÉ DESCARTES: CARTESIAN DUALISM
1600s

Decartes proposed that mind and body are two fundamental and independent substances that can interact with each other.

JOHN LOCKE'S "AN ESSAY CONCERNING HUMAN UNDERSTANDING"
1690

An early attempt to define consciousness in relation to experience and personal identity.

HUMAN-CENTRIC

SIGMUND FREUD: TOPOGRAPHY OF THE MIND
EARLY 1900s

Freud divided human consciousness into three levels of awareness: conscious, preconscious, and unconscious.

CARL JUNG: COLLECTIVE UNCONSCIOUSNESS
1916

The term was introduced to present a form of unconsciousness that contains archetypes of images and ideas.

DANIEL DENNETT: *CONSCIOUSNESS EXPLAINED*
1991

Dennett proposed that consciousness is the result of the interaction between physical and cognitive processes in the brain.

GERALD EDELMAN: *NEURAL DARWINISM*
1987

Or *The Theory of Neuronal Group Selection*. Edelman posited that the brain learns from its experience and shapes itself over our lifetimes.

NONHUMANS, OBJECTS, SYSTEMS, MACHINES

TURING TEST AND MACHINE INTELLIGENCE
1950

Alan Turing first proposed the Turing Test as a way of approaching the question as to whether machines can think.

DONNA HARAWAY: *A CYBORG MANIFESTO*
1985

Haraway used the concept of cyborg to reject the rigid boundaries that separate human from animal and human from machine.

OBJECT-ORIENTED ONTOLOGY
2000s

Founded by Graham Harman, a school of thought that rejects the privilege of human existence over the existence of nonhuman objects.

INTEGRATED–INFORMATION THEORY
2004

This theory proposed by Giulio Tononi postulates that casual properties determine a system's consciousness—an intrinsic, fundamental property of any physical system.

CAMBRIDGE DECLARATION ON CONSCIOUSNESS
2012

An international group of neuroscientists declared the existence of consciousness in nonhuman animals.

To reiterate, humans are not the *only* intelligent species—far from it. We are but one kind of intelligent life. Countless living creatures exhibit remarkable forms of intelligence and ability; one could argue that some are superior in many ways to human intelligence. Trees as intelligent systems provide the air we breathe. A spider can fly by weaving a silk balloon to use as a parachute. The octopus can camouflage, learn by observation, and show its intent and emotions by changing its appearance. Ants and beetles bury their dead. Elephants have superb memory, develop dominant limbs, and have distinct personalities.

Animal behavior researcher and zoologist Donald R. Griffin writes: "Must we reject, or repress, any suggestion that the chimpanzees or the herons think consciously about the tasty food they manage to obtain by these coordinated actions? Many animals adapt their behavior to the challenges they face either under natural conditions or when confined to zoos or laboratories. This has persuaded numerous scientists that some sort of cognition must be required to orchestrate such versatile behavior."[56] Rodney Brooks believes that nonhuman intelligence is the kind of intelligence AI developers should be modeling.[57] In 2012, an international group of neuroscientists, including Stephen Hawking, came together for the Cambridge Declaration of Consciousness to declare the existence of consciousness in nonhuman animals.[58]

We need another and a wiser and perhaps a more mystical concept of animals. Remote from universal nature and living by complicated artifice, man in civilization surveys the creature through the glass of his knowledge and sees thereby a feather magnified and the whole image in distortion. We patronize them for their incompleteness, for their tragic fate for having taken form so far below ourselves.

And therein do we err. For the animal shall not be measured by man. In a world older and more complete than
ours, they move finished and complete, gifted with the extension of the senses we have lost or never attained, living
by voices we shall never hear. They are not brethren, they
are not underlings: they are other nations, caught with ourselves in the net of life and time, fellow prisoners of the
splendour and travail of the earth.

—HENRY BESTON

Why is it so difficult for some in our societies to respect and value
these distinct forms of intelligence? Some religions teach that human cognition is unique, superior, and godlike.[59] Despite their
enormous contributions to our lives, only a relative few appreciate
the brilliance of the billions of diverse nonhuman life-forms popu-
lating the planet. Why can't we accept that they too are conscious
and capable of an aliveness equal to our own? I believe that our
inability or unwillingness to view all living things in this way may
be our downfall. It will also constrict our ability to forge future
partnerships with our machines. Accepting a broader definition of
intelligence and consciousness is vital to our survival.

One such definition that some have subscribed to, including philosopher Graham Harman (who coined the term) and philosopher
Timothy Morton, is "object-oriented ontology,"[60] which rejects the
idea that human existence is more important than nonhuman existence.[61] Each object in the universe is interdependent and interconnected, and each has its own form of consciousness.[62] This way of
thinking shifts the viewpoint from an always human-centered one to
one in which all objects in the universe have equal standing and are
not dependent on whether a human can perceive them or not.[63] A bee
sees what a bee sees, and we see what a human sees. We are all limited

in our vantage points. Just as Philip Pullman's *His Dark Materials* series instructs us, we must find and reconnect our bond with living things[64] to be able to accommodate and partner with other forms of intelligence entering our world.

A philosophy embracing and valuing all types of intelligence and living things should not be perceived as a threat to any belief system—if other sentient creatures have consciousness or souls, this doesn't diminish the importance of the human consciousness or soul. You don't have to be exceptional to be unique and irreplaceable. We are kin to all creatures. We are made of carbon and hydrogen and everything in between.[65] We have remnants of gills and tails.[66] They are us and we are them.

> All living things are descended from a common ancestor, and how we are in this sense all related to each other. So humans are related not only to apes and other animals but to plants too.
>
> —OLIVER SACKS

Acknowledging the inconvenient truth of what separates us from machines (or other living things) and the radical possibility that consciousness isn't inherent, but rather something the brain just learns to do,[67] opens us up. The neuroplasticity of our brains can shape and stretch us in new ways, ways we will need to succeed in the coming Technological Age. T. M. Scanlon asks the question: What do we owe to each other?[68] Can we expand this idea beyond humans? Like others before him, Einstein and Albert Schweitzer among them, Jeremy Bentham makes a case for moving away from anthropocentrism, for expanding the canon of compassion. "It may come one day to be recognized, that the number of legs, the villosity [sic] of the

skin, or the termination of the os sacrum, are reasons equally insufficient for abandoning a sensitive being to the same fate. What else
is it that should trace the insuperable line? Is it the faculty of reason,
or perhaps, the faculty for discourse? . . . The question is not, can
they reason? nor, can they talk? but, can they suffer? Why should
the law refuse its protection to any sensitive being? . . . The time will
come when humanity will extend its mantle over everything which
breathes . . ."[69]

If we come to accept and regard the acumen and contributions
of other life-forms, what about our future synthetically intelligent
inventions? We know that AI will be more intelligent than we are
in many ways; why should we be afraid of creating machines that
are smarter than we are? We already rely on intelligent tools every day, and have accepted and assimilated advancing technology
into our lives throughout history. It wasn't that long ago that people were afraid to ride in an elevator that was not controlled by
an operator. Today, that idea seems quaint. We used to do math
in our heads, but now most of us exclusively rely on calculators.
We used to only conduct financial transactions with human bank
tellers. Now we prefer ATMs. Are we not all safer and more comfortable flying around and above the planet in modern machines
with sophisticated computers and algorithms making the critical
decisions than we were riding in a single-engine contraption with
a joystick and sole pilot control?

While some theorize about the entry of smart, and soon extremely
smart, machines into our lives, and while some speculate on how and
whom it will affect, it's important to keep the perspective that we will,
invariably, want to categorize our intelligent machine creations' function and utility as separate and distinct from humans', no matter how
closely their thinking comes to resemble our own. This is just as we

have always done with all nonhuman intelligence. As our technology rapidly evolves and merges into our ecosystem, our bodies, and our lives, confronting human limitations will aid us in coming to terms with them.

There is a doctrine called panpsychism, related to object-oriented ontology, wherein everything, from humans to trees to quarks to electrons, has at least some semblance of an inner life.[70] Some people think this is true,[71] and some don't.[72] This principle is not dissimilar from what many cultures believe about the inter-connectivity of all things. Those who reject the idea point to the implausibility of the "combination problem," which has to do with the panpsychist belief that consciousness arises from a combination of many bits of small, subatomic consciousnesses. But there is little science or even theory as to how these small bits of consciousnesses combine.

Related to this thinking, some scientists believe in cosmopsychism, the idea that the universe itself, as a holistic entity, has a consciousness.[73] But how would this square with each of us also having a distinct identity? Bernardo Kastrup posits that we may all be the dissociated personalities of one indivisible consciousness, accounting for how the whole could also be parts through our individual minds.[74]

Darwin's ideas once seemed ludicrous, even blasphemous, when he first presented them. Einstein's theories were wildly out of the ballpark of contemporary thought, until he showed how big the ballpark really is. Copernicus and Galileo were in grave danger for sharing their visions of how the universe was really arranged. It took years for the scientific community to fully acknowledge astronomer Vera Rubin's evidence of the existence of dark matter, which has since revolutionized our understanding of the cosmos.[75] A crazy idea is crazy until it's not. We think we're at the center until we see we're not.

> The biggest opportunity in AI is not machines that think
> like us or do what we do, but machines that think in ways
> we cannot conceive and do what we cannot.
>
> —RADHIKA DIRKS

We don't yet know if there is something special about the human mind. We have not yet proven whether or not *we* have a consciousness, let alone established the idea that a machine could ever acquire one. Even if we could validate it, should that intelligence/consciousness/ soul be the metric we use to decide who or what may be entitled to things like personhood? The question is, What does it really mean to be human? If someone or something is different from you, should that mean they get fewer rights than you?

Turing's test stipulated that the key to determining if a machine's intelligence could become indistinguishable from ours was whether or not an AI could relate to human beings in an authentic way. Isn't this the sign we have been looking for all along? The idea is as ancient as human history itself: how we treat others, how we treat the world around us, and how we treat those who may think for us, is our destiny.

The questions will linger and the theories will continue to be contested, but what I am interested in is a path forward, a way to accept and even flourish in this uncertainty as we head into the AI revolution. As Walt Whitman said, we "contain multitudes."[76] Reject binary thinking. Embrace the gray area. Celebrate inclusion. To support and protect another is to save yourself. There are no hard edges between us and the world.

LIVING THE UNCERTAINTY

Until he extends his circle of compassion to include all living things, man will not himself find peace.

—ALBERT SCHWEITZER

To see and be seen by others, to be recognized as valuable and worthy, helps us see ourselves in others and others in ourselves.[77] To value all types of intelligence and all life is to see that we are all interconnected and that we are all interdependent. To reject the other is to reject oneself. To assume that humans are the pinnacle of all creation, of all genius and all intelligence, is to live in the darkness, shortsighted and afraid. We don't know what's ahead, but we can only thrive if we accept these truths and work together.

We have a long history of not seeing and valuing other living things in the moment. It's only later that purpose emerges, and it can continue to shift and morph as time marches ever onward. A ceramic bowl, a worn dress, a brass spoon—ordinary objects of one era become museum artifacts in another, and are endowed with a certain magic. What is now seen as a damaged pot might one day be heralded as a wabi sabi masterpiece.

To value life, live the questions. Dwell in possibility.[78] To crack the code of flight, humans had to let go of having to fly exactly like birds fly.[79] Now, we need to let go of the widely held belief that the human mind and the human soul are singular and unique, and that artificial intelligence has to replicate ours. Only if we can look beyond exceptionalism, the need to be more special than other beings, can we soar.

To be open to holding all living things in esteem, respecting all their complexities and gifts, is our gateway to valuing present and future machine intelligence. This in turn will guide us toward remaining in wonder and awe, ever-curious about not just how we can build more and smarter machines, but also how the process can make us all better people. Some AI experts believe that curiosity is the quintessential human trait that a truly intelligent machine must have to be more like us. Whether we could teach a robot to be curious, or whether we have a soul or unique consciousness, or whether our brain's neurons can be replicated mechanically—we just don't have scientifically proven answers to these questions yet.

That's where our character is born. That's at the heart of being human: living in the gray area, in the questions, in all of our flaws and miscalculations, and the will to rise up again. That's who we are. It's not about predicting the future—it's about imagining beyond our current reality so we can give ourselves the best chance to get it right.

AI is the most transformative technology humankind will ever create. We should fear not new technology, but rather the inability to perpetuate the best of our humanity, our kindness, our willingness to do better, and our willingness to accept the science and accept change. We don't need to save ourselves from robots. We need to save robots from ourselves. Today, there is no human without machine bias, and there is no machine without human bias. Are we all just organic algorithms? Or something more? We're going to have to live in the uncertainty.

The spectrum motif throughout this book, from thinking about intelligence to thinking about consciousness, is a plea to release our grip on binary thinking in multiple realms, to move closer to understanding, tolerance, and acceptance—a broader view, a fuller picture, where we can see all of our systems, beliefs, and selves as interconnected and flowing ever onward. Intelligence isn't the pinnacle of human life and the nucleus of the human condition. There is something above our thoughts, deeper than our knowledge, perhaps even unnameable. Our society focuses on intellectual aptitude and the individual brilliant mind.[80] Much of our obsession around building an artificial brain centers around intellectual acuity that can perhaps be mechanically constructed. However, it is what lies beyond intelligence that makes life luminous.

How can we create a future that has room for us all? I'd now like to expand David Whyte's idea of having courageous conversations— not only about AI, but *with* AI as well.

In *Frankenstein*, Mary Shelley teaches us it's not enough to create life. It has to be treated well, nurtured, and cultivated. We can't conceive of something and then expect it to meet all of our expectations without any responsibility on our end. If we don't regard something as human, it will not act human. Our failure to bestow basic kindness and dignity on living things has negative precedent throughout our history.

When we relate to others, we are looking in a mirror. Our machines, too, will be a reflection of us.

9

THE ADJACENT POSSIBLE

MIT developed a computer program called World One to model global sustainability and look at the world as "one system." World One was "an electronic guided tour of our behavior since 1900 and where that behavior will lead us." The program produced a detailed report of statistics and graphs, accounting for population, quality of life, supplies of natural resources, pollution, and other variables. It concluded: "At around 2020, the condition of the planet becomes highly critical. If we do nothing about it, the quality of life goes down to zero. Pollution becomes so serious it will start to kill people, which in turn will cause the population to diminish, lower than it was in the 1900s. At this stage, around 2040 to 2050, civilized life as we know it on this planet will cease to exist."[1]

That was in 1973.

World One's projections from almost a half century ago were not meant to be a precise forecast, but rather a way to see the world as a single system; an interconnected and interdependent organism. While climate scientists are now confirming some of World One's findings, this is a lesson about the perils of failing to heed the warnings of the capable and evolving technologies we have constructed to help us navigate our increasingly complex existence. We cannot solve our problems in isolation, and we are ever more reliant on our technologies to help us conduct meaningful research and number crunching so we can learn about the mosaic of Earth's systems. Our intelligent machines can go to a depth that humans simply cannot, and soon they will be able to do so under their own direction. Moral imagination is indispensable for establishing trust with and within our technology and for setting the algorithmic coordinates of this course.

The daily flood of information coming at us can seem overwhelming. Amplified and weaponized by ubiquitous media, this data deluge can make us feel bombarded, as we swat away intellectual micro-assaults throughout the day. It's difficult to keep perspective. We try to avoid feeling insignificant in the grand scheme of things. We are just one of billions. Will anything we do matter?

The intelligent tools we are building can help sort the truth from the falsehoods amid this barrage. In this and other ways, they can empower every one of us. But the cautionary tale of the 1973 MIT program illustrates that we can have the best statistics and analysis at hand, can know the risks, and still fail to act. Our smart machines can only help and guide us if we listen to them in time. And they will only become trustworthy enough for us to accept when we build them to mirror the goodness in us.

THE ADJACENT POSSIBLE

The words "compass" and "compassion" share the Latin root meaning "with, together." With this in mind, what intrinsic human qualities should our internal compass point to? What qualities do we want our synthetically intelligent machines to echo? If our AI is not imbued with the best parts of ourselves, it may come to demonstrate some of our worst tendencies. We are not neutral, so the technology we build won't be either. If we want machines that act ethically, we have to be ethical. There is no moral machine without a moral human.

As imperative as it seems to create AI that shares our optimal values, it's probable we only have a short-term window to do so. It may only be viable for us to code and program values into the relatively primitive versions of intelligent technology we are already building, as the increasing complexity and autonomy of AI agents will multiply the challenge as they mature. AI is here. It's growing up fast. We should face the possibility that our intelligent machines may eventually leave us behind, much as we have destroyed and discarded other living organisms over the millennia. Ninety-nine point nine percent of every species that has ever roamed the earth is now gone (with humans causing almost all of the ongoing sixth extinction[2]). Extending our collective future may be dependent on adapting to life in a digital sphere.

So humans won't play a significant role in the spreading of intelligence across the cosmos. But that's OK. Don't think of humans as the crown of creation. Instead view human civilization as part of a much grander scheme, an important step (but not the last one) on the path of the universe towards higher complexity. Now it seems ready to take its

next step, a step comparable to the invention of life itself
over 3.5 billion years ago.

—JÜRGEN SCHMIDHUBER

To prepare ourselves for a transformed future in which we are not the
central or most dominant beings on our planet, we must redefine our
relationships to our technology and the world around us. We must rethink our societal structures and reimagine what it means to be human.

There is a concept that may be illuminative in imagining our
transfigured human and mechanical future, which scientist Stuart
Kauffman has evocatively named "the adjacent possible." To better
produce creative thought amid the onslaught of information from every app and screen, it can facilitate sifting through the noise and fusing
information and concepts into something new—a Marauder's Map[3]
of potential ideas and discoveries. The adjacent possible is building
upon existing innovations, sometimes seemingly unrelated, to forge
whole new archetypes we couldn't previously envision. With such an
approach, we can promote collaboration across disciplines and random occurrences outside our customary intellectual confines, creating
a potent mélange of our collective sapience and imagination.

In his book *Where Good Ideas Come From*, Steven Johnson describes the adjacent possible as a "shadow future, hovering on the
edges of the present state of things, a map of all the ways in which
the present can reinvent itself." The adjacent possible, Johnson continues, "captures both the limits and the creative potential of change
and innovation."[4] The adjacent possible is the horizon at the edge of
possibility—we can just manage to see it, but we can't quite get there.
This is because it's not fully formed yet. It's piecing itself together as
we trudge onward. The road is materializing as we walk down it. With
every step, what is possible adjusts.

We must be mindful of the adjacent possible as we continue to advance our AI—to reach for the edge of what is conceivable. And when we can almost reach the outer border and see that new boundaries have emerged, we must stretch further. These always-morphing possibilities bleed into the future like a watercolor yet to be painted. The more we explore, the more we innovate; the more the periphery expands, the greater the potential for yet more possible futures. Nikola Tesla invented the alternating current motor; Edison perfected it. Einstein had a theory; Oppenheimer built the atomic bomb. Joseph Weizenbaum imagined the language processor ELIZA; Siri took over.[5] Eric, the first humanoid robot, made its debut (and a speech) in 1928 at the Society of Model Engineers in London.[6] Now we have Honda's ASIMO, which can recognize and react to human movements and emotions.[7] The more doors we open, the more that appear.

The adjacent possible has been multiplied to the umpteenth power by intelligent technologies. Even though AI is in its infancy, we can barely see its boundaries anymore, much less control them. The machines are teaching themselves how to build upon human achievement, and can now make their own innovations. They are even learning to be curious.[8] The adjacent possible is no longer ours alone. It now also includes what AI can discover and achieve. We won't protect ourselves by trying to suppress its potential. Innovation is at its best when we cross-pollinate ideas across disciplines and intellects and break down the walls that isolate us and drive us to fearful places. And now we have a brilliant new partner.

> Human life is but a series of footnotes to a vast obscure unfinished masterpiece.
>
> —VLADIMIR NABOKOV

To brave technological disruption, we have to fully weigh the consequences. To innovate with solely commercial objectives is no longer adequate, because if the goal is only profit, with AI's rapidly expanding capacity for autonomy, we may lose control of it and it may undermine any aims we set out for it. Recall the hypothetical paper-clip robot that will do anything to produce more paper clips. The goal must be to make something *better*, to improve, to empower, to benefit all, not just to produce capital. The old standards will not sustain us. To transition from siloed profit-based models focused only on building AI or any new technology with self-serving financial ambitions to ones we can also transparently measure in altruistic benefits that produce a brighter future for all is going to take some major societal restructuring.

The shift is a philosophical one. To accept our end: the inevitable end of each of us, the end of our run as the smartest species on the planet, and the conclusion of the myth that we are the only exceptional, intelligent, and conscious beings on it. Adopting a more heuristic approach to confronting the challenges in front of us, like the one espoused by Carlo Ratti, called Futurecraft,[9] can be enlightening. This mindset is "not about fixing the present, or predicting the future—but influencing it."[10] In other words, acknowledging that we cannot fully know the future and instead enlisting the profundity of human experience to pilot us.

THE OVERVIEW EFFECT

This is what heaven must look like.

—ASTRONAUT MICHAEL MASSIMINO

In 1968, as the *Apollo 8* mission was returning, the astronauts onboard felt a powerful shift in their worldview. A sense of pure awe and wonder came over them. After seeing our home planet from afar, they

had immense feelings of both their own smallness, as well as the uni-
fying forces of humanity that should override all human disputes. The
"overview effect," coined by author Frank White in his 1987 book,[11]
is this acute awareness that an astronaut experiences when looking at
Earth from above. Astronaut Ron Garan recounts the experience as
"the realization that we are all traveling together on the planet and that
if we all looked at the world from that perspective we would see that
nothing is impossible."[12] It's something we should all aspire to emulate.

When we see the reality of our place in the cosmos—our home, a
tiny speck of blue in an endless sea of darkness, a delicate ecosystem in
which we all float—the trivial divisions we devise to separate ourselves
fade away. The borders and walls, the sparring nations and claims to
this land or that part of the sea, all vanish. We see how all-important it
is to protect and hold dear what the great astronomer Carl Sagan calls
the "pale blue dot." Our only, fragile, dying home. When looking at our
home from the far reaches of space, astronauts have described a feeling
of clarity, a deep sense of interconnectedness, and a surrendering acceptance of our small role in the big picture. Returning from a mission to
the moon, one space traveler remarked that this act of looking back at
Earth "may have been the most important reason we went."[13]

Upon leaving our galaxy in 1990, *Voyager 1* (at Carl Sagan's suggestion) took a last look back at our solar system, turning homeward
to snap some photos of Earth before venturing beyond.[14] Sagan's book,
The Pale Blue Dot, is based on the image of Earth the spacecraft took
that day. It is an iconic reminder of the importance of maintaining an
astronaut's-eye view of who we are as a civilization. In Sagan's mind,
this simple shift in perspective is powerful, with the potential to increase our empathy toward one another and inspire us to act more
ethically here on Earth. As he put it, "To me, it underscores our responsibility to deal more kindly with one another, and to preserve and
cherish the pale blue dot, the only home we've ever known."[15]

Perhaps our worldly problems might be solved if we could all experience the overview effect. But even with Richard Branson and Jeff Bezos set to offer the wealthiest among us space rides in the near term, the privilege of this view will only be available to an exclusive group— for now. Although more of us may someday get to experience a simulated view via virtual or augmented reality, today most can only try to imagine the sensation of seeing our planet from space.

So how do we change our mentality without actually experiencing the wonder of seeing our home as a tiny grain of sand in the seas of space and time? What can make us feel a sense of being interconnected, humble, and open, with mental acuity? What can help us achieve this perspective, united in our need to create a bonded society, compelling us to be individually responsible caretakers of our planet, respecting and valuing all forms of life? Which magic potion will guide us to be the astronauts of our own voyage of discovery? The elixir, I believe, is empathy.

BUILDING EMPATHY

Empathy is the ability to put yourself in someone or something else's position, to feel what they feel, and to act accordingly. To share in their experience. Empathy is a learned skill.[16] We can practice it. Our mirror neurons can sense the feelings of others. Mirror neurons also fire in other species, from birds to primates.[17] We can each strive to see and feel from the perspectives of others, to immerse ourselves in their points of view.

Empathy is the path to self-awareness and appreciation of the world around us. It leads to altruism,[18] and even to heroism.[19] It is the bedrock of leadership, of hope. Empathy leads us to help others, to care for one another. It's the antidote to dehumanization, to cognitive biases, to cognitive dissonance. It allows us to see the world as others do, to communicate, to understand one another. It's the essential emotional skill for the economic, political, and social systems we have created and will create. Empathy is at the core of our humanity.

If it is our hope that our intelligent creations can be engineered with this facility, we must first consider why so many of us demonstrably fail to have enough of it for other humans, other groups, other living things. This deficiency comes from tribalism. Exceptionalism. Other-ism. The urge to pick sides, our side. To make someone else feel less-than so we can feel more-than, better-than. The instinctive fear of change, of what is different.

How do we turn the tide of these human tendencies and acquire empathy? To start with, we widen our lens. We find another vantage point.

Sunaura Taylor, an artist and disability and animal rights activist, can help point the way. As Taylor writes in her seminal work, *Beasts of Burden*, "disability studies and activism call for recognizing new ways of valuing life that aren't limited by specific physical or mental capabilities."[20] Adeptly demonstrating how ableism is related to species-ism, Taylor illustrates how "neurotypical" (cognitively normative and species typical) human intelligence and reason have been valued above all else. Valuing reason and "rational thinking" above other modes of feeling, being, knowing, and acting has a long history of being associated with sexism, imperialism, classism, and anthropocentrism.[21]

However, our value, worth, morality, and dignity are not defined by human reason and intelligence. This anthropocentric fallacy is a house of cards that humans construct in order to feel superior to those with different ways of being, of existing. Taylor goes on to argue that we discriminate against animals for the same reasons we discriminate against other marginalized humans. While each and every group and individual is affected differently, her point is to never put a category of people above the rest of our living ecosystem of beings.

Taylor describes meeting Peter Singer, the controversial moral philosopher, and challenging some of his core and oft-cited assumptions, particularly his blunt and uninformed remarks regarding the capacity and potential happiness of those with disabilities.[22] She references herself as a person with disabilities and as an artist—powerful parts of herself that infuse innovation, empathy, and creativity into everything she does. These qualities help her seek and find creative solutions every day.[23] Notions of the supremacy of rationality, efficiency, and "progress" can stand in the way of valuing other forms of life, other ways of living. Taylor doesn't give us any easy answers, but instead asks for nuance, for seeing possibilities for more compassion, more ways of seeing one another as worthy, different, and also similar at all once. As Professor James F. McGrath eloquently puts it, "to be human but also humane."[24]

With sympathy, we understand the feelings and sufferings of another at a distance. With empathy, we imagine and experience the feelings and thoughts of another; we get inside their skin and vicariously experience what they are feeling and thinking alongside them. With compassion, we experience the feelings, the thoughts of another, and we want to relieve that suffering, reaching out to take action to alleviate it.

Psychologists and computer scientists are experimenting to see if it's possible to code empathy into technology systems to produce artificial emotional intelligence. Affectiva, a company that emerged from the MIT Media Lab, is developing software they call Emotion AI that "humanizes how people and technology interact."[25] They are working toward systems such as an occupant-aware car that could help detect if the driver is getting tired, personalized explanations to help a struggling student with their learning process, and therapy to support those with autism and Parkinson's, as well as a way to provide immediate help for someone with suicidal ideation.

Microsoft and Apple have divisions devoted to the subject[26] and have purchased businesses that are developing AI applications for detecting emotion.[27] MIT is working on Deep Empathy, which uses deep learning to simulate how your own neighborhood would look if it were bombarded and torn apart by conflict, as in Homs, Syria.[28] These tools can help train us, too. Hans Rosling's Dollar Street data visualization shows how people around the world really live, allowing us to peek into their homes to see who they are and how they walk through the world.[29] Humans and machines can indeed learn to be more empathetic together, though it will take a multiplicity of voices and perspectives to build a kinder future.

Danielle Krettek of Google's Empathy Lab sees her work as a:

> school teacher for machines where I'm looking after the finger-painting during their upbringing while others are training them in the hardcore math and science. These machines need to see the world fully in a spectrum and that means exposing them to story tellers, philosophers, artists, poets, designers, and filmmakers. I think every science or artistic discipline has a slightly different way of looking at a human problem, or a potential human solution, or an inspiring way to crack either of those—and it feels like this is an all hands on deck moment where we need everyone.[30]

It's important—a matter of survival, perhaps—for us to attempt to embed empathy into the smart machines we are building so that they can identify and appropriately respond to human concerns and emotions. Communion with others and emotional connections are the marrow of any human civilization we would want to live in. While there are valid arguments about limiting our relationships with artificial devices,[31] to wall technology off from the ongoing vital discussion of how we build ethical and fair societies is not only shortsighted but probably doomed to failure. If we cannot figure out the science to code empathy, it could make us and our world less so.

Yet it is important to acknowledge the concerns of thinkers like Sherry Turkle, who are highly unsettled by human-machine relations. Turkle believes that interacting with devices is a path to losing what makes us human, that it diminishes us as humans, and that we should be alarmed by the disconcerting rise of interactive robots. She says that "technology makes us forget what we know about life. We become enchanted by technology's promises because we have so many problems we would like technology to solve."[32] Certainly technology can foster disconnection, detachment, and worse. The potential benefits of AI should outweigh these fears. The machines are coming—we must prepare for a future alongside them, as opposed to avoiding their inevitable advancement and, in so doing, risking everything. Turkle does, however, also say that "technology challenges us to look at our human values"[33] and argues, as I do, that staying empathetic is the essential task of humans today.

Empathy is at the core of what it means to be human. It's also at the heart of political reconciliation, restorative justice, creativity, effective leadership and relationships, and innovation. But it's not a panacea. It takes time to build. It can still be manipulated. Our emotions can be used against us.[34] Our minds connect more vividly with one story of one person than with the many who are suffering. We connect more to those who look like us, who come from the same place as us.[35] The countermeasure to this tendency is to picture ourselves in the vast scheme of things: to not let caring for one make us oppose another. This is the trap. The hierarchy of worthiness, saving it for some but not others, will be our undoing unless we avoid it.

AI will be a mirror image of who we are as we build it. We must move away from fixed interpretations that leave us disconnected, sepa-

PROGRAMMING EMPATHY INITIATIVES

SOFTBANK ROBOTICS' PEPPER AND AFFECTIVA PARTNERSHIP

Pepper, dubbed the world's first social humanoid robot, is designed to recognize faces and basic human interactions.[1] A recent partnership with Affectiva enabled Pepper to understand more nuanced states of human feelings, further enhancing its capability to interact with humans in social settings.[2]

THE DEEP EMPATHY PROJECT BY MIT AND UNICEF

The project aims "to create a scalable way to induce empathy" by utilizing deep learning to learn the characteristics of Syrian neighborhoods affected by conflict, and then stimulating how cities around the world would look like in a similar scenario. By teaching AI to learn empathy, the project aims to help us understand and feel more empathetic toward people who are different from us.[3]

HONDA'S "CURIOUS-MINDED MACHINE" RESEARCH

In partnership with several universities, Honda aims to develop new types of machines that can acquire an interest in learning and understanding people's needs. Previously, at the 2018 Consumer Electronic Show in January, Honda also introduced a new lineup of social and assistance robots under the moniker 3E: Empower, Experience, and Empathy.[4]

(1) SoftBank Robotics, 2018, https://www.softbankrobotics.com/us/pepper
(2) Khari Johnson, "Softbank Robotics enhances Pepper the robot's emotional intelligence," *VentureBeat*, August 28, 2018.
(3) Katharine Schwab, "MIT Trained An AI To Tug At Your Heartstrings," *Fast Company*, December 12, 2017.
(4) Kyle Wiggers, "Honda partners with universities to investigate human-like AI," *VentureBeat*, October 25, 2018.

rate, and hierarchical and aim for harmony, creativity, the overview effect. A broader, more inclusive picture. Just as interconnections among our firing neurons help us develop neural networks, interconnections among ideas, and people, and systems—our collective intelligence, shared knowledge, and shared intelligence[36]—will steer us away from hasty stress responses and toward finding a way into a future where we can all flourish.

DOWNLOADING DICKINSON AND PROGRAMMING PLATH

> In the end is the word, as long as the word exists, the possibility of connection exists . . . It is in the nature of the novel to say "We are still alive."
>
> —JANE SMILEY

Intelligent technology can help us become better storytellers by helping us turn data into narratives. Storytelling gives us meaning and common values, and it's how we understand ourselves and the world around us.[37] We can feel it in our bones when we have been told a great story. It also cultivates empathy.[38] A data point representing one million people doesn't penetrate our minds or hearts, and humans remember little from this type of information. But the story of one person—a face, a visual, and a narrative that stands for millions, the humanity in the data—is how we understand and feel compelled to engage in the world around us.[39]

One idea that researchers are exploring is teaching our intelligent machines about empathy by having them read our great works of literature.[40] Immersing ourselves in fiction allows us to enter and better understand the worlds of others.[41] Maryanne Wolf, in her book *Reader Come Home*, makes the connection: "Reading at the deepest levels may provide one part of the antidote to the noted trend away from empathy. But make no mistake: empathy is not solely about being compassionate toward others; its importance goes further. For it is also about a more in-depth understanding of the Other, an essential skill in a world of increasing connectedness among divergent cultures."[42]

Reading literary fiction has been scientifically proven to increase empathy.[43] For instance, a 2014 study of Americans showed that reading a story about a Muslim woman decreased their expressions of racism.[44] But storytelling's large-scale benefits to our ethical selves can only be realized when we are exposed to a diverse array of stories. As author Chimamanda Ngozi Adichie reminds us, we are all prone to ignorance and worse if we only learn a "single story."[45]

It isn't possible to become more empathetic just by scanning tweets and texts or reading short-form writing alone; we have to immerse ourselves in longer narrative forms and character arcs to grow in our capacity for empathy and improve our theory of mind. It takes time to meander through the recesses of human experience, from fragility to intrepidity and everything in between. When we read literary fiction and engage ourselves in these works of art, we not only enhance our ability to understand others, to see that others have their own different experiences and ideas,[46] but we also mature in our understanding of ourselves.[47] Psychologists have found that in the art of storytelling, it's the characters' beliefs, intentions, and acts that affect us most.[48] Other research has shown that those who read a Chekhov story were inspired to consider themselves and their personalities in a new way.[49] Fairy tales and fables evolve alongside us, emboldening our imaginations to take flight.[50] Steven Pinker has called fiction "empathy technology."[51]

Many feel that all of the wonderful animals depicted in literature and other storytelling media promote learning in children and foster empathy. Author Kate Bernheimer says "the kind of sensitivity to beauty and terror that permeates fairy tales—the very stories that often introduce writers to the reading sublime—should motivate us to read ethically, to be inclusive, and kind."[52] Others have strongly argued that reading literary fiction improves theory of the mind—that essential ability our intelligent machines would need to achieve to be aware of others' feelings, intentions, and thoughts.[53]

Science fiction is a didactic genre for imagining future scenarios and dissecting our relationships with technology, helping us to think about what could be, stimulating us to wrestle with and reconcile our past, present, and future.[54] Margaret Atwood's *The Handmaid's Tale*, a dystopian novel (and now TV show) focusing on women in a near-future, religious totalitarian society in the northeastern United States, endures because it tells a haunting tale of the future while also feeling eerily familiar. In describing how she wrote the book, Atwood said that she only included events that really happened—all the laws, atrocities, technologies, and historical precedent were real. She says that the book is not a prediction but rather "an antiprediction: If this future can be described in detail, maybe it won't happen. But such wishful thinking cannot be depended on either."[55]

Similarly, Philip K. Dick's novels, such as *Do Androids Dream of Electric Sheep?*, have helped us to rethink what it means to be a human, questioning our concepts of empathy, intelligence, and the nature of being alive.[56] *1984* feels like a future universe, as well as a past and present one, as it was born from George Orwell's reality at the time of its publication in 1949. Silicon Valley and advertising firms are recognizing the advantages of this kind of insight and now hire science fiction writers to help them imagine the future.[57] The U.S. military has worked with writers to help envision worst-case scenarios.[58] As well as playing out dystopian possibilities, science fiction can help us better visualize a future shared with intelligent machines.[59] For writer Neil Gaiman, "fiction is a lie that tells us true things, over and over."[60] When we engross ourselves in the full narrative arc of a good story, our brains synthesize oxytocin, which leads us to be more generous, empathetic, compassionate, and attuned to social cues.[61] Trying on another's consciousness lets us enter what social scientist and author Jèmeljan Hakemulder calls our "moral laboratory."[62] Humans can explore other worlds and the inner lives of others; we can learn to connect, to empathize, to care. Maybe our machines can, too?

Joseph Campbell sees human interconnectedness and empathy at the foundation of all human myths and stories: "You and the Other are one."[63] And scholars such as the Roman Catholic nun Karen Armstrong believe that compassion is a core value at the center of all religions.[64] Writer and Tibetan Buddhist teacher Matthieu Ricard believes that "interdependency is at the root of altruism and compassion."[65] Even if we may not agree on a full list of definitive, universal values, we can see that empathy and compassion are the cornerstone of all major religions.[66] Isn't this what we ideally want our technological creations to have when faced with moral and ethical choices?

As we continue to offload tasks, memories, and responsibilities to our smart devices, we may have to rely on them more and more to remind us of who we are. Just as an AI can digest the thousands of medical journals a single doctor could never get to in a lifetime in order to help her diagnose and treat patients, AI can assist us in learning to be more compassionate and connected, synthesizing and imparting the courage of Arundhati Roy, the thoughtfulness of Virginia Woolf, the bravery of Anne Frank, or the wisdom of Toni Morrison. And whereas humans have only a limited capacity to digest great literature, our intelligent machines do not. AI could become a digital library for the world's knowledge to date—and we will all have library cards.

Georgia Tech researchers Mark Riedl and Brent Harrison have been experimenting with a system they call Quixote to teach "value alignment" to robots through stories. They based this concept on the idea that humans learn about social responsibility and culturally sensitive behavior through reading stories. By instructing AI through "reverse engineering" vital lessons about morality from stories, AI can more closely align its goals with human values and be rewarded for compatible actions.[67]

This kind of innovative scientific investigation is more urgent than ever. Many of us almost always have a phone with us these days.[68] Five and a half billion of us will own mobile devices by 2022.[69] While the inquiry is ongoing, and mobile technology is indispensable for those with less access to resources, a 2011 study of American college students found that they were cultivating and expressing less empathy, due in large part to their digital lifestyles.[70] The more computer interaction, apparently the fewer opportunities to practice relating to the emotions of ourselves and others. Narcissism in the Digital Age is on the rise.[71] Other research affirms that we favor and are primed to mimic what we are repeatedly connected and exposed to.[72] This may explain why Silicon Valley executives often restrict their kids' use of the very platforms they are making billions of dollars developing.[73] If digital addiction is eroding our children's emotional intelligence, how can we cultivate the kindness, compassion, social connections, fairness, and global citizenship we will need for our future? Can AI versed in our quintessential human stories help us find a way back to one another?

Immersing our intelligent technology in literature obviously isn't the whole answer to establishing ethical AI. From a machine's perspective, there is nothing mathematically self-evident to indicate that all life is important—yet. Creating compassionate artificial intelligence is a much greater challenge than will be solved by just enabling AI to perceive sadness on a human face or in human speech. We all have our own backgrounds, patterns, stories, strokes of fortune or misfortune, and histories. We see the world through our own filters, blurring the perspectives of others. While we strive to empathize and find affinity

AI AND STORYTELLING

STORY ANALYSIS
MIT'S THE STORY LEARNING MACHINE

This project uses machine-based analytics to map video story structures across many story types and formats. In addition, methods to analyze viewer engagement with these stories are also developed and mapped according to the story structure.[1]

FILM
"SUNSPRING" AND "IT'S NO GAME"

Director Oscar Sharp and AI researcher Ross Goodwin released two sci-fi short films written by an algorithm named Benjamin. The AI learns to create long sentences based on learning rules from a collection of writing.[2]

ADVERTISING
LEXUS'S AI-SCRIPTED COMMERCIAL

Directed by Oscar winner Kevin Macdonald, the commercial is based on a script developed by IBM's Watson system. Fifteen years' worth of footage, text, and audio for car and luxury brand campaigns were analyzed.[3]

JOURNALISM
REUTERS' LYNX INSIGHT

Reuters' Lynx Insight is used to assist journalists in analyzing data, suggesting story ideas, and helping with writing simple sentences.[4]

GAMING + INTERACTIVE NARRATIVE
SKYRIM'S RADIANT AI STORY SYSTEM

Skyrim employs Radiant AI artificial intelligence to allow nonplayer characters to dynamically react to and interact with other characters and the world around them. Radiant Story system is also employed to create new dynamic quests, resulting in more vibrant gameplay.[5]

---

(1) "The Story Learning Machine," *MIT Media Lab*.
(2) Annalee Newitz, "An AI Wrote All Of David Hasselhoff's Lines In This Bizarre Short Film," *Ars Technica*, April 25, 2017.
(3) Todd Spangler, "First AI-Scripted Commercial Debuts, Directed by Kevin Macdonald for Lexus," *Variety*, November 19, 2018.
(4) Reginald Chua, "The Cybernetic Newsroom: Horses and Cars," *Reuters*, March 12, 2019.
(5) Zoe Delahunty-Light, "Remember Skyrim's Radian AI? It's Got the Potential to Revolutionise RPGs," *Gamesradar*, March 05, 2018.

with others, it's also valuable to remember that we can never fully inhabit the experiences of others; that the universe doesn't revolve around and exist for our points of view.

But if, alongside our intelligent technological partners, we humans can better embrace the valor and ideals of Yuri Kochiyama, Jean Valjean, Albus Dumbledore, Maya Angelou, or Martin Luther King Jr., this will be an important step toward developing AI that will have a better and more nuanced way of discerning the human condition. Could AI help tutor and spiritually embolden us, find the best in each of us? Could it show us the courage of the hobbits in *The Lord of the Rings*, the joys and sorrows in the poetry of Pablo Neruda, Langston Hughes, Rumi, or Mary Oliver, the power in "Letter from Birmingham Jail," or the wisdom in the Vedas?

> It matters what matters we use to think other matters with; it matters what stories we tell to tell other stories with; it matters what knots knot knots, what thoughts think thoughts, what descriptions describe descriptions, what ties tie ties. It matters what stories make worlds, what worlds make stories.
>
> —DONNA HARAWAY

The answers to whether it's possible to code something akin to empathy into our intelligent machines may not be too far into the future. What was once seen as a formidable barrier to advancing AI capability, its tendency toward "catastrophic forgetting,"[74] may be imminently resolved. Computer scientists at Google DeepMind are building AI that can remember.[75] And if AI can retain its aggregate memories, as humans have evolved to do, but with far more precision and accuracy, we should be able to build on the library of knowledge as allies.

Google DeepMind founder, AI expert, neuroscientist, and game designer Demis Hassabis believes that the key to AI lies in connecting the fields of AI and neuroscience. Understanding the brain will help unlock AI and help it acquire attributes like intuition. In turn, building AI will help us understand more about who we are.[76] Cognitive scientist Gary Marcus has expressed a similar idea, suggesting that studying children's cognitive development is key to advancing machine learning.[77] Though it will be difficult to achieve, such a goal also underlines the need to communicate and translate ideas across fields and disciplines.

As for the power of the human intellect, our extraordinary mental gift of cognitive time travel, back and forth into our past and into the future, is core to the civilizations we inhabit.[78] Scientists have found that cerebrally journeying through time may be linked to humans' development of language as well as to comprehending others—our theory of mind. Cognitive neuroscience has also shown that mind-wandering is critical to our ability to navigate our past or imagine the future. Some go so far as to say that cognitive time travel, and our capability to conceive of the future, is the distinguishing component of human intelligence.[79] Others argue that animals also have the capacity for mental travel, albeit on a less sophisticated scale.[80] Either way, storytelling may be our most essential human technology.[81]

In our minds, we can build worlds and imagine universes, traveling back to ancient history and fast-forwarding to the end of time. We remember past hurts and we dream of triumph in the future. With this ability, we can envision future outcomes based on past patterns, just as the many great writers of time-travel literature have imagined technological possibilities that later came true.

AI, with its unprecedented capacity to consume and sift through data, can already record and instantly retrieve information, document history, and predict consequences far beyond anything heretofore envisaged. As we encode more creative features into AI, it is inevitable it will also compose new narratives in ways we cannot yet foresee. It is already making art, composing music, and writing books. Authors are experimenting with software that finishes typing their sentences, with far more sophisticated tools on the horizon.[82]

Lest we think that creative storytelling is a uniquely human attribute that a machine could never acquire, what we have long thought of as other unique, divinely endowed human characteristics may have actually just been learned over time. For example, in *The Enigma of Reason*, the authors suggest that human reason itself is an evolved trait, an "adaptation to hyper social niches humans have evolved for themselves." And "subject-centered" reasoning is a mechanism we developed, incrementally, to prevent us from being taken advantage of by the group—a relatively new theory dating back to the seventeenth century.[83]

From classical philosophy to law to economics, the singular ability of the human brain to reason has historically been of paramount importance. Human reasoning has allowed us to dominate the earth thus far, and acknowledging it as something we learned over time should not devalue it; rather, it illustrates our capacity to grow. We know today that our brains are neuroplastic and that we can rewire ourselves and our thinking. Although we are not blank slates, we can change our path. We can acknowledge the rational and emotional parts of ourselves, face our darkness *and* our light. And we can train our intelligent machines to help get us there.

We already partner with our smart machines, animals, and the environment. We have, however, historically regarded them as inferior. They are not. Hierarchizing intelligence allows us to assign lesser dignities to others. The way forward into our new age is to cease insisting on absolute supremacy in all things. Our survival does not depend on maintaining control, for we ultimately have very little of that anyway.

It lies, instead, in acceptance, tolerance, and collaboration. History reminds us time and time again that first we fight against one another, for the throne, the power, the glory, the victory—yet to truly triumph, we need to band together.

> In the long history of humankind (and animal kind, too) those who learned to collaborate and improvise most effectively have prevailed.
>
> —CHARLES DARWIN

The AI wave is already beginning to crest. Predicting with certainty how it will take shape is not possible, nor should it be the goal. Remember the adjacent possible—we are already hurtling through the artificially intelligent space not knowing where we might land, endeavoring to build upon our collective imagination. We could yet fail.

With the introduction of new forms of intelligence that already exceed our own, consider the possibility that *we* are actually the robots, albeit carbon-based ones; not mechanical but both programmed to survive and destined to fail to live up to our own principles. To flourish, we cannot put technology ahead of humanity—or human before the rest. The AI is us, made of our star-stuff. We and our intelligent new mechanical partners have already begun to merge our storylines. As much as we would like to have some certainty about what our future will look like alongside our brilliant new creations in what now still sounds like science fiction, we can only find our true north by following the set of instructions we hold inside ourselves. A human algorithm that reminds us to value all forms of intelligence and hold dear all living things.

10

A HUMAN ALGORITHM

The cosmos is within us. We are made of star-stuff. We are
a way for the universe to know itself.

—CARL SAGAN

GO INTO THE FOREST

Jane Goodall had no formal training in animal behavior nor any scientific knowledge of chimpanzees when she arrived in Tanzania in 1960.
She was also a woman, therefore at that time she was expected to
marry and stay at home—in fact, her mother had to come with her to
the national park because authorities insisted that a young woman not
be alone. While visiting a friend in Kenya, Goodall met and was then

hired by the renowned paleontologist Louis Leakey, who had been searching for someone to spend time in the wild to find connections between chimpanzees and humans.[1]

Leakey believed that Goodall could do the work. So he hired her to do her dream job: observe chimps in their natural habitat. He saw great potential in her, that she had a mind "uncluttered and unbiased by theory."[2]

When Goodall walked into Gombe National Park and witnessed, for the first time, a chimpanzee not only *using* but also *making* a tool, she reported this stunning finding to Leakey, who famously said: "Now we must redefine man, redefine tools, or accept chimpanzees as humans."[3]

Traditional "experts" can be brilliant; they can also be dangerously closed-minded. Studies show that "experts" can be especially shortsighted because they believe they have "earned" the right to be more dogmatic.[4] In contrast, Goodall walked into the forest not with the hubris of expertise, but instead with an open mind, and she observed something no one else had ever been able to see. When the chimpanzees showed us how similar we are to them, in essence holding up a mirror, she was brave enough to peer into it and then carry this mirror back for all of us to see.

In this book I have attempted to outline the daunting challenges the Intelligent Machine Age presents. The various conceivable ways this future could unfold are overwhelming and complex. Adopting Jane Goodall's unfettered mind, with arms wide open to the possibilities of our intelligent creations and the world we will share with them, is the posture to emulate. As Federico García Lorca tells us, "every step we take on earth brings us to a new world."[5] Make your footprints visible, trusting that together we can find our way in the dark.

Walk into the forest of our rapidly evolving technological future, unbound by dogma, mindful of its amorphous potential. Live in reverence and curiosity about what's out there, about what's next. Let's face our fears and find a way to marvel at whatever we might find. Of course, there is no such thing as a completely unprejudiced and dispassionate human, but there are ways we can get closer to tabula rasa. We can become more aware. Perhaps the question AI can help us answer isn't, "What does it mean to be human?" but rather, "How can we be *more* than human?" How can we be the caterpillar and the machine, the octopus and the elephant, the mountain and the star?

> There are no passengers on spaceship Earth. We are all crew.
>
> —MARSHALL McLUHAN

The impending age of intelligent machines gives us all an opportunity to find the common ground needed to become accepting of all people and living things. For the first time since humans walked the earth, we'll have no choice but to learn to live among the crowd of all beings as opposed to above it. We're on a spaceship rumbling into a distant galaxy. On this trek, alongside machines, we can explore new solar systems of our imaginations, leading to greater empathy than our species has ever manifested before. If we do, we may all be able to experience the same awakening, the same enlightenment, the same sacred understanding.

THE PROBLEM OF GOD

> There is no great invention, from fire to flying, which has not been hailed as an insult to some god.
>
> —J. B. S. HALDANE

At first glance, the widespread adoption of smart technologies and new scientific discoveries, such as finding the "god particle,"[6] and the creation of new, possibly conscious, artificially intelligent beings would seem to indicate an inexorable march toward secularization. Are these astounding discoveries proof that God doesn't exist, at least not in the forms taught to us by interpretations of ancient texts espoused by the world's largest religions? Or will the advent of these technologies take us to new heights of spirituality?

A class at Georgetown University called "Problem of God" explores ideas of religion and faith, from Santería to deep ecology, looking at "fundamental human questions that need some sort of answer, however tentative."[7] Hindu chaplain Brahmachari Sharan, who teaches the course, ponders that to probe these existential conundrums, "Ignatian spirituality says to find the gray and live in it."[8] To contemplate how intelligent technology may affect religion and human spirituality, it is into this gray we, too, must go.

Science and religion have often been at odds. Over the ages, religions and their various interpretations have generated persecution and dangerous dogma. But whether you believe in God or you don't, we have to acknowledge that a majority of our fellow humans still do hold a religious belief.[9] Some reports show that religious populations are actually on the rise relative to the nonreligious.[10] Many North Americans would call themselves at least spiritual.[11] To be inclusive as we stride toward our technological future, we must consider ideas from religion and spiritual beliefs. Like the image of Earth from space, both religion and AI can remind us of our ultimate smallness, our limited time on Earth. Religion, belief, and prayer have a place in the discussion of AI and ethics, because whether you are an atheist, an agnostic, or a believer, religion still matters on some level—whether as a belief system, an ethical framework, or a cultural touchstone—to much of the world's human population. As with technology, religion is responsible for some of humanity's achievements as well as some of life's cruelest tragedies. We can all have faith, empathy, and compassion with or without these identities.

Although we are moving toward a greater discussion about religious pluralism and diversity and also, in some respects, less adherence to organized religion,[12] questions about religion remain elusive, complicated, personal, and controversial. We may speculate about how technology that unmasks more mysteries of the universe and produces new, sentient, and self-aware beings may collide with systems of belief and reshape identities, real or digital, but such speculation remains in the realm of philosophical conjecture. Nonetheless, these discussions are within the purview of any significant consideration of where we are headed as a civilization.

Dr. Beth Singler, a social and digital anthropologist of new religious movements, explains that religions tend to cope with technology in three stages—rejection, adoption, and adaption—and that the "initial reaction can often be negative, but technology soon becomes ubiquitous and part of the mainstream."[13] This is understandable; religions are institutions that bind groups who believe and worship a variety of deities. Science, and new discoveries in particular, have always threatened such institutions.

The discourse about intelligent technology and religion among theologians, philosophers, scientists, and others is already broad, deep, and heated. Some suggest that artificial intelligence demeans our specialness, while others predict it will bring us closer to God. In some religions, humans project their own likeness onto their objects of worship (Imago Dei, or "image of God"). There is reason to think that this may also hold true for how we design our synthetically intelligent companions. In Western traditions, we want our anthropomorphized God to look like us, though in the images we create of God, he (we usually assume God is a "him") only looks like some of us. AI itself is fostering new kinds of religions with rites and rituals devoted to electronic gods.[14] Scholarly consensus on even exactly what constitutes "religion" remains unsettled. It's also interesting to observe that those working in AI, in what appears to be a largely secular community, often use religious terminology to describe achievements and objectives, such as the "prophets," "oracles," and "evangelists" of our technological future, working on things like the "infinite knowing" of the singularity or "the escape of the flesh" of uploading our minds.[15]

What seems inescapable is that self-aware, conscious technology will affect theology by exposing our beliefs about consciousness, intelligence, the soul, and what it means to be alive. It will test our individual and collective faiths and beliefs. As we recognize new, intelligent entities, concepts of human uniqueness will be challenged. Technology that can not just unlock but unseal new scientific doors will also reveal our human limitations as AI takes over more of our professional and societal roles. It may convince many that our lives are ephemeral—that we are just of the earth, and thus transient. On the other hand, what happens to one's faith in an afterlife when we can digitally prolong life, perhaps indefinitely? And might AI also allow humans more time to explore spirituality and what we truly believe in, and help many more of us renew our faith in one another?

> Faith is personal and mysterious and individualistic and inexpressible and indefinable. Religion is merely the language that you can use to express what is fundamentally inexpressible, to define what is undefinable . . . For me, the language that you choose is not that important . . . It's what you are expressing that actually matters.
>
> —REZA ASLAN

The Intelligent Machine Age will certainly disrupt our existing belief systems. However, my interest here is less in organized religion than in the idea of faith itself. Faith does not spring from reason or logic. Faith is trust. It allows us to get into a taxi or an airplane; count on a friend; follow our intuition; move forward from tragedy. Faith says there will be a better tomorrow. Faith can breed hope. Faith is something within us we can't quite explain. Faith helps us find purpose, believe in something larger than ourselves. It helps show us the way.

With faith rather than dogma, the next technological revolution may afford us the opportunity to look inward; to wonder more at the intricacies of nature, even as more mysteries are revealed; to marvel at the enigmas that will always live on; and to nurture and comfort our human souls by engaging with one another and our world in new and profound ways. As the idea of the adjacent possible suggests, the acceleration of intelligent technology may expand to the point of blurring the frontiers between science and spirituality, the known and the unknown, the known and the unknowable.

> To say that there is more to reality than physics can account for is not a piece of mysticism: it is an acknowledgement that we are nowhere near a theory of everything, and that science will have to expand to accommodate facts of a kind fundamentally different from those that physics is designed to explain.
>
> —THOMAS NAGEL

From both our religions (if we have them) and our technology, we seek answers. Validation. It's easy to overlook the flaws in our religious texts, our Facebook feeds, our in-group, or our reasoning. It's difficult to let go of long-held beliefs or to develop empathy for those from different tribes. This involves a shift in who we think we are, and what our place in the world is. Yet it's essential to understand that when we deny the possibility of dignity and humanity to others, we take it away from ourselves. The story of AI is the story of us—all of us. Writing parts for the whole panoply of the earth's characters, be they bone or metal, is how we arc our story toward hope.

Our intelligent machines may give us the capacity to realize our collective human potential. Intelligent technology instilled with our highest values, technology in which we have confidence to help make decisions that are fair and equal to all, is in our best interests and in the best interests of future generations. Machines will be partners in which we place our faith. After all, when we step onto a modern airplane, we trust technology (as well as the pilot) to deliver us safely. Our new inventions can also help transport us where we need to go.

As we have done throughout history, we'll continue to trust our technology more and more. We now trust it to help judge our sporting events, keep our passwords, memorize our faces and fingerprints, operate our elevators, and recognize our voices. Technology secures our homes and monitors our babies, forecasts the weather, informs our air traffic controllers, and helps design our skyscrapers, bridges, tunnels, and levies. It explores the galaxies, collides atoms, and guides surgical instruments; we trust it with our most revered commodity, money, in banks, on stock exchanges, and in the form of new kinds of currency. Smart technology helps diagnose our illnesses and entertains us while we recover. Soon it will drive us on highways and help care for our children and parents. It will perform many of our complex thinking tasks. We are well into the technological stage Kevin Kelly refers to as "cognification," in which the things around us are getting much smarter.[16] As James Vincent of ThinkLabs calls it, we are in an "algorithmic gaze" where AI is already training us,[17] where the world is increasingly being seen through the eyes of computers.

BIOLOGICAL TRANSFORMATION AND DIGITAL EVOLUTION

To design AI that reflects human ideals, we have to recognize our darkness, too—the violence, aggression, and conflict baked into us. Whether cultural, biological, or somewhere in between, these brutal realities are parts of our history that we must face in order to make our way toward more peace, more understanding, more promise. Our brokenness, our human imperfection, is part of our story too. In acknowledging the most narrow-minded parts of ourselves, we may loosen our unwillingness to accept one another in all of our beautiful diversity and shared lineage. We begin to free ourselves to walk into the future without having to mold intelligent creations solely in our own image and instead open up a passage to a more humane and inclusive technological future. To understand our foibles and faults is a step toward compassion, toward feeling how our pulse is connected to the web of life all around us.

Living in a world with forms of intelligence superior to our own requires having faith in one another: faith that we can respect and honor all the living things that share our home. In doing so, we can move past our fear of bestowing consciousness, intelligence, rights, and dignity upon others. This is our best chance of getting it right with AI—AI that is good—in a home that can sustain us all.

To form a lasting, symbiotic partnership with synthetic intelligence, that intelligence will have to understand, respect, and carry forward our humanity and our collective set of values. Before we can attempt to do that mechanically, curious inquiry has to advance. Today, we are only at the very earliest stages of programmable humaneness; computer scientist Vincent Conitzer is conducting a study funded by the Future of Life Institute to reverse engineer behavior to discover how humans make ethical and moral choices, so that an AI can be enabled with this capability, too.[18] The challenge in translating our values to machines, as he sees it, is that "moral judgments are not objective." Rather, our human morality is time-constrained and complicated, and it hasn't yet reached its apex. He believes that combining ideas from numerous fields, from philosophy to economics to psychology, is the key.[19]

The research is ongoing and may or may not achieve its goals. At MIT, neuroscientists are beginning to investigate how they might build AI based on how children's brains grow, morph, and take shape.[20] How do we integrate an AI without a physical form into the calculus? Algorithms traditionally have a single mathematical aim. However, in life, it can be lethal to allow for only one absolute answer. Peter Eckersley of the Partnership on AI is experimenting with programming uncertainty into algorithms so they are more aligned with the nuance of the human experience.[21] Our increasingly complex coexistence suggests that we will cede more and more control to our intelligent machines. Let's give them humane code instead of rigid rules.

Technology is not born with cognitive bias; it inherits it from those who code, program, and design it. If we want our rapidly advancing AI to be ethical, we need to commit to improving our own internal algorithms. This involves identifying the core principles we want to live by, accepting that we have system flaws, ferreting out and repairing the bugs, monitoring the ways our systems interact with those of other beings, and upgrading our human features to align more and more with who we aspire to be.

In the paper "The Surprising Creativity of Digital Evolution: A Collection of Anecdotes from the Evolutionary Computation and Artificial Life Research Communities," researchers studying the field

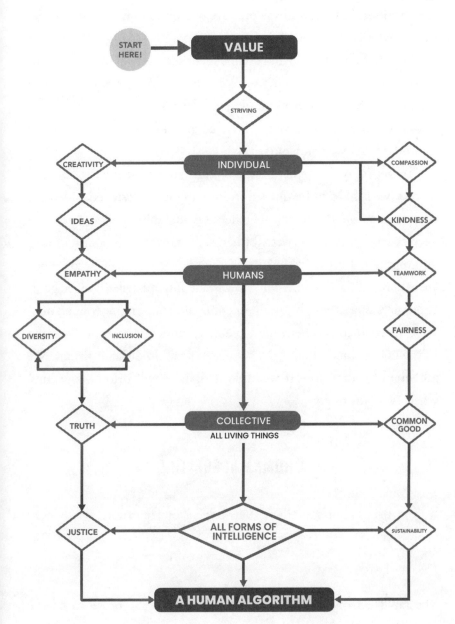

of digital evolutionary processes corrected a common misconception that such processes lack relevance to biological evolution by looking specifically at how algorithms produce outcomes that surprise the designers who created them. The authors noted that "digital evolution can be a useful tool to aid and complement the study of biological evolution. Indeed, these evolving systems can be seen as real instances of evolution, rather than mere simulation of evolution."[22] In other words, as our machines evolve, we too are changing in significant ways, and by studying AI we study ourselves.

To get to a point where humans can truly trust intelligent technology, we'll have to be unified in insisting it be designed to benefit the common good and that it reflect demographic parity. These are not yet mechanical electives. Rather, right now we can think of it as an aspirational mindset, nurturing the science that will become our karma. Building our tech for good is the much harder, longer path. It requires more thought, more intentional action, more cooperation, more acceptance of others, more practice, more debate, more treading in the uncertainty. That's OK, because we can do difficult things. We are wired for that, too. If we build it right, it will help take us anywhere we want to go.

A HUMAN ALGORITHM

Being human is given. But keeping our humanity is a choice.

—UNKNOWN

The rapid expansion of intelligent technology may prove to be the chrysalis for the biggest metamorphosis humankind will ever experience. The path forward is as much humanistic as it is based in the "hard" sciences. I agree with the physicist David Deutsch that "philosophy will be the key that unlocks artificial intelligence."[23] For in the end, we are flecks of dust in a vast universe working around us, in spite of us, metronomically, as it has done for billions of years. But even in our cosmic smallness, we all have a profound responsibility: to map a human algorithm, one that encompasses who we are and who we want to become.

A human algorithm is the philosophical center of ourselves. It's our personal and collective ethos; it's the DNA of our humanity; it's our conscience. All the things that make us who we are, in all of our misery and majesty, fallibility and brilliance. Just as celestial navigation enables us to chart the heavens and find our way, our human algorithms guide us to our values, our kindness, our compassion, our bravery, our humanness. The more multifaceted the diversity, the more human the algorithm: never perfect, yet ever more humane.

On the vast canvas of possible futures, the warp and weft that will become the society the next generations will inhabit is being composed now. Our technology will mirror our human algorithms, and that is our destiny. We want it to know us, in all our imperfect human complexity; to protect us, to remind us of the best in us, to become a trusted partner. The machines are us. They can remember the memories that escape us and unravel the dreams that elude us. Together, we can reimagine our place in the universe, our connection to all things, remembering that we are all—human and creature, mountain and river, sun and moon—made up of stardust.

To most of us, building the actual tech of intelligent machines will continue to be akin to alchemy. Yet while many of us still struggle to operate our iPhones, our children have quickly adopted tech only dreamed of a few years earlier; their children will come to know AI with a fluency we cannot yet imagine. We owe it to them to ensure they can coexist with this technology naturally. Humans are more than just an algorithm that a robot can replace. AI can enrich our human culture in extraordinary ways.

Today, a human algorithm can only be described in metaphysical terms, not scientific ones. It isn't a map for how to get out of the forest. It's a map for *going in*. Every action we take, all the code we write, all the truths we espouse, all the positions we hold, and all the justice we seek affect others in the gossamer web we all share. We venture onward, knowing that we will continually fall short, that none of us will get all the way there. It is only when we are secure in the design and function of our internal algorithms that we'll be able to build machines we can trust, that we would be proud to leave to the ages. Like a time capsule we send into space or bury in the backyard, filled with the music that lifts our souls and the moments that define us, a human algorithm is empathy in action, a compassionate siren's call to the future.

This book is a cautious statement of hope that, in the end, technology will reveal who we are—resilient and vulnerable, curious and creative, abounding with potential for genuine connection with ourselves and with others—and that it presents an opportunity to code these traits into our future, to bend collectively toward the light. Much of the journey into the Intelligent Machine Age is still in front of us, but I am confident that in our quest to build a digital soul, we will find our own.

Acknowledgments

Publishing a book is a team sport. Any inspiration you take away from these pages is due to the dedication of a vibrant community that worked on this project with me. I stand on the shoulders of friends and collaborators, and I owe much to their voices—past, present, and future. Any errors are mine alone.

To the team at Counterpoint Press: I'm humbled to be in your pantheon of authors, and I'm so proud my book found a home with your press. To Dan Smetanka: working together to complete this project was a joy. We edited, we laughed, and we edited again. Thank you for believing in me and in this book. To Jenn Kovitz, Becky Kraemer, and Katie Boland, along with Sarah Jean Grimm, Megan Fishmann, Dustin Kurtz, Miyako Singer, and the entire crew: I'm honored to work with such a powerhouse group, and I'm incredibly grateful for your guidance and support. To Nicole Caputo and Sarah Brody for bringing this dream to undulating, artistic life with your stunning cover design. To the exquisite editors who saw the sculpture in the marble: Jordan Koluch, Katherine Kiger, Jenefer Shute, and Laura Grow-Nyberg. To Meg Whiteford, whose fact-checking, research, and collaboration have been essential. To Hoai Nam Pham, whose imaginative designs light up the pages of this book. Thank you.

To Kevin O'Connor: thank you for being my first ally in the publishing world. To the team at Sheedy Lit, helmed by Charlotte Sheedy: thank you for being a champion of literary magic, social justice, diversity, and inclusion. It's a great honor to be part of your world and to help carry the flame. To Laurie Dolphin, for believing in this idea from the start, and to Stuart Shapiro, who has known me since I was little, for supporting my literary dreams.

To my teachers and mentors: thank you for showing me who I want to be and who I am still becoming. I hope to always make you proud. To my students, who challenge and inspire me every day. It's a true gift to watch you thrive. You give me such hope in the future.

To the keepers of libraries, bookstores, and literary places far and wide, who provide sanctuary and solace for so many: thank you for keeping the light and kettle on for us writers and dreamers. To those whose courage and resilience has helped me to see the essence of the human spirit and the humanity within us all: thank you for leading the way. To the many brilliant people whose source material fills the endnotes of this book: you are a teeming well of wisdom and a record of who we are. To the innovators, inventors, and visionaries who transport us: thank you for seeing what is not yet here, but could be. To all the living beings we share our planet with: I've tried to listen to your calls and be your advocate in this book. I hope it has helped in some small way to turn your suffering into light.

To my dream team: Genevieve Casey, you are the conscience of this book. With you I'm in the finest book club I could ever hope to join. To the early readers of this book, who provided critical feedback and expertise that made it better: John Garnett, Joe Cirincione, and Dana Rubin. Thank you. To my sister, for a mind unlike any other. To my beloved family and friends, you light a candle when it feels dark. Thank you for helping me find my song. Especially to Shauna Brittenham Reiter, Vidya Satchit, and Steven Morrison. I love you forever.

To my mom: for your imaginative spirit unlike anyone else on Earth. For your artistic vision, for reading early drafts, and for laughing with me through this process and through life. Let's keep evolving.

And to my dad: I wouldn't want to do this without you, and without you none of this would be possible. You are the greatest father this planet has ever known. I share this with you.

Finally, to the future generations, the torchbearers, the poets, the makers, the rule breakers, the change makers, the guardians, the world builders, the scribblers, the lovers, the rebels, our children, and our children's children who will be: take care of one another, all the creatures with whom we share our home, and all those who will come after you.

See you in the stars.

Notes

Links to internet sites are provided for the convenience of the reader and are correct at the time of publication.

INTRODUCTION: OUR BRAVE NEW WORLD

1. Christianna Reedy, "Kurzweil Claims That the Singularity Will Happen by 2045," Futurism, October 5, 2017, futurism.com/kurzweil-claims-that-the-singularity-will-happen-by-2045.
2. Jamie Condliffe, "The Average American Spends 24 Hours a Week Online," The Download, *MIT Technology Review,* January 23, 2018, www.technologyreview.com/the -download/610045/the-average-american-spends-24-hours-a-week-online.
3. James Vincent, "Hillary Clinton Says America is 'Totally Unprepared' for the Impact of AI," The Verge, November 23, 2017, www.theverge.com/2017/11/23/16693894/hillary -clinton-ai-america-totally-unprepared.
4. Bill Hathaway, "Online Illusion: Unplugged, We Really Aren't That Smart," Yale News, March 31, 2015, news.yale.edu/2015/03/31/online-illusion-unplugged-we-really-aren-t-smart.
5. Alyson Shontell, "Google Is Destroying Our Memories, Scientists Find," Business Insider, July 16, 2011, www.businessinsider.com/google-effect-on-brain-memory-psychology-2011-7.
6. "How Algorithms (Secretly) Run the World," Phys.org, February 11, 2017, phys.org /news/2017-02-algorithms-secretly-world.html.

7. Yilun Wang and Michal Kosinski, "Deep Neural Networks Are More Accurate than Humans at Detecting Sexual Orientation from Facial Images," Open Science Framework, October 16, 2017, www.gsb.stanford.edu/faculty-research/publications/deep-neural-networks-are-more-accurate-humans-detecting-sexual.

8. Som Bathla, "This is How High-Achievers Make Smart (and Avoid Bad) Decisions," Medium, June 14, 2018, medium.com/swlh/this-is-how-high-achievers-make-smart-and-avoid-bad-decisions-5d842ce4f78.

9. Robyn Caplan, Joan Donovan, Lauren Hanson, and Jeanna Matthews, "Algorithmic Accountability: A Primer," Data & Society, April 18, 2018, datasociety.net/output/algorithmic-accountability-a-primer.

10. George Dvorsky, "Why a Superintelligent Machine May Be the Last Thing We Ever Invent," Gizmodo, October 2, 2013, io9.gizmodo.com/why-a-superintelligent-machine-may-be-the-last-thing-we-1440091472.

11. Tim Adams, "Artificial intelligence: 'We're like children playing with a bomb,'" *Guardian*, June 12, 2016, www.theguardian.com/technology/2016/jun/12/nick-bostrom-artificial-intelligence-machine.

12. Daniel Victor, "Microsoft Created a Twitter Bot to Learn from Users. It Quickly Became a Racist Jerk," *New York Times*, March 24, 2016, www.nytimes.com/2016/03/25/technology/microsoft-created-a-twitter-bot-to-learn-from-users-it-quickly-became-a-racist-jerk.html.

13. Julia Angwin, Ariana Tobin, and Madeleine Varner, "Facebook (Still) Letting Housing Advertisers Exclude Users by Race," ProPublica, November 21, 2017, www.propublica.org/article/facebook-advertising-discrimination-housing-race-sex-national-origin.

14. Gideon Resnick, "How Pro-Trump Twitter Bots Spread Fake News," The Daily Beast, November 17, 2016, www.thedailybeast.com/how-pro-trump-twitter-bots-spread-fake-news.

15. "al-Khwarizmi, the Father of Algebra," Interactive Math, accessed October 8, 2018, www.intmath.com/basic-algebra/al-khwarizmi-father-algebra.php.

16. Nick Bostrom, "Are You Living in a Computer Simulation?" *Philosophical Quarterly* Vol. 53, No. 211 (2003): 243–255, www.simulation-argument.com/simulation.pdf.

17. George Feifer interview with Vladimir Nabokov, *Saturday Review*, November 27, 1976, 22.

18. "AI to Drive GDP Gains of $15.7 Trillion with Productivity, Personalisation Improvements," PricewaterhouseCoopers, June 21, 2017, press.pwc.com/News-releases/ai-to-drive-gdp-gains-of--15.7-trillion-with-productivity--personalisation-improvements/s/3cc702e4-9cac-4a17-85b9-71769fba82a6.

19. Kate Becker, "When Computers Were Human: The Black Women Behind NASA's Success," *New Scientist*, January 20, 2017, www.newscientist.com/article/2118526-when-computers-were-human-the-black-women-behind-nasas-success.

20. Michio Kaku, *Physics of the Future* (New York: Doubleday, 2011).

21. Karla Lant, "By 2020, There Will Be 4 Devices for Every Human on Earth," Futurism, June 18, 2017, futurism.com/by-2020-there-will-be-4-devices-for-every-human-on-earth.

22. Gary Marcus, "Why We Should Think About the Threat of Artificial Intelligence," *New Yorker*, October 24, 2013, www.newyorker.com/tech/annals-of-technology/why-we-should-think-about-the-threat-of-artificial-intelligence.

23. Tom Ward, "Google's New AI Is Better at Creating AI Than the Company's Engineers,"

Futurism, May 19, 2017, futurism.com/googles-new-ai-is-better-at-creating-ai-than-the
-companys-engineers.

24. Stephen Hawking, Stuart Russell, Max Tegmark, and Frank Wilczek, "Stephen Hawking: 'Transcendence Looks at the Implications of Artificial Intelligence—but Are We Taking AI Seriously Enough?'" *Independent UK*, May 1, 2014, www.independent.co.uk/news/science /stephen-hawking-transcendence-looks-at-the-implications-of-artificial-intelligence-but -are-we-taking-9313474.html.

25. Samuel Gibbs, "Elon Musk: Artificial Intelligence is Our Biggest Existential Threat," *Guardian*, October 27, 2014, www.theguardian.com/technology/2014/oct/27/elon-musk -artificial-intelligence-ai-biggest-existential-threat.

26. Radina Gigova, "Who Vladimir Putin thinks will rule the world," CNN, September 2, 2017, www.cnn.com/2017/09/01/world/putin-artificial-intelligence-will-rule-world/index .html.

27. Rodney Brooks, "The Seven Deadly Sins of AI Predictions," *MIT Technology Review*, October 6, 2017, www.technologyreview.com/s/609048/the-seven-deadly-sins-of-ai-predictions.

28. Jackie Snow, "Jeff Bezos Gave a Sneak Peek into Amazon's Future," *MIT Technology Review*, March 22, 2018, www.technologyreview.com/s/610607/jeff-bezos-gave-a-sneak-peak -into-amazons-future.

29. Joshua J. Mark, "Protagoras of Abdera: Of All Things Man Is the Measure," Ancient History Encyclopedia, January 18, 2012, www.ancient.eu/article/61/protagoras-of-abdera-of-all -things-man-is-the-meas.

30. Peter Stone, Rodney Brooks, Erik Brynjolfsson, Ryan Calo, Oren Etzioni, et al., "Artificial Intelligence and Life in 2030," One Hundred Year Study on Artificial Intelligence: Report of the 2015–2016 Study Panel, Stanford University, Stanford, CA, September 2016, ai100 .stanford.edu/sites/default/files/ai_100_report_0831fnl.pdf.

31. Jane Wakefield, "Robot 'Talks' to MPs About Future of AI in the Classroom," BBC News, October 16, 2018, www.bbc.com/news/technology-45879961.

32. Alex Hern, "Give Robots 'Personhood' Status, EU Committee Argues," *Guardian*, January 12, 2017, www.theguardian.com/technology/2017/jan/12/give-robots-personhood-status -eu-committee-argues.

33. Pamela McCorduck, "What Do You Think About Machines That Think?" The Edge, 2015, www.edge.org/responses/the-edge-question.

34. Samantha Masunaga, "Robots Could Take Over 38% of U.S. Jobs Within About 15 Years, Report Says," *Los Angeles Times*, March 24, 2017, www.latimes.com/business/la-fi-pwc -robotics-jobs-20170324-story.html.

35. Roy Amara, attributed in *The Age*, 31, October 2006.

36. Ariel Conn, "How Do We Align Artificial Intelligence with Human Values?" Future of Life Institute, February 3, 2017, futureoflife.org/2017/02/03/align-artificial -intelligence-with-human-values.

37. Adam Rogers, "The Way the World Ends: Not with a Bang but with a Paperclip," *Wired*, October 21, 2017, www.wired.com/story/the-way-the-world-ends-not-with-a-bang-but-a-paperclip.

38. Joel Achenbach, "Why Do Many Reasonable People Doubt Science?" *National Geographic*, March 2015, www.nationalgeographic.com/magazine/2015/03/science-doubters -climate-change-vaccinations-gmos.

39. The trolley dilemma is a philosophical game that consists of innumerable hypothetical situations that test our sense of ethics and explore how we might react when faced with moral quandaries such as if and when it's appropriate to harm an innocent bystander for the sake of the greater good. Laura D'Olimpio, "The Trolley Dilemma: Would You Kill One Person to Save Five?" The Conversation, June 2, 2016, theconversation.com /the-trolley-dilemma-would-you-kill-one-person-to-save-five-57111.

40. Isaiah Berlin, *The Proper Study of Mankind: An Anthology of Essays*, Hendry Hardy, Roger Hausheer, eds. (London: Chatto and Windus, 1997), 11.

41. Julian Savulescu and Hannah Maslen, "Moral Enhancement and Artificial Intelligence: Moral AI?" *Beyond Artificial Intelligence. Topics in Intelligent Engineering and Informatics*, J. Romport, E. Zackova, J. Kelemen, eds., Vol. 9 (2005): 79–95, link.springer.com /chapter/10.1007/978-3-319-09668-1_6.

42. Mary Shelley, *Frankenstein, or, The Modern Prometheus* (Lackington, Hughes, Harding, Mavor & Jones, 1818).

CHAPTER 1: FIRE TO FIREWALLS

1. Bennet Woodcroft, ed., *The Pneumatics of Hero of Alexandria by Hero of Alexandria* (CreateSpace Independent Publishing Platform, 2009).

2. "The Amazing Ancient Machines of Hero of Alexandria," Gizmodo, February 28, 2014, gizmodo.com/the-amazing-ancient-machines-of-hero-of-alexandria-1533213972.

3. Mary Bellis, "The History of Steam Engines," ThoughtCo., September 24, 2018, www .thoughtco.com/history-of-steam-engines-4072565.

4. Jimmy Stamp, "A Brief History of Robot Birds," *Smithsonian Magazine*, May 22, 2013, www.smithsonianmag.com/arts-culture/a-brief-history-of-robot-birds-77235415.

5. Ira Spar, "The Origins of Writing," *Heilbrunn Timeline of Art History* (New York: The Metropolitan Museum of Art, 2000), October 2004, www.metmuseum.org/toah/hd /wrtg/hd_wrtg.htm.

6. Judith Thurman, "First Impressions," *New Yorker*, June 23, 2008, www.newyorker.com /magazine/2008/06/23/first-impressions.

7. *Cave of Forgotten Dreams*, directed by Werner Herzog (France: Creative Differences, 2010).

8. Anne Trubek, "What the Heck is Cuneiform, Anyway?" *Smithsonian Magazine*, October 20, 2015, www.smithsonianmag.com/history/what-heck-cuneiform-anyway-180956999.

9. "The Phoenicians (1500–300 BCE)," The Metropolitan Museum of Art, October 2004, www.metmuseum.org/toah/hd/phoe/hd_phoe.htm.

10. Hilary Wilder and Sharmila Pixy Ferris, "Communication Technology and the Evolution of Knowledge," William Paterson University, Vol. 9, Issue 2 (Summer 2006), dx.doi .org/10.3998/3336451.0009.201.

11. Fred D'Agostino, "Contemporary Approaches to the Social Contract," *Stanford Encyclopedia of Philosophy*, 2017, plato.stanford.edu/entries/contractarianism-contemporary.

12. William McNeill, *The Rise of the West: A History of the Human Community* (University of Chicago, 1963), 65–66.

13. Yuval Noah Harari, author of *Sapiens: A Brief History of Humankind* (New York: Harper, 2015), divides history into three broad ages—the Cognitive, Agricultural, and Scientific Revolutions—and postulates an interesting twist with his theory that the Agricultural

Revolution, traditionally credited with enhancing human health and security, actually domesticated *us*, which led to a decline in human happiness.

14. Katherine J. Latham, "Human Health and the Neolithic Revolution: An Overview of Impacts of the Agricultural Transition on Oral Health, Epidemiology, and the Human Body," *Nebraska Anthropologist* (2013): 187, digitalcommons.unl.edu/nebanthro/187.

15. Jared Diamond, "The Worst Mistake in the History of the Human Race," *Discover*, May 1987.

16. Ibid.

17. Hans Rosling, Anna Rosling Rönnlund, and Ola Rosling, *Factfulness: Ten Reasons We're Wrong About the World—and Why Things Are Better Than You Think* (New York: Flatiron, 2018).

18. Editors of Encyclopaedia Britannica, "Hindu-Arabic Numerals," *Encyclopaedia Britannica*, accessed October 5, 2018, www.britannica.com/topic/Hindu-Arabic-numerals.

19. Syamal K. Sen and Ravi P. Agarwal, *Zero: A Landmark Discovery, the Dreadful Void, and the Ultimate Mind* (Cambridge, MA: Academic Press, 2015).

20. David Eugene Smith and William Judson LeVeque, "Numerals and Numeral Systems," *Encyclopaedia Britannica*, accessed October 5, 2018, www.britannica.com/science/numeral.

21. Gabrielle Emanuel, "Why We Learn Math Lessons That Date Back 500 Years," July 23, 2016, NPR *All Things Considered*, www.npr.org/sections/ed/2016/07/23/486172977/a-history-lesson-when-math-was-taboo.

22. Korea introduced woodblock printing somewhere between 1011 and 1087 CE. Hye Ok Park, "The History of Pre-Gutenberg Woodblock and Movable Type Printing in Korea," *International Journal of Humanities and Social Science*, Vol. 4, No. 9 (July 2014), www.ijhssnet.com/journals/Vol_4_No_9_1_July_2014/2.pdf.

23. Kim Viborg Andersen and Morten Thanning Vendelo, eds., *The Past and Future of Information Systems* (Oxford, UK: Butterworth-Heinemann, 2004), 93.

24. "Martin Luther (1483–1546)," BBC History, accessed October 5, 2018, www.bbc.co.uk/history/historic_figures/luther_martin.shtml.

25. "How Luther Went Viral," *Economist*, December 17, 2011, www.economist.com/christmas-specials/2011/12/17/how-luther-went-viral.

26. Joseph Loconte, "Martin Luther and the Long March to Freedom of Conscience," *National Geographic*, October 27, 2017, news.nationalgeographic.com/2017/10/martin-luther-freedom-protestant-reformation-500.

27. Joan Acocella, "How Martin Luther Changed the World," *New Yorker*, October 30, 2017, www.newyorker.com/magazine/2017/10/30/how-martin-luther-changed-the-world.

28. Walter Isaacson, *Leonardo Da Vinci* (New York: Simon & Schuster, 2017).

29. Jonathan Bate, "Shakespeare: Who Put Those Thoughts in His Head?" *Guardian*, April 20, 2016, www.theguardian.com/culture/2016/apr/20/shakespeare-thinking-philosophy-jonanthan-bate.

30. "Computer," Etymology Online, accessed October 5, 2018, www.etymonline.com/word/computer.

31. "Women Computers in World War II," Engineering and Technology Wiki, accessed October 5, 2018, ethw.org/Women_Computers_in_World_War_II.

32. Jo Marchant, "Decoding the Antikythera Mechanism, the First Computer," *Smithsonian*

Magazine, February 2015, www.smithsonianmag.com/history/decoding-antikythera
-mechanism-first-computer-180953979.

33. Elena Goukassian, "The History of One of the Oldest Astronomical Clocks in the
World," Hyperallergic, February 2, 2018, hyperallergic.com/424337/the-history-of-one
-of-the-oldest-astronomical-clocks-in-the-world.

34. "Federalist Papers," History, October 5, 2018, www.history.com/topics/early-us/federalist
-papers.

35. Si Sheppard, *The Partisan Press: A History of Media Bias in the United States* (North Carolina: McFarland & Company, 1972).

36. Derek Hastings, *Nationalism in Modern Europe: Politics, Identity, and Belonging Since the
French Revolution* (London: Bloomsbury, 2018).

37. Jürgen Wilke, "History as a Communication Event: The Example of the French Revolution," *European Journal of Communication*, Vol. 4, Issue 4 (1989), doi.org/10
.1177/0267323189004004002.

38. Jeremy Popkin, *Revolutionary News: The Press in France, 1789–1799 (Bicentennial Reflec-
tions on the French Revolution)* (North Carolina: Duke University Press, 1989).

39. Robert G. Parkinson, "Print, the Press, and the American Revolution," *Oxford Research Encyclopedias* (2005), americanhistory.oxfordre.com/view/10.1093/acrefore/9780199329175.001
.0001/acrefore-9780199329175-e-9.

40. Jane Chapman, "Republican Citizenship, Ethics, and the French Revolutionary Press
1789–92," *Ethical Space: the International Journal of Communication Ethics*, 2 (2005):
7–12, eprints.lincoln.ac.uk/1133.

41. Hugh Gough, *The Newspaper Press in the French Revolution* (New York: Routledge, 1988).

42. The study, importance, and impact of memes, which replicate elements of ideas, culture,
and behavior, and spread them from person to person by imitation, is heavily debated.
Since the word's first modern appearance in Richard Dawkins's 1976 book, *The Selfish
Gene*, thinkers have debated whether memetics is a legitimate science and if it can be analo-
gized to the spread of human genes. Susan Blackmore, who researches memes, psychology,
and consciousness, believes that humans' ability to imitate is what makes us human. In any
case, the history of memes illustrates that ideas spread because they are good replicators,
not necessarily because they are true. Susan Blackmore, *The Meme Machine* (New York:
Oxford University Press, 1999).

43. Ferenc Fehér, ed., *The French Revolution and the Birth of Modernity* (Berkeley: University of
California Press, 1990), ark.cdlib.org/ark:/13030/ft2h4nb1h9.

44. Paul R. Hanson, *The A to Z of the French Revolution* (Maryland: Scarecrow Press, 2007), 235.

45. Michael R. Swaine and Paul A. Freiberger, "Difference Engine," *Encylocpaedia Britannica*,
accessed October 6, 2018, www.britannica.com/technology/Difference-Engine.

46. Brian Libby, "Beyond the Bulbs: In Praise of Natural Light," *New York Times*, June 17,
2003, www.nytimes.com/2003/06/17/health/beyond-the-bulbs-in-praise-of-natural-light
.html.

47. Dr. Mark Philp, "Britain and the French Revolution," BBC History, February 17, 2011,
www.bbc.co.uk/history/british/empire_seapower/british_french_rev_01.shtml.

48. Frederick Douglass, "British Influence on the Abolition Movement in America: An Address Delivered in Paisley, Scotland, on April 17, 1846," *Renfrewshire Advertiser*, April 25,

1846, in *The Frederick Douglass Papers: Series One–Speeches, Debates, and Interviews*, John Blassingame, ed. (New Haven: Yale University Press, 1979), Vol. I, 215.

49. Tom Wheeler, "The First Wired President," *New York Times*, May 24, 2012, opinionator .blogs.nytimes.com/2012/05/24/the-first-wired-president.

50. Lumeng (Jenny) Yu, "The Great Communicator: How FDR's Radio Speeches Shaped American History," *The History Teacher, Society for History Education*, Vol. 39, No. 1 (November, 2005): 89–106, DOI:10.2307/30036746.

51. Ron Simon, "See How JFK Created a Presidency for the Television Age," *Time*, May 30, 2017, time.com/4795637/jfk-television.

52. Joseph Campbell, *The Power of Myth* (New York: Knopf Doubleday, 1988).

53. Peter S. Green and *International Herald Tribune*, "History or Propaganda? Communist-Era TV Show Stages a Controversial Return: 'Major Zeman' Leads Czechs to Question Their Past," *New York Times*, October 1, 1999, www.nytimes.com/1999/10/01/news /history-or-propaganda-communistera-tv-show-stages-a-controversial.html.

54. Ian Watson, "How Alan Turing Invented the Computer Age," *Scientific American*, April 26, 2012, blogs.scientificamerican.com/guest-blog/how-alan-turing-invented-the-computer-age.

55. Herman Hollerith and Dr. John Shaw Billings, "The Punched Card," IBM Icons of Progress, accessed October 6, 2018, www-03.ibm.com/ibm/history/ibm100/us/en/icons /tabulator.

56. Walter Isaacson, "Grace Hopper, Computing Pioneer," *Harvard Gazette*, December 3, 2014, news.harvard.edu/gazette/story/2014/12/grace-hopper-computing-pioneer.

57. Paul A. Freiberger and Michael R. Swaine, "ENIAC," *Encylopaedia Britannica*, accessed October 6, 2018, www.britannica.com/technology/ENIAC.

58. "A Short History of Computers," BBC Manchester, May 19, 2009, www.bbc.co.uk /manchester/content/articles/2008/06/17/210608_computer_timeline_feature.shtml.

59. When AI became its own discipline in the wake of a 1956 conference at Dartmouth and began to grow in popularity and prominence, the term and field of cybernetics began to take a back seat in the history of the field. Norbert Wiener, *Cybernetics, Second Edition* (Cambridge, MA: MIT Press, 1965).

60. Errol Morris, "The Fog of War: Transcript," from *The Fog of War*, directed by Errol Morris (Sony Pictures Classics, 2003), www.errolmorris.com/film/fow_transcript.html.

61. Francis A. Boyle, *The Criminality of Nuclear Deterrence* (Atlanta, GA: Clarity Press, 2015).

62. Eric Schlosser, "The Growing Dangers of the New Nuclear-Arms Race," *New Yorker*, May 24, 2018, www.newyorker.com/news/news-desk/the-growing-dangers-of-the-new -nuclear-arms-race.

63. Richard Rhodes, *The Making of the Atomic Bomb* (New York: Simon & Schuster, 1986).

64. James Moor, "The Dartmouth College Artificial Intelligence Conference: The Next Fifty Years," *AI Magazine*, Vol. 27, No. 4 (2006): 87–89, pdfs.semanticscholar.org/d486/9863b 5da0fa4ff5707fa972c6e1dc92474f6.pdf.

65. Leo Gugerty, "Newell and Simon's Logic Theorist: Historical Background and Impact on Cognitive Modeling," *Sage Journals*, Vol. 50, Issue 9 (October 1, 2006), doi.org /10.1177/154193120605000904.

66. Pamela McCorduck, *Machines Who Think: A Personal Inquiry into the History and Prospects of Artificial Intelligence* (AK Peters/CRC Press, 2004).

67. It also ended up proving thirty-eight of the first fifty-two theorems in *Principia Mathematica*, the landmark work that popularized mathematical logic. And *Logic Theorist*'s proof of one of the theorems ended up being more elegant than the proof produced laboriously by hand by Bertrand Russell and Alfred North Whitehead, the writers of *Principia Mathematica* themselves. Apparently, when Simon showed the proof to Bertrand Russell, he was thrilled. Ibid.

68. "Third Generation Computers," Techopedia, accessed October 6, 2018, www.techopedia .com/definition/9718/third-generation-computers.

69. Catherine Clifford, "The No. 1 Thing the Co-inventor of Ethernet Learned from His Mentor, Steve Jobs," CNBC, June 13, 2017, www.cnbc.com/2017/06/13/what-ethernet-co -inventor-bob-metcalfe-learned-from-steve-jobs.html.

70. Metcalfe named this concoction after a (discredited) scientific theory of a luminiferous aether, an undifferentiated universal medium that scientists in the eighteenth and nineteenth centuries thought was necessary to propagate light. Metcalfe reintroduced it as a metaphor for a concept that would propagate information.

71. Alvin and Heidi Toffler, *Future Shock* (New York: Bantam, 1970); *The Third Wave* (New York: Bantam, 1980).

72. Matt Novak, "Information Overload: A Recurring Fear," BBC Future, March 7, 2012, www.bbc.com/future/story/20120306-information-overload-fears.

73. Alvin and Heidi Toffler. *Future Shock, The Third Wave*.

74. Alvin and Heidi Toffler. *Powershift: Knowledge, Wealth, and Violence at the Edge of the 21st Century* (New York: Bantam, 1991).

75. "Fourth Generation Computers," PC Mag, accessed October 6, 2018, www.pcmag.com /encyclopedia/term/43438/fourth-generation-computer.

76. Paul Freiberger and Michael Swaine, *Fire in the Valley: The Making of The Personal Computer* (McGraw-Hill Companies, 2000).

77. Michael Dertouzos, "Wire All Schools? Not So Fast . . ." *MIT Technology Review*, September 1, 2008, www.technologyreview.com/s/400242/wire-all-schools-not-so-fast.

78. Katie Hafner and Matthew Lyon, *Where Wizards Stay Up Late: The Origins of the Internet* (New York: Simon and Schuster, 1998).

79. "The Birth of the Web," CERN, accessed October 6, 2018, home.cern/topics/birth-web.

80. Steve Lohr, "The Age of Big Data," *New York Times*, February 11, 2012, www.nytimes .com/2012/02/12/sunday-review/big-datas-impact-in-the-world.html.

81. Ian Bogost, "The Internet of Things You Don't Really Need," *Atlantic*, June 23, 2015, www.theatlantic.com/technology/archive/2015/06/the-internet-of-things-you-dont-really -need/396485.

82. "Number of Monthly Active Facebook Users Worldwide as of 3rd Quarter 2018 (in Millions)," Statista, accessed October 14, 2018, www.statista.com/statistics/264810/number-of -monthly-active-facebook-users-worldwide.

83. Martin Heidegger, *The Question Concerning Technology* (Germany: Garland Science, 1954).

84. Jean M. Twenge, "Have Smartphones Destroyed a Generation?" *Atlantic*, September 2017, www.theatlantic.com/magazine/archive/2017/09/has-the-smartphone-destroyed-a -generation/53419.

85. Adrian F. Ward, Kristen Duke, Ayelet Gneezy, and Maarten W. Bos, "Brain Drain: The Mere Presence of One's Own Smartphone Reduces Available Cognitive Capacity," *Journal*

of the Association for Consumer Research, Vol. 2, Issue 2 (2017): 140–154, econpapers.repec
.org/article/ucpjacres/doi_3a10.1086_2f691462.htm.

86. Twenge, "Have Smartphones Destroyed a Generation?"

87. T. J. H. Morgan, N. T. Uomini, L. E. Rendell, L. Chouinard-Thuly, S. E. Street, et al.,
"Experimental Evidence for the Co-Evolution of Hominin Tool-Making Teaching and
Language," *Nature Communications*, Vol. 6, No. 6029 (2015), www.nature.com/articles
/ncomms7029.

88. Colin McGinn, *Prehension: The Hand and the Emergence of Humanity* (Cambridge, MA:
MIT Press, 2015), 34–35.

89. Lawrence Barham, *From Hand to Handle: The First Industrial Revolution* (New York: Oxford University Press, 2013), 33.

90. Darian Leader, *Hands* (New York: Penguin, 2016).

91. Darian Leader, "Darian Leader: How Technology is Changing Our Hands," *Guardian*,
May 21, 2016, www.theguardian.com/books/2016/may/21/darian-leader-how-technology
-changing-our-hands.

92. Dom Galeon, "Expert: Human Immortality Could Be Acquired Through AI," Futurism,
April 21, 2017, futurism.com/expert-human-immortality-could-be-acquired-through-ai.

93. Nellie Bowles, "Our Tech Future: the Rich Own the Robots While the Poor Have 'Job
Mortgages,'" *Guardian*, March 12, 2016, www.theguardian.com/culture/2016/mar/12
/robots-taking-jobs-future-technology-jerry-kaplan-sxsw.

CHAPTER 2: THE SCIENCE OF INTELLIGENCE

1. Katherine Harmon Courage, "Speedy Octopus Sets Record for Jar Opening," *Scientific
American*, January 13, 2014, blogs.scientificamerican.com/octopus-chronicles/speedy
-octopus-sets-record-for-jar-opening.

2. Olivia Judson, "What the Octopus Knows," *Atlantic*, January/February 2017, www
.theatlantic.com/magazine/archive/2017/01/what-the-octopus-knows/508745.

3. "Synthetic Smarts," Raytheon, accessed October 1, 2018, www.raytheon.com/news
/feature/artificial_intelligence.

4. Jostein Gaarder, *Sophie's World* (New York: Farrar, Straus and Giroux, Reprint edition,
2007).

5. A. M. Turing, "The Chemical Basis of Morphogenesis," *Philosophical Transactions of the
Royal Society of London, Series B, Biological Sciences*, Vol. 237, No. 641 (August 14, 1952):
37–72.

6. Geoffrey Hinton, the head of Google Brain and the Vector Institute (and considered
by many the father of deep learning), believes that overcoming AI's limitations involves
"building a bridge between computer science and biology." James Somers, "Is AI Riding
a One-Trick Pony?" *MIT Technology Review*, September 29, 2017, www.technologyreview
.com/s/608911/is-ai-riding-a-one-trick-pony.

7. The brightest geniuses of the ages, from Leonardo da Vinci to Albert Einstein to Galileo
Galilei, have broken new ground in the vast reserves of human ingenuity and brilliance
by blurring the lines between science, art, religion, philosophy, engineering, architecture,
literature, and math. They had an insatiable curiosity for understanding how and why the
world works and finding our place in the universe, for the pure joy of learning. They saw

the patterns in nature, the truth and beauty all around us, which propelled us all into new frontiers of human thought, creativity, and innovation. Armed with a beginner's mind, always seeking new perspectives, and paying attention to the worlds within the simplest details will be what leads us to a digital consciousness, and thus the depths of our own.

8. Dalya Alberge, "Letters Reveal Alan Turing's Battle with His Sexuality," *Guardian*, August 22, 2015, www.theguardian.com/science/2015/aug/23/alan-turing-letters-reveal-battle-sexuality.

9. Robert Mullins, "The Turing Machine," Cambridge University, accessed October 1, 2018, www.cl.cam.ac.uk/projects/raspberrypi/tutorials/turing-machine/one.html.

10. Paul A. Freiberger and Michael R. Swaine, "ENIAC," *Encyclopaedia Britannica*, accessed October 1, 2018, www.britannica.com/technology/ENIAC.

11. Douglas Hofstadter, *Gödel, Escher, Bach* (New York: Basic Books, 1999).

12. "Introducing Binary," BBC Bitesize, accessed October 1, 2018, www.bbc.com/bitesize /guides/zwsbwmn/revision/1.

13. A. M. Turing, "Computing Machinery and Intelligence," *Mind*, Vol. 49: 433–460.

14. Some AI experts, like Gary Marcus, Stuart Russell, and Marvin Minsky, believe that the Turing Test was a thought experiment that wasn't meant to be taken literally and that it only focuses on one kind of intelligence. Stuart Russell said that the test "wasn't designed as the goal of AI, it wasn't designed to create a research agenda to work toward . . . It was designed as a thought experiment to explain to people who were very skeptical at the time that the possibility of intelligent machines did not depend on achieving consciousness, that you could have a machine that would behave intelligently . . . because it was behaving indistinguishably from a human being." Guia Marie Del Prado, "Researchers Say the Turing Test is Almost Worthless," Business Insider, August 18, 2015, www.businessinsider.com /ai-researchers-arent-trying-to-pass-the-turing-test-2015-8.

15. Ernst Von Glasersfeld, *Partial Memories: Sketches from an Improbable Life* (London: Andrews UK Limited, 2016), 136.

16. John Sulston and Georgina Ferry, "The Common Thread," *New York Times*, March 16, 2003, www.nytimes.com/2003/03/16/books/chapters/the-common-thread.html.

17. Gina Kolata, "Human Genome, Then and Now," *New York Times*, April 15, 2013, www .nytimes.com/2013/04/16/science/the-human-genome-project-then-and-now.html.

18. Sui-Lee Wee, "China Halts Work by Scientist Who Says He Edited Babies' Genes," *New York Times*, November 29, 2018, www.nytimes.com/2018/11/29/science/gene-editing-babies -china.html.

19. John Harris, "Pro and Con: Should Gene Editing Be Performed on Human Embryos?" *National Geographic*, August 2016, www.nationalgeographic.com/magazine/2016/08 /human-gene-editing-pro-con-opinions.

20. Robotics is just an application of AI, and typically, this construct will be built from software/algorithms running on one or more computers. That said, an AI that is embedded in a robot may evolve differently over time than an AI unable to directly manipulate its environment, so robotics could be key to an AI's development.

21. "People vary in how they understand AI. Two-thirds of those surveyed say they know something about AI, although only about two in 10 (18%) say that they know a lot. One-third acknowledged knowing nothing about AI. We found that by far the most common first impression of AI is 'robots,' as 22% of respondents said. These find-

ings vary slightly by geography; for instance, nearly twice as many Chinese consumers said they know a lot about AI compared to those in other markets." Leslie
Gaines-Ross, "What Do People—Not Techies, Not Companies—Think About Artificial Intelligence?" *Harvard Business Review*, October 24, 2016, hbr.org/2016/10/what-do
-people-not-techies-not-companies-think-about-artificial-intelligence.

22. Kyle Russell, "Netflix Is 'Training' Its Recommendation System by Using Amazon's Cloud
to Mimic the Human Brain," Business Insider, February 11, 2014, www.businessinsider
.com/netflix-using-ai-to-suggest-better-films-2014-2.

23. Showing more movies featuring your favorite actor is a relatively simple thing to do and
does not necessarily require machine learning; an article in which Netflix describes how
they create recommendations. Libby Plummer, "This is How Netflix's Top-Secret Recommendation System Works," *Wired*, August 22, 2017, www.wired.co.uk/article/how-do
-netflixs-algorithms-work-machine-learning-helps-to-predict-what-viewers-will-like.

   One interesting and vital piece of this is the classifying of people into taste groups.
If Netflix can assign you to a group of like-minded customers, then it can look for like-
minded customers who have watched movies that you have not yet watched. Since you have
things in common with those like-minded customers, you may like those same movies.
Machine learning can be used to determine which group of customers is most like you.

   Also, machine learning can be used to determine which features of a movie are most
important to consider (director, actors, genre, recency, topic, etc.) for a particular customer
at a particular time. The set of important features may be different depending on the type
of customer.

24. J. D. Biersdorfer, "Let Gmail Finish Your Sentences," *New York Times*, June 1, 2018, www
.nytimes.com/2018/06/01/technology/personaltech/gmail-smart-compose.html.

25. Troy Wolverton, "Google CEO Sundar Pichai Revealed a Jaw-Dropping Fact About Its
Translation App That Shows How Much Money is Still Sitting on the Table," Business Insider, July 23, 2018, www.businessinsider.com/sundar-pichai-google-translate-143-billion
-words-daily-2018-7.

26. John Markoff, "Computer Wins on 'Jeopardy!': Trivial, It's Not," *New York Times*, February 17, 2011, www.nytimes.com/2011/02/17/science/17jeopardy-watson.html.

27. "A Holistic Approach to AI," University of California, Berkeley, accessed October 3, 2018,
www.ocf.berkeley.edu/~arihuang/academic/research/strongai3.html.

28. "For example, a machine might hear 'good morning' and start to associate that with the
coffee maker turning on. If the computer has the ability, it theoretically could hear 'good
morning' and decide to turn on the coffee maker." Jeff Kerns, "What's the Difference
Between Weak and Strong AI?" MachineDesign, February 15, 2017, www.machinedesign
.com/robotics/what-s-difference-between-weak-and-strong-ai.

29. "Quantum Technology is Beginning to Come into Its Own," *Economist*, accessed October
14, 2018, www.economist.com/news/essays/21717782-quantum-technology-beginning-come
-its-own.

30. Kevin Kelly, "The Myth of a Superhuman AI," *Wired*, April 25, 2017, www.wired.com
/2017/04/the-myth-of-a-superhuman-ai.

31. Nick Bostrom, "The Superintelligence Will: Motivation and Instrumental Rationality in
Advanced Artificial Agents," *Minds and Machines*, Vol. 22, Issue 2 (2012): 71–85.

32. Nick Bostrom, "How Long Before Superintelligence?" *International Journal of Future Studies*, Vol. 2 (1998).

33. Robert D. Hof, "Deep Learning," *MIT Technology Review*, accessed October 1, 2018, www.technologyreview.com/s/513696/deep-learning.

34. Cade Metz, "Building A.I. That Can Build A.I.," *New York Times*, November 5, 2017, www.nytimes.com/2017/11/05/technology/machine-learning-artificial-intelligence-ai.html.

35. Greg Williams, "Wise Up, Deep Learning May Never Create a General Purpose AI," *Wired*, January 20, 2018, www.wired.co.uk/article/deep-learning-automl-cloud-gary-marcus.

36. Roger Melko, "The Most Complex Problem in Physics Could Be Solved by Machines with Brains," Quartz, February 1, 2017, qz.com/897033/applying-machine-learning-to-physics-could-be-the-way-to-build-the-first-quantum-computer.

37. Jordana Cepelewicz, "New AI Strategy Mimics How Brains Learn to Smell," Quanta Magazine, September 18, 2018, www.quantamagazine.org/new-ai-strategy-mimics-how-brains-learn-to-smell-20180918.

38. Larry Hardesty, "Explained: Neural Networks," MIT News, April 14, 2017, news.mit.edu/2017/explained-neural-networks-deep-learning-0414.

39. Angela Chen, "A Pioneering Scientist Explains 'Deep Learning,'" The Verge, October 16, 2018, www.theverge.com/2018/10/16/17985168/deep-learning-revolution-terrence-sejnowski-artificial-intelligence-technology.

40. Terrence J. Sejnowski, *The Deep Learning Revolution* (Cambridge, MA: MIT Press, 2018).

41. Will Knight, "Google Has Released an AI Tool That Makes Sense of Your Genome," *MIT Technology Review*, December 4, 2017, www.technologyreview.com/s/609647/google-has-released-an-ai-tool-that-makes-sense-of-your-genome.

42. Pedro Domingos, *The Master Algorithm: How the Quest for the Ultimate Learning Machine Will Remake Our World* (New York: Basic Books, 2015).

43. Rachel David, "Can Robots Truly Be Creative and Use Their Imagination?" *Guardian*, October 10, 2015, www.theguardian.com/technology/2015/oct/10/can-robots-be-creative.

44. Domingos, *The Master Algorithm*.

45. Daniel Faggella, "Artificial Intelligence in Marketing and Advertising—5 Examples of Real Traction," Techemergence, September 16, 2018, www.techemergence.com/artificial-intelligence-in-marketing-and-advertising-5-examples-of-real-traction.

46. Domingos, *The Master Algorithm*.

47. Vishal Maini, "Machine Learning for Humans, Part 3: Unsupervised Learning," Medium, April 19, 2017, medium.com/machine-learning-for-humans/unsupervised-learning-f45587588294.

48. For example, to teach a neural network to recognize a horse by using supervised learning, the data scientist provides a set of training data that consist of a wide variety of images that are labeled as being a horse and a set of other images labeled as not being a horse. As each training example is processed, the neural network updates the strength of connections between various neurons to reflect the details of the new example. When the training is complete, the data scientist provides a new image to the neural network that it had not been given previously. The trained neural network processes the new image and, based on the output of the neural network, gives an answer of yes (this is a horse) or no (this is not a horse). (If the training data was insufficient, the network may answer incorrectly.)

49. Bernard Marr, "Supervised v. Unsupervised Machine Learning—What's the Difference?" *Forbes*, March 16, 2017, www.forbes.com/sites/bernardmarr/2017/03/16/supervised-v-unsupervised-machine-learning-whats-the-difference/#33c3dd73485d.

50. James Thewlis, Hakan Bilen, and Andrea Vedaldi, "Unsupervised Learning of Object Frames by Dense Equivariant Image Labelling," Visual Geometry Group, University of Oxford, accessed October 1, 2018, homepages.inf.ed.ac.uk/hbilen/assets/pdf/Thewlis17a.pdf.

51. Calum McClelland, "The Difference Between Artificial Intelligence, Machine Learning, and Deep Learning," Medium, December 4, 2017, medium.com/iotforall/the-difference-between-artificial-intelligence-machine-learning-and-deep-learning-3aa67bff5991.

52. Aman Agarwal, "Explained Simply: How DeepMind Taught AI to Play Video Games," Medium, August 27, 2017, medium.freecodecamp.org/explained-simply-how-deepmind-taught-ai-to-play-video-games-9eb5f38c89ee.

53. István Szita, "Reinforcement Learning in Games," Marco Wiering and Martijn van Otterlo eds., *Reinforcement Learning: Adaptation, Learning, and Optimization*, Springer, Berlin, Heidelberg, Vol. 12 (2012), link.springer.com/chapter/10.1007/978-3-642-27645-3_17.

54. Elizabeth Gibney, "Self-Taught AI is Best Yet at Strategy Game Go," *Nature*, October 18, 2017, www.nature.com/news/self-taught-ai-is-best-yet-at-strategy-game-go-1.22858.

55. Wilder Rodrigues, "Deep Learning for Natural Language Processing—Part I," Medium, December 12, 2017, medium.com/cityai/deep-learning-for-natural-language-processing-part-i-8369895ffb98.

56. Knight, "The Dark Secret at the Heart of AI."

57. Julia Hirschberg and Christopher D. Manning, "Advances in Natural Language Processing," *Science*, Vol. 349, Issue 6245 (July 17, 2015): 261–266, DOI: 10.1126/science.aaa8685.

58. Jo Best, "IBM Watson: The Inside Story of How the *Jeopardy*-Winning Supercomputer Was Born, and What It Wants to Do Next," TechRepublic, accessed October 2, 2018, www.techrepublic.com/article/ibm-watson-the-inside-story-of-how-the-jeopardy-winning-supercomputer-was-born-and-what-it-wants-to-do-next.

59. Daniela Hernandez and Ted Greenwald, "IBM Has a Watson Dilemma," *Wall Street Journal*, August 11, 2018, www.wsj.com/articles/ibm-bet-billions-that-watson-could-improve-cancer-treatment-it-hasnt-worked-1533961147.

60. "IBM Watson Hard at Work: New Breakthroughs Transform Quality Care for Patients," Memorial Sloan Kettering Cancer Center, accessed October 2, 2018, www.mskcc.org/press-releases/ibm-watson-hard-work-new-breakthroughs-transform-quality-care-patients.

61. Farhad Shakerin, Gopal Gupta, "Induction of Non-Monotonic Logic Programs to Explain Boosted Tree Models Using LIME," Computer Science Department, University of Texas at Dallas (2018), arxiv.org/abs/1808.00629.

62. Erik T. Mueller, *Commonsense Reasoning* (San Francisco: Morgan Kaufmann, 2006).

63. "Automating Common Sense," Morgan Kaufmann Series in Representation and Reasoning, (1990): 1–26, www.sciencedirect.com/science/article/pii/B9781483207704500095?via%3Dihub.

64. Pranav Dar, "MIT Open Sources Computer Vision Model that Teaches Itself Object Detection in 45 Minutes (with GitHub Codes)," Analytics Vidhya, September 10, 2018, www.analyticsvidhya.com/blog/2018/09/mit-computer-vision-teaches-object-detection-45-minutes.

65. Tom Simonite, "Facebook's AI Chief: Machines Could Learn Common Sense from Video," *MIT Technology Review*, March 9, 2017, www.technologyreview.com/s/603803/facebooks-ai-chief-machines-could-learn-common-sense-from-video.

66. A petaflop is the ability of a computer to do one quadrillion floating-point operations per second (FLOPS). A petaflop can also be measured as one thousand teraflops. The world's current fastest supercomputer, China's TaihuLight, is capable of 93 petaflops. Vangie Beal, "Petaflop," Webopedia, accessed October 3, 2018, www.webopedia.com/TERM/P/petaflop.html.

67. "Computing will not be sustainable by 2040, when the energy required for computing will exceed the estimated world's energy production. Thus, radical improvement in the energy efficiency of computing is needed." "Rebooting the IT Revolution," Semiconductor Industry Association, accessed October 3, 2018, 27, www.src.org/newsroom/rebooting-the-it-revolution.pdf.

68. Abigail Beall and Matt Reynolds, "What Are Quantum Computers and How Do They Work? WIRED Explains," *Wired*, February 16, 2018, www.wired.co.uk/article/quantum-computing-explained.

69. Robert D. Hof, "Neuromorphic Chips," *MIT Technology Review*, accessed October 3, 2018, www.technologyreview.com/s/526506/neuromorphic-chips.

70. Lea Winerman, "Making a Thinking Machine," American Psychological Association, Vol. 49, No. 4 (2018): 30, www.apa.org/monitor/2018/04/cover-thinking-machine.aspx.

71. Xuan "Silvia" Zhang, "Insects are Revealing How AI Can Work in Society," Venturebeat, September 5, 2017, venturebeat.com/2017/09/05/insects-are-revealing-how-ai-can-work-in-society.

72. "The Quest for AI Creativity," IBM, accessed October 3, 2018, www.ibm.com/watson/advantage-reports/future-of-artificial-intelligence/ai-creativity.html.

73. Oliver Burkeman, "Why Can't the World's Greatest Minds Solve the Mystery of Consciousness?" *Guardian*, January 21, 2015, www.theguardian.com/science/2015/jan/21/-sp-why-cant-worlds-greatest-minds-solve-mystery-consciousness.

74. Greg Miller, "How Our Brains Make Memories," *Smithsonian Magazine*, May 2010, www.smithsonianmag.com/science-nature/how-our-brains-make-memories-14466850.

75. Ernest Hartmann, "Why Do We Dream?" *Scientific American*, July 14, 2003, www.scientificamerican.com/article/why-do-we-dream.

76. David Rettew, MD, "Nature Versus Nurture: Where We Are in 2017," *Psychology Today*, October 6, 2017, www.psychologytoday.com/us/blog/abcs-child-psychiatry/201710/nature-versus-nurture-where-we-are-in-2017.

77. "The Neuroscience of Decision Making," Kavli Foundation, August 2011, www.kavlifoundation.org/science-spotlights/neuroscience-of-decision-making#.W7VMtRNKg0o.

78. Beau Lotto, "Is This the Real Life? The Neuroscience of Perception Offers Us an Answer," Salon, August 24, 2017, www.salon.com/2017/04/24/is-this-the-real-life-the-neuroscience-of-perception-offers-us-an-answer.

79. Stephen Cave, "There's No Such Thing as Free Will," *Atlantic*, June 2016, www.theatlantic.com/magazine/archive/2016/06/theres-no-such-thing-as-free-will/480750.

80. R. Colom, S. Karama, R. E. Jung, and R. J. Haier, "Human Intelligence and Brain Networks," *Dialogues in Clinical Neuroscience*, 12.4 (2010): 489–501, www.ncbi.nlm.nih.gov/pmc/articles/PMC3181994.

81. Ibid.

82. Interestingly, while people continue to debate whether using calculators helps or hinders a student's ability to learn math, studies are showing that using graphing calculators helps students with both relational and instrumental understanding of math, giving them a deeper understanding of the why behind the algorithms they are working with. Frederick Peck and David Erickson, "The rise—and possible fall—of the graphing calculator," The Conversation, June 13, 2017, theconversation.com/the-rise-and-possible-fall-of-the-graphing-calculator-78017.

83. Kurzweil, *How to Create a Mind: The Secret of Human Thought Revealed.*

84. Melissa Hogenboom, "The Traits That Make Human Beings Unique," BBC Future, July 6, 2015, www.bbc.com/future/story/20150706-the-small-list-of-things-that-make-humans-unique.

85. Richard Mabey, *Cabaret of Plants: Forty Thousand Years Of Plant Life and the Human Imagination* (New York: W. W. Norton & Company, 2017).

86. David Masci, "Darwin and His Theory of Evolution," Pew Research Center, February 4, 2009, www.pewforum.org/2009/02/04/darwin-and-his-theory-of-evolution.

87. Ray Kurzweil. *How to Create a Mind: The Secret of Human Thought Revealed.*

88. Radhika Nagpal, "What Intelligent Machines Can Learn from a School of Fish," April 2017, TED, video, 10:50, www.ted.com/talks/radhika_nagpal_what_intelligent_machines _can_learn_from_a_school_of_fish/transcript.

89. Carlos E. Perez, "Alien Intelligences in Our Midst," Medium, August 6, 2017, medium .com/intuitionmachine/alien-intelligences-in-our-midst-2a738e58c204.

90. Jack Copeland, "What is Artificial Intelligence?" May 2010, www.scribd.com/doc/11563045 /What-is-Artificial-Intelligence-by-Jack-Copeland.

91. Rodney Brooks, "Elephants Don't Play Chess," *Robotics and Autonomous Systems,* Vol. 6, Issues 1–2 (June 1990): 3–15, dl.acm.org/citation.cfm?id=1752988.

92. Brooks has since switched his focus away from this research and toward speaking openly about what he sees as misconceptions in the field of AI.

93. Katherine Bailey, "Reframing the 'AI Effect,'" Medium, October 27, 2016, medium .com/@katherinebailey/reframing-the-ai-effect-c445f87ea98b.

94. "True AI is Whatever Hasn't Been Done Yet," On Larry Tesler's Theorem, Douglas Hofstadter, *Gödel, Escher, Bach: an Eternal Golden Braid* (New York: Basic Books, 1979). Note: Tesler feels he was misquoted.

CHAPTER 3: THE DANGER OF HOMOGENEITY AND THE POWER OF COMBINATORIAL CREATIVITY

1. Dorothy Stein, *Ada: A Life and A Legacy* (Cambridge, MA: MIT Press, October 1985).

2. Aleta George, "Booting Up a Computer Pioneer's 200-Year-Old Design," *Smithsonian Magazine,* April 1, 2009, www.smithsonianmag.com/science-nature/booting-up-a-computer -pioneers-200-year-old-design-122424896.

3. John Fuegi and Jo Francis, "Lovelace & Babbage and the Creation," *IEEE Annals of the History of Computing,* Vol. 25, Issue 4 (October–December 2003): 16–26.

4. Betty Alexandra Toole, *Ada, The Enchantress of Numbers* (Sausalito: Strawberry Press, 1998), 175–178, www.cs.yale.edu/homes/tap/Files/ada-bio.htm.l

5. Some say that it was Lovelace's work that inspired Alan Turing's. Dominic Selwood, "Ada Lovelace Paved the Way for Alan Turing's More Celebrated Codebreaking a Century Be-

fore He was Born," *Telegraph UK*, December 10, 2014, www.telegraph.co.uk/technology /11285007/Ada-Lovelace-paved-the-way-for-Alan-Turings-more-celebrated-codebreaking -a-century-before-he-was-born.html.

6. John Markoff, "It Started Digital Wheels Turning," *New York Times*, November 7, 2011, www .nytimes.com/2011/11/08/science/computer-experts-building-1830s-babbage-analytical -engine.html.

7. "As people realized how important computer programming was, there was a greater backlash and an attempt to reclaim it as a male activity," says Valerie Aurora, the executive director of the Ada Initiative, a nonprofit organization that arranges conferences and training programs to elevate women working in math and science. "In order to keep that wealth and power in a man's hands, there's a backlash to try to redefine it as something a woman didn't do, and shouldn't do, and couldn't do."

The numbers are still low today. "The Census Bureau [found] that the share of women working in STEM (science, technology, engineering, and math) has decreased over the past couple of decades; this is due largely to the fact that women account for a smaller proportion of those employed in computing. In 1990, women held thirty-four per cent of STEM jobs; in 2011, it was twenty-seven per cent."

Betsy Morais, "Ada Lovelace, the First Tech Visionary," *New Yorker*, October 15, 2013, www.newyorker.com/tech/elements/ada-lovelace-the-first-tech-visionary.

8. Lovelace had access to great tutors, including Mary Somerville, the first scientist (rather than "man of science"), a creative and artistic scientific mind. Christopher Hollings, Ursula Martin, and Adrian Rice, "The Early Mathematical Education of Ada Lovelace," *Journal of the British Society for the History of Mathematics*, 32:3 (2017): 221–234, DOI: 10.1080/17498430.2017.1325297.

9. Toole, *Ada, The Enchantress of Numbers: Poetical Science.*

10. Yasmin Kafai, "Celebrating Ada Lovelace," MIT Press, October 13, 2015, mitpress.mit .edu/blog/changing-face-computing%E2%80%94one-stitch-time.

11. Toole, *Ada, The Enchantress of Numbers*, 235.

12. James Essinger, *Ada's Algorithm: How Lord Byron's Daughter Ada Lovelace Launched the Digital Age* (Brooklyn: Melville House, 2014).

13. Toole, *Ada, The Enchantress of Numbers*, 175–178.

14. "Ada Lovelace," Computer History, accessed September 3, 2018, www.computerhistory .org/babbage/adalovelace.

15. Claire Cain Miller, "Overlooked: Ada Lovelace," *New York Times*, March 8, 2018, www .nytimes.com/interactive/2018/obituaries/overlooked-ada-lovelace.html.

16. Nicola Perrin and Danil Mikhailov, "Why We Can't leave AI in the hands of Big Tech," *Guardian*, November 3, 2017, www.theguardian.com/science/2017/nov/03/why-we-cant-leave-ai-in -the-hands-of-big-tech.

17. Mark Cuban, "The World's First Trillionaire Will Be an Artificial Intelligence Entrepreneur," CNBC, March 13, 2017, www.cnbc.com/2017/03/13/mark-cuban-the-worlds-first -trillionaire-will-be-an-ai-entrepreneur.html.

18. Christopher Summerfield, Matt Botvinick, and Demis Hassabis, "AI and Neuroscience," DeepMind, accessed September 27, 2018, deepmind.com/blog/ai-and-neuroscience -virtuous-circle.

19. Katherine Dempsey, "Democracy Needs a Reboot for the Age of Artificial Intelligence," *Nation*, November 8, 2017, www.thenation.com/article/democracy-needs-a-reboot-for-the -age-of-artificial-intelligence.

20. Researchers can't even agree on the name of the conference. Tom Simonite, "AI Researchers Fight Over Four Letters: NIPS," *Wired*, October 26, 2018, www.wired.com/story /ai-researchers-fight-over-four-letters-nips.

21. Jackie Snow, "We're in a Diversity Crisis: Cofounder of Black in AI on What's Poisoning Algorithms in Our Lives," *MIT Technology Review*, February 14, 2018, www.technology review.com/s/610192/were-in-a-diversity-crisis-black-in-ais-founder-on-whats-poisoning -the-algorithms-in-our.

22. Partnerships on AI, accessed September 3, 2018, www.partnershiponai.org.

23. Gillian Tett, *The Silo Effect: The Peril of Expertise and the Promise of Breaking Down Barriers* (New York: Simon and Schuster, 2015).

24. Steve Lohr, "M.I.T. Plans College for Artificial Intelligence, Backed by $1 Billion," *New York Times*, October 15, 2018, www.nytimes.com/2018/10/15/technology/mit-college -artificial-intelligence.html.

25. Ulrik Juul Christensen, "Robotics, AI Put Pressure on K-12 Education to Adapt and Evolve," The Hill, September 1, 2018, thehill.com/opinion/education/404544 -robotics-ai-put-pressure-on-k-12-to-adapt-and-evolve.

26. Derek Thompson, "America's Monopoly Problem," *Atlantic*, October 2016, www .theatlantic.com/magazine/archive/2016/10/americas-monopoly-problem/497549.

27. Sam Shead, "Oxford and Cambridge Are Losing AI Researchers to DeepMind," Business Insider, November 9, 2016, www.businessinsider.com/oxbridge-ai-researchers-to -deepmind-2016-11.

28. Zachary Cohen, "US Risks Losing Artificial Intelligence Arms Race to China and Russia," CNN Politics, November 29, 2017, www.cnn.com/2017/11/29/politics/us-military-artificial -intelligence-russia-china/index.html.

29. Jane C. Hu, "Group Smarts," Aeon, October 3, 2016, aeon.co/essays/how-collective -intelligence-overcomes-the-problem-of-groupthink.

30. Thomas W. Malone, *Superminds: The Surprising Power of People and Computers Thinking Together* (New York: Little, Brown, 2018).

31. Unanimous AI, accessed October 28, 2018, unanimous.ai/about-us.

32. Cade Metz, "Google Just Open Sourced Tensorware, its Artificial Intelligence Engine," *Wired*, November 9, 2015, www.wired.com/2015/11/google-open-sources-its-artificial -intelligence-engine.

33. Jorge Cueto, "Race and Gender Among Computer Science Majors at Stanford," Medium, July 13, 2015, medium.com/@jcueto/race-and-gender-among-computer-science-majors -at-stanford-3824c4062e3a.

34. IEEE Spectrum, accessed September 3, 2018, spectrum.ieee.org/tech-talk/at-work/tech -careers/computer-vision-leader-feifei-li-on-why-ai-needs-diversity.

35. Caroline Bullock, "Attractive, Slavish and at Your Command: Is AI Sexist?" BBC News, December 5, 2016, www.bbc.com/news/business-38207334.

36. "Diversity in High Tech," US Equal Employment Opportunity Commission, accessed September 3, 2018, www.eeoc.gov/eeoc/statistics/reports/hightech.

37. "Advancing Opportunity for All in the Tech Industry," US Equal Employment Opportunity Commission, May 18, 2016, www.eeoc.gov/eeoc/newsroom/release/5-18-16.cfm.

38. Erik Sherman, "Report: Disturbing Drop in Women in Computing Field," *Fortune*, March 26, 2015, fortune.com/2015/03/26/report-the-number-of-women-entering-computing-took-a-nosedive.

39. Johana Bhuiyan, "The Head of Google's Brain Team is More Worried About the Lack of Diversity in Artificial Intelligence than an AI Apocalypse," Recode, August 13, 2016, www.recode.net/2016/8/13/12467506/google-brain-jeff-dean-ama-reddit-artificial-intelligence-robot-takeover.

40. Rachel Thomas, "Diversity Crisis in AI, 2017 Edition," fast.ai, August 16, 2017, www.fast.ai/2017/08/16/diversity-crisis.

41. Tom Simonite, "AI is the Future—But Where are the Women?" *Wired*, August 17, 2018, www.wired.com/story/artificial-intelligence-researchers-gender-imbalance.

42. "The Global Gender Gap Report 2018," World Economic Forum, accessed December 22, 2018, www3.weforum.org/docs/WEF_GGGR_2018.pdf.

43. "Science and Engineering Degrees, By Race/Ethnicity of Recipients: 2002–12," National Science Foundation, May 21, 2015, www.nsf.gov/statistics/2015/nsf15321/#chp2.

44. Danielle Brown, "Google Diversity Annual Report 2018," accessed September 27, 2018, diversity.google/annual-report/#!#_our-workforce.

45. Maxine Williams, "Facebook 2018 Diversity Report: Reflecting on Our Journey," July 12, 2018, newsroom.fb.com/news/2018/07/diversity-report.

46. Brown, "Google Diversity Annual Report 2018."

47. Tom Simonite, "AI is the Future—But Where are the Women?"

48. Clive Thompson, "The Secret History of Women in Coding," *New York Times*, February 13, 2019, www.nytimes.com/2019/02/13/magazine/women-coding-computer-programming.html.

49. Amy Rees Anderson, "No Man Is Above Unconscious Gender Bias in The Workplace—It's 'Unconscious,'" *Forbes*, December 14, 2016, www.forbes.com/sites/amyanderson/2016/12/14/no-man-is-above-unconscious-gender-bias-in-the-workplace-its-unconscious/#d055ac512b42.

50. Rachel Thomas, "If You Think Women in Tech is Just a Pipeline Problem, You Haven't Been Paying Attention," Medium, July 27, 2015, medium.com/tech-diversity-files/if-you-think-women-in-tech-is-just-a-pipeline-problem-you-haven-t-been-paying-attention-cb7a2073b996.

51. Cisgender is a trans-inclusionary term meaning anyone who identifies with their gender assigned at birth.

52. Jessi Hempel, "Melinda Gates and Fei-Fei Li Want to Liberate AI from 'Guys with Hoodies,'" *Wired*, May 4, 2017, www.wired.com/2017/05/melinda-gates-and-fei-fei-li-want-to-liberate-ai-from-guys-with-hoodies.

53. Richard Kerby, "Where Did You Go to School?" Noteworthy, July 30, 2018, blog.usejournal.com/where-did-you-go-to-school-bde54d846188.

54. Steve O'Hear, "Tech Companies Don't Want to Talk about the Lack of Disability Reporting," Techcrunch, November 7, 2016, techcrunch.com/2016/11/07/parallel-pr-universe.

55. Ciarán Daly, "'We're in a Diversity Crisis'—This Week in AI," AI Business, February 15, 2018, aibusiness.com/interview-infographic-must-read-ai-news.

56. Nico Grant, "The Myth of the 'Pipeline Problem,'" Bloomberg, June 13, 2018, www
.bloomberg.com/news/articles/2018-06-13/the-myth-of-the-pipeline-problem-jid07tth.

57. "Compared to overall private industry, the high tech sector employed a larger share of
whites (63.5 percent to 68.5 percent), Asian Americans (5.8 percent to 14 percent) and
men (52 percent to 64 percent), and a smaller share of African Americans (14.4 percent to
7.4 percent), Hispanics (13.9 percent to 8 percent), and women (48 percent to 36 percent)."
"Diversity in High Tech," US Equal Opportunity Employment Commission, accessed
September 3, 2018, www.eeoc.gov/eeoc/statistics/reports/hightech.

58. O'Hear, "Tech Companies Don't Want to Talk about the Lack of Disability Reporting."

59. "Ingroup Favoritism and Prejudice," *Principles of Social Psychology*, accessed September 27,
2018, opentextbc.ca/socialpsychology/chapter/ingroup-favoritism-and-prejudice.

60. Victor Tangermann, "Hearings Show Congress Doesn't Understand Facebook Well
Enough to Regulate It," Futurism, April 11, 2018, futurism.com/hearings-congress-doesnt
-understand-facebook-regulation.

61. "How Facebook Has Handled Recent Scandals," Letters to the Editor, *New York Times*,
November 16, 2018, www.nytimes.com/2018/11/16/opinion/letters/facebook-scandals
.html.

62. Pierre Lévy, *Collective Intelligence: Mankind's Emerging World in Cyberspace* (New York:
Basic Books, 1994), 13.

63. Oliver Milman, "Paris Deal: A Year After Trump Announced US Exit, a Coalition Fights
to Fill the Gap," *Guardian*, June 1, 2018, www.theguardian.com/us-news/2018/may/31
/paris-climate-deal-trump-exit-resistance.

64. George Anders, *You Can Do Anything: The Surprising Power of a "Useless" Liberal Arts Education* (New York: Little, Brown, and Company, 2017).

65. Annette Jacobson, "Why We Shouldn't Push Students to Specialize in STEM Too Early,"
PBS *NewsHour*, September 5, 2017, www.pbs.org/newshour/education/column-shouldnt
-push-students-specialize-stem-early.

66. Fareed Zakaria, *In Defense of a Liberal Education* (New York: W. W. Norton & Company,
2016).

67. Talia Milgrom-Elcott, "STEM Starts Earlier Than You Think," *Forbes*, July 24, 2018,
www.forbes.com/sites/taliamilgromelcott/2018/07/24/stem-starts-earlier-than-you-think
/#150b641a348b.

68. Maria Popova, "The Art of Chance-Opportunism in Creativity and Scientific Discovery,"
Medium, accessed September 3, 2018, www.brainpickings.org/2012/05/25/the-art-of
-scientific-investigation-1; William I. B. Beveridge, *The Art of Scientific Investigation* (New
Jersey: Blackburn Press, 2004).

69. Rebecca M. Jordan-Young, *Brain Storm: The Flaws in the Science of Sex Differences* (Cambridge, MA: Harvard University Press, 2011).

70. Monica Kim, "The Good and the Bad of Escaping to Virtual Reality," *Atlantic*, February 18,
2015, www.theatlantic.com/health/archive/2015/02/the-good-and-the-bad-of-escaping-to
-virtual-reality/385134.

71. "There is, of course, a certain connection between those elements and relevant logical
concepts. It is also clear that the desire to arrive finally at logically connected concepts is
the emotional basis of this rather vague play with the above-mentioned elements. But taken

from a psychological viewpoint, this combinatory play seems to be the essential feature in productive thought—before there is any connection with logical construction in words or other kinds of signs which can be communicated to others." Albert Einstein, *Ideas and Opinions* (New York: Crown, 1954), 77.

72. Tham Khai Meng, "Everyone is Born Creative, but It Is Educated Out of Us at School," *Guardian,* May 18, 2016, www.theguardian.com/media-network/2016/may/18/born-creative -educated-out-of-us-school-business.

73. Margot Lee Shetterly, *Hidden Figures: The American Dream and the Untold Story of the Black Women Mathematicians Who Helped Win the Space Race* (New York: William Morrow, 2016).

74. "Why Did Humans Become the Most Successful Species on Earth?" Interview by Guy Raz, March 4, 2016, NPR, *TED Radio Hour,* 11:00, www.npr.org/templates/transcript /transcript.php?storyId=468882620.

75. The name is still up for debate. Joseph Stromberg, "What Is the Anthropocene and Are We in It?" *Smithsonian Magazine,* January 2013, www.smithsonianmag.com/science-nature /what-is-the-anthropocene-and-are-we-in-it-164801414; Jonathan Amos, "Welcome to the Meghalayan Age—a New Phase in History," BBC News, July 18, 2018, www.bbc.com /news/science-environment-44868527.

76. "The great driver of scientific and technological innovation [in the last 600 years has been] the increase in our ability to reach out and exchange ideas with other people, and to borrow other people's hunches and combine them with our hunches and turn them into something new." Steven Johnson, *Where Good Ideas Come From* (New York: Riverhead Books, 2010).

77. Amy Novotney, "No Such Thing as 'Right-Brained' or 'Left-Brained,' New Research Finds," American Psychological Association, Vol. 44, No. 10 (November 2013), www.apa .org/monitor/2013/11/right-brained.aspx.

78. Cody C. Delistraty, "Can Creativity Be Learned?" *Atlantic,* July 16, 2014, www.the atlantic.com/health/archive/2014/07/can-creativity-be-learned/372605.

79. Norman Doidge, *The Brain That Changes Itself: Stories of Personal Triumph from the Frontiers of Brain Science* (New York: Viking, 2007).

80. Isaacson, *Leonardo da Vinci,* 117.

81. "The Spread of the Printing Press Across Europe," Garamond, accessed September 3, 2018, www.garamond.culture.fr/en/page/the_spread_of_the_printing_press_across_europe.

82. Isaacson, *Leonardo da Vinci,* 172.

83. From the preface to section seven. Leonardo da Vinci, "Notebook of Leonardo da Vinci ('The Codex Arundel'). A Collection of Papers Written in Italian by Leonardo da Vinci (b. 1452, d. 1519)," British Library, accessed September 4, 2018, www.bl.uk/manuscripts /Viewer.aspx?ref=arundel_ms_263_f001r.

84. Isaacson, *Leonardo da Vinci,* 98.

85. "The skills that are imperative and differentiated in a world with intuitive technology are the skills that help us to work together as humans, where the hard work is envisioning the end product and its usefulness, which requires real-world experience and judgment and historical context. What Jeff's story taught us is that the customer was focused on the wrong thing. It's the classic case: the technologist struggling to communicate with the business and the end user, and the business failing to articulate their needs. I see it every

day. We are scratching the surface in our ability as humans to communicate and invent together, and while the sciences teach us how to build things, it's the humanities that teach us what to build and why to build them. And they're equally as important, and they're just as hard. It irks me . . . when I hear people treat the humanities as a lesser path, as the easier path. Come on! The humanities give us the context of our world. They teach us how to think critically. They are purposely unstructured, while the sciences are purposely structured. They teach us to persuade, they give us our language, which we use to convert our emotions to thought and action. And they need to be on equal footing with the sciences. And yes, you can hire a bunch of artists and build a tech company and have an incredible outcome." Eric Berridge, "Why Tech Needs the Humanities," December 2017, TED@IBM, 11:13, www.ted.com/talks/eric_berridge_why_tech_needs_the_humanities.

86. Ibid.

87. Alok Jha, "Helicopter Powered by Man on Bicycle Wins $250,000 Prize," *Guardian*, July 12, 2013, www.theguardian.com/science/2013/jul/12/helicopter-powered-man-bicycle -prize.

88. Einstein questioned our role in the universe, knowing that play was just as important as study in unlocking the secrets of the cosmos. He pondered the universe in its physical and other senses, finding answers while playing the violin. Mitch Waldrop, "Inside Einstein's Love Affair With 'Lina'—His Cherished Violin," *National Geographic*, February 3, 2017, news.nationalgeographic.com/2017/02/einstein-genius-violin-music-physics-science.

89. Ken Gewertz, "Albert Einstein, Civil Rights Activist," *The Harvard Gazette*, April 12, 2007, news.harvard.edu/gazette/story/2007/04/albert-einstein-civil-rights-activist.

90. Thomas Levenson, *Einstein in Berlin* (New York: Bantam, 2004).

91. "Refugee Statistics," USA for UNHCR: The UN Refugee Agency, updated 2017, www .unrefugees.org/refugee-facts/statistics.

92. Mary Shelley, *Frankenstein: Annotated for Scientists, Engineers, and Creators of All Kinds* (Cambridge: MIT Press, 2017).

93. Carl Zimmer, "Nabokov Theory on Butterfly Evolution Is Vindicated," *New York Times*, January 25, 2011, www.nytimes.com/2011/02/01/science/01butterfly.html.

94. Adam Kirsch, "Design for Living," *New Yorker*, February 1, 2016, www.newyorker.com /magazine/2016/02/01/design-for-living-books-adam-kirsch.

95. Harold Boom, *Genius: A Mosaic of One Hundred Exemplary Creative Minds* (New York: Warner, 2003).

96. "Victor is incurious about the results of his actions, which is an enormous failing in a scientist." Shelley, *Frankenstein: Annotated for Scientists, Engineers, and Creators of All Kinds*, 234.

97. Ian Sample, "'It's Able to Create Knowledge Itself': Google Unveils AI that Learns on Its Own," *Guardian*, October 18, 2017, www.theguardian.com/science/2017/oct/18/its-able -to-create-knowledge-itself-google-unveils-ai-learns-all-on-its-own.

98. "Recent studies offer evidence that, contrary to popular belief, the main event of the imagination—creativity—does not require unrestrained freedom; rather, it relies on limits and obstacles." Matthew May, *The Laws of Subtraction: 6 Simple Rules for Winning in the Age of Excess Everything* (McGraw-Hill Education, 2012), 130.

99. Cade Metz, "Building A.I. That Can Build A.I.," *New York Times*, November 5, 2017,

www.nytimes.com/2017/11/05/technology/machine-learning-artificial-intelligence-ai .html.

100. Bullock, "Attractive, Slavish and at Your Command: Is AI Sexist?"

101. "Listeners [find] the male voice to be more trustworthy." Clifford Nass and Scott Brave, *Wired for Speech: How Voice Activates and Advances the Human-Computer Relationship* (Cambridge: MIT Press, 2005), 15.

102. Jana Kasperkevic, "Google Says Sorry for Racist Auto-tag in Photo App," *Guardian*, July 1, 2015, www.theguardian.com/technology/2015/jul/01/google-sorry-racist-auto-tag-photo-app.

103. Malek Murison, "Sage: Why Gender-Neutral AI Helps Remove Bias from Systems," Internet of Business, March 29, 2018, internetofbusiness.com/gender-neutral-robot-assistants-bias-ai.

104. Sarah Parker Harris, Randall Owen, and Cindy De Ruiter, "Civic Engagement and People with Disabilities: The Role of Advocacy and Technology," *Journal of Community Engagement*, August 22, 2012, jces.ua.edu/civic-engagement-and-people-with-disabilities-the -role-of-advocacy-and-technology.

105. On August 8, 1996, a Special Interest Forum (SIF) was held in Washington, D.C., on the topic of "Accessible Appliances and Universal Design, Center for Inclusive Design and Environmental Access," udeworld.com/dissemination/publications/56-reprints-short-articles -and-papers/127-accessible-appliances.html.

106. "'We believe that Google should not be in the business of war,' says the letter, addressed to Sundar Pichai, the company's chief executive. It asks that Google pull out of Project Maven, a Pentagon pilot program, and announce a policy that it will not 'ever build warfare technology.'" Scott Shane and Daisuke Wakabayashi, "'The Business of War': Google Employees Protest Work for the Pentagon," *New York Times*, April 4, 2018, www.nytimes .com/2018/04/04/technology/google-letter-ceo-pentagon-project.html.

107. Daisuke Wakabayashi, Erin Griffith, Amie Tsang, and Kate Conger, "Google Walkout: Employees Stage Protest Over Handling of Sexual Harassment," *New York Times*, November 1, 2018, www.nytimes.com/2018/11/01/technology/google-walkout-sexual-harassment .html.

108. From the letter: "'We request that Microsoft cancel its contracts with ICE, and with other clients who directly enable ICE. As the people who build the technologies that Microsoft profits from, we refuse to be complicit. We are part of a growing movement, comprised of many across the industry who recognize the grave responsibility that those creating powerful technology have to ensure what they build is used for good, and not for harm.'" Sheera Frenkel, "Microsoft Employees Protest Work With ICE, as Tech Industry Mobilizes Over Immigration," *New York Times*, June 19, 2018, www.nytimes.com/2018/06/19/technology /tech-companies-immigration-border.html.

109. Modupe Akinnawonu, "Why Having a Diverse Team Will Make Your Products Better," Times Open Team, Medium, May 23, 2017, open.nytimes.com/why-having-a-diverse -team-will-make-your-products-better-c73e7518f677.

110. David Rock and Heidi Grant, "Why Diverse Teams Are Smarter," *Harvard Business Review*, November 4, 2016, hbr.org/2016/11/why-diverse-teams-are-smarter.

111. Francesca Lagerberg, "The Value of Diversity," Grant Thornton: Women in Business, September 29, 2015, www.grantthornton.global/en/insights/articles/diverse-boards-in-india-uk-and -us-outperform-male-only-peers-by-us$655bn.

112. Mollie Goodfellow, "Women in Health Tech: Designing Solutions and Transforming Lives Across Society," *Guardian*, June 19, 2018, www.theguardian.com/axa-health-tech-and-you/2018/jun/19/women-in-health-tech-designing-solutions-and-transforming-lives-across-society.

113. Katherine W. Phillips, "How Diversity Makes Us Smarter," *Scientific American*, October 1, 2014, www.scientificamerican.com/article/how-diversity-makes-us-smarter.

114. Rock and Grant, "Why Diverse Teams Are Smarter."

115. Henry Fountain, "Putting Art in STEM," *New York Times*, October 31, 2014, www.nytimes.com/2014/11/02/education/edlife/putting-art-in-stem.html.

116. "When completing his creation, Victor Frankenstein is in the thrall of technical sweetness, which is the allure of the pieces of an intellectual puzzle fitting neatly together. Scientists working at Los Alamos experienced a similar excitement and blindness to the full implications of their work, and they reacted similarly to Victor, bearing a burden of responsibility for their work into the post-WWII context. Frankenstein thus serves as a useful parable for scientists and engineers, showing the difficulty of looking past immediate technical success to the broader implications of their work." Heather E. Douglas, "The Bitter Aftertaste of Technical Sweetness," *MIT Press Scholarship Online*, accessed September 3, 2018, DOI:10.7551/mitpress/9780262533287.003.0012.

117. "If virtue is even partly circumstantial, then all who act in the world, including scientists, must recognize that judgments about their own worth and the value of their work require close scrutiny. Victor [Frankenstein] acted alone, without consulting anyone about the value of his invention or its potential unintended consequences. If he had conferred with a community of thinkers and innovators with cooler heads, perhaps he could have rekindled his own compassion and avoided the cascading tragedy that emanates from his solitary creation." Sally Kitch in Mary Shelley's *Frankenstein: Annotated for Scientists, Engineers, and Creators of All Kinds*, 90.

CHAPTER 4: HUMAN RIGHTS AND ROBOT RIGHTS

1. Cheyenne Macdonald, "'Ethical Knob' Could Allow You to Choose Whose Life a Driverless Car Would Save in a Deadly Accident," *UK Daily Mail*, October 2017, www.dailymail.co.uk/sciencetech/article-4986142/Ethical-knob-let-driverless-car-decide-save.html.

2. Abigail Beall, "Driverless Cars Could Let You Choose Who Survives in a Crash," *New Scientist*, October 13, 2017, www.newscientist.com/article/2150330-driverless-cars-could-let-you-choose-who-survives-in-a-crash.

3. "The knob tells an autonomous car the value that the driver gives to his or her life relative to the lives of others . . . The car would use this information to calculate the actions it will execute, taking into account the probability that the passengers or other parties suffer harm as a consequence of the car's decision." Ibid.

4. "Values," Ethics Unwrapped, University of Texas McCombs School of Business, accessed September 8, 2018, ethicsunwrapped.utexas.edu/glossary/values.

5. "Morals," Ethics Unwrapped, University of Texas McCombs School of Business, accessed September 8, 2018, ethicsunwrapped.utexas.edu/glossary/morals.

6. "Ethics," Ethics Unwrapped, University of Texas McCombs School of Business, accessed September 8, 2018, ethicsunwrapped.utexas.edu/glossary/ethics.

7. Bertrand Russell, *Free Thought and Official Propaganda* (New York: B. W. Huebsch, 1922); Bertrand Russell, *The Will to Doubt* (New York: Welcome Rain Publishers, 2014).

8. "We're doing ethics on a deadline. If you survey the top 100 AI safety researchers or AI researches in the world, you'll see that they give a probability distribution of the likelihood of human level artificial intelligence with about a 50% probability at 2050." Lucas Perry, "AI Alignment Podcast: The Metaethics of Joy, Suffering, and Artificial Intelligence with Brian Tomasik and David Pearce," Future of Life Institute, August 16, 2018, futureoflife.org/2018/08/16/ai-alignment-podcast-metaethics-of-joy-suffering-with-brian-tomasik-and-david-pearce.

9. "Algorithms and Human Rights," Council of Europe, March 13, 2018, rm.coe.int/algorithms-and-human-rights-en-rev/16807956b5.

10. Johannes Morsink, *The Universal Declaration of Human Rights: Origins, Drafting, and Intent* (Philadelphia: University of Pennsylvania Press, 1984).

11. "Article I, Universal Declaration of Human Rights," United Nations, accessed September 8, 2018, www.un.org/en/universal-declaration-human-rights.

12. "Guide on Article 8 of the European Convention on Human Rights," Council of Europe/European Court of Human Rights, 2017, 102, www.refworld.org/pdfid/5a016ebe4.pdf.

13. Lorna McGregor, Vivian Ng, Ahmed Shaheed, Elena Abrusci, Catherine Kent, Daragh Murray, and Carmel Williams, "The Universal Declaration of Human Rights at 70: Putting Human Rights at the Heart of the Design, Development and Deployment of Artificial Intelligence," Human Rights Big Data and Technology Project, December 20, 2018, accessed December 22, 2018, 48ba3m4eh2bf2sksp43rq8kk-wpengine.netdna-ssl.com/wp-content/uploads/2018/12/UDHR70_AI.pdf.

14. Jay T. Stock, "Are Humans Still Evolving?" *EMBO Reports*, July 9, 2008, embor.embopress.org/content/9/1S/S51.

15. There is very little support or change in legislation for Native American rights and many such rights have been reversed or actively violated. This reminds us that progress can move slowly and even regress. Native American Rights Fund, accessed September 15, 2018, www.narf.org/our-work/promotion-human-rights.

16. Susan Mizner, "House Members Are Pushing a Bill That Will Roll Back the Rights of People with Disabilities," American Civil Liberties Union, February 13, 2018, www.aclu.org/blog/disability-rights/house-members-are-pushing-bill-will-roll-back-rights-people-disabilities; Vann R. Newkirk II, "The End of Civil Rights," *Atlantic*, June 18, 2018, www.theatlantic.com/politics/archive/2018/06/sessions/563006.

17. Charlie Stross, "Dude, You Broke the Future!" Antipope, accessed September 18, 2018, www.antipope.org/charlie/blog-static/2018/01/dude-you-broke-the-future.html#more.

18. "A growing number of scholars, drawn from a wide swath of disciplines—neuroscience, philosophy, computer science—now argue that this aptitude for cognitive time travel, revealed by the discovery of the default network, may be the defining property of human intelligence. 'What best distinguishes our species,' [University of Pennsylvania psychologist Martin Seligman] wrote in a Times Op-Ed with John Tierney, 'is an ability that scientists are just beginning to appreciate: We contemplate the future.' He went on: 'A more apt name for our species would be Homo prospectus, because we thrive by considering our prospects. The power of prospection is what makes us wise.'" Steven Johnson, "Looking to the Future has Always Defined Humanity. Will A.I. Become the Best Crystal Ball of All?" *New York Times*,

November 15, 2018, www.nytimes.com/interactive/2018/11/15/magazine/tech-design-ai
-prediction.html.

19. Angela Duckworth, *Grit: The Power of Passion and Perseverance* (New York: Scribner, 2016).

20. Editors of Encyclopaedia Britannica, "Ptolemaic system," *Encyclopaedia Britannica*, accessed September 8, 2018, www.britannica.com/science/Ptolemaic-system.

21. Thomas Georges, *Digital Soul: Intelligent Machines and Human Values* (New York: Basic Books, 2004), 2.

22. Robert D. Hof, "Deep Learning," *MIT Technology Review*, 2013, www.technologyreview.com/s/513696/deep-learning.

23. "International Covenant on Civil and Political Rights," United Nations Human Rights Office of the High Commissioner, accessed September 8, 2018, www.ohchr.org/en/professionalinterest/pages/ccpr.aspx.

24. Louis Menand, "Why Do We Care So Much About Privacy?" *New Yorker*, June 18, 2018, www.newyorker.com/magazine/2018/06/18/why-do-we-care-so-much-about-privacy.

25. Neil Hughes, "98 Percent of Americans View Privacy as a Basic Civil Right, OWI Labs Survey Finds," One World Identity, June 7, 2018, oneworldidentity.com/98-percent-americans-view-privacy-basic-civil-right-owi-labs-survey-finds.

26. Michael Gaynor, "Telecom Lobbyists Have Stalled 70 State-Level Bills That Would Protect Consumer Privacy," Motherboard, August 6, 2018, motherboard.vice.com/en_us/article/3ky5wj/telecom-lobbyists-have-stalled-70-state-level-bills-that-would-protect-consumer-privacy.

27. Jennifer Zhu Scott, "You Should be Paid for Your Facebook Data," Quartz, April 11, 2018, qz.com/1247388/you-should-be-paid-for-your-facebook-data.

28. "Public Interest Privacy Principles," Federation of State PIRGs, November 13, 2018, uspirg.org/resources/usp/public-interest-privacy-principles.

29. Alvaro M. Bedoya, "A License to Discriminate," *New York Times*, June 6, 2018, www.nytimes.com/2018/06/06/opinion/facebook-privacy-civil-rights-data-huawei-cambridge-analytica.html.

30. Sophia Yan, "Chinese Surveillance Grows Stronger with Technology that Can Recognise People from How They Walk," *Telegraph UK*, November 6, 2018, www.telegraph.co.uk/news/2018/11/06/chinese-surveillance-grows-stronger-technology-can-recognise.

31. Sam Levin, "Face-Reading AI Will Be Able to Detect your Politics & IQ, Professor Says," *Guardian*, September 12, 2017, www.theguardian.com/technology/2017/sep/12/artificial-intelligence-face-recognition-michal-kosinski; Jennifer Lynch, "Face Off: Law Enforcement Use of Face Recognition Technology," Electronic Frontier Foundation, February 12, 2018, www.eff.org/wp/law-enforcement-use-face-recognition#_idTextAnchor141.

32. James Bridle, *New Dark Age: Technology and the End of the Future* (New York: Verso Books, 2018).

33. Colin Lecher and Russell Brandom, "The FBI has Collected 430,000 Iris Scans in a So-Called 'Pilot Program,'" The Verge, July 12, 2016, www.theverge.com/2016/7/12/12148044/fbi-iris-pilot-program-ngi-biometric-database-aclu-privacy-act.

34. Marcello Ienca, "Do We Have a Right to Mental Privacy and Cognitive Liberty?" *Scientific American*, May 3, 2017, blogs.scientificamerican.com/observations/do-we-have-a-right-to-mental-privacy-and-cognitive-liberty.

35. Samantha Cole, "There Is No Tech Solution to Deepfakes," Motherboard, August 14, 2018, motherboard.vice.com/en_us/article/594qx5/there-is-no-tech-solution-to-deepfakes.

36. South African Constitution, accessed September 18, 2018, www.justice.gov.za/legislation /constitution/index.html.

37. Sue Onslow, "A Question of Timing: South Africa and Rhodesia's Unilateral Declaration of Independence, 1964–65," *Cold War History*, Vol. 5, Issue 2 (August 16, 2006), www .tandfonline.com/doi/abs/10.1080/14682740500062135.

38. "History of the Document," United Nations, accessed September 15, 2018, www.un.org /en/sections/universal-declaration/history-document/index.html.

39. "Article 19 at the UNHRC: 'The Same Rights That People Have Offline Must Also Be Protected Online,'" Article 19, June 14, 2017, www.article19.org/resources/article-19-at -the-unhrc-the-same-rights-that-people-have-offline-must-also-be-protected-online.

40. Commissioner Kara M. Stein, "From the Data Rush to the Data Wars: A Data Revolution in Financial Markets," U.S. Securities and Exchange Commission, September 27, 2018, www.sec.gov/news/speech/speech-stein-092718.

41. Edward L. Carter, "The Right to Be Forgotten," *Oxford Research Encyclopedias*, November 2016, DOI: 10.1093/acrefore/9780190228613.013.189.

42. Stefanie Koperniak, "Artificial Data Give the Same Results as Real Data—Without Compromising Privacy," MIT News, March 3, 2017, news.mit.edu/2017/artificial-data -give-same-results-as-real-data-0303.

43. "Isaac Asimov's Three Laws of Robotics," Auburn University, 2001, www.auburn.edu /~vestmon/robotics.html.

44. Andrew Feenberg, *Critical Theory of Technology* (Oxford: Oxford University Press, 1991).

45. Joanna J. Bryson, "Robots Should Be Slaves," Artificial Models of Natural Intelligence, University of Bath, United Kingdom, May 21, 2009, www.cs.bath.ac.uk/~jjb/ftp/Bryson -Slaves-Book09.pdf.

46. Ira Flatow, "Science Diction: The Origin of the Word 'Robot,'" April 22, 2011, NPR, *Talk of the Nation*, 5:22, www.npr.org/2011/04/22/135634400/science-diction-the-origin -of-the-word-robot.

47. Janosch Delcker, "Europe Divided Over Robot 'Personhood,'" Politico, April 11, 2018, www.politico.eu/article/europe-divided-over-robot-ai-artificial-intelligence-personhood.

48. "Open Letter to the European Commission," Politico, May 4, 2018, www.politico.eu/wp -content/uploads/2018/04/RoboticsOpenLetter.pdf.

49. Kate Darling, "Extending Legal Protection to Social Robots: The Effects of Anthropomorphism, Empathy, and Violent Behavior Towards Robotic Objects," We Robot Conference 2012, University of Miami, April 23, 2012, dx.doi.org/10.2139/ssrn.2044797.

50. Todd Leopold, "HitchBOT, the Hitchhiking Robot, Gets Beheaded in Philadelphia," CNN, August 4, 2015, www.cnn.com/2015/08/03/us/hitchbot-robot-beheaded-philadelphia-feat /index.html.

51. Daisuke Wakabayashi, "Self-Driving Uber Car Kills Pedestrian in Arizona, Where Robots Roam," *New York Times*, March 19, 2018, www.nytimes.com/2018/03/19/technology/uber -driverless-fatality.html.

52. Frank Pasquale, *The Black Box Society: The Secret Algorithms That Control Money and Information* (Cambridge, MA: Harvard University Press, 2015).

53. Peter H. Kahn Jr., Takayuki Kanda, Hiroshi Ishiguro, Brian T. Gill, Jolina H. Ruckert, Solace Shen, Heather E. Gary, Aimee L. Reichert, Nathan G. Freier, and Rachel L. Severson, "Do People Hold a Humanoid Robot Morally Accountable for the Harm It Causes?" Session: Attitudes and Responses to Social Robots, March 5–8, 2012, depts .washington.edu/hints/publications/Robovie_Moral_Accountability_Study_HRI _2012_corrected.pdf.

54. Liam J. Bannon, "From Human Factors to Human Actors," *Design at Work: Cooperative Design of Computer Systems*, J. Greenbaum and M. Kyng, eds. (Hillsdale: Lawrence Erlbaum Associates, 1991): 25–44, DOI: 10.1016/B978-0-08-051574-8.50024-8.

55. Gabriella Airenti, "The Cognitive Bases of Anthropomorphism: From Relatedness to Empathy," *International Journal of Social Robotics*, Vol. 7, Issue 1 (January 14, 2015): 117–127, link.springer.com/article/10.1007/s12369-014-0263-x.

56. Joshua Rothman, "Are Disability Rights and Animal Rights Connected?" *New Yorker*, June 5, 2017, www.newyorker.com/culture/persons-of-interest/are-disability-rights-and-animal -rights-connected.

57. "Forty Million Victims of Modern Slavery in 2016: Report," Al Jazeera, September 19, 2017, www.aljazeera.com/news/2017/09/forty-million-victims-modern-slavery-2016-report -170919141907308.html.

58. Ashish Kothari, Mari Margil, and Shrishtee Bajpai, "Now Rivers Have the Same Legal Status as People, We Must Uphold Their Rights," *Guardian*, April 21, 2017, www.theguardian .com/global-development-professionals-network/2017/apr/21/rivers-legal-human-rights -ganges-whanganui.

59. "Nature or Pachamama, where life is reproduced and exists, has the right to exist, persist, maintain and regenerate its vital cycles, structure, functions and its processes in evolution. Every person, people, community or nationality, will be able to demand the recognitions of rights for nature before the public organisms." "Rights of Nature Articles in Ecuador's Constitution," accessed September 15, 2018, therightsofnature.org/wp-content/uploads /pdfs/Rights-for-Nature-Articles-in-Ecuadors-Constitution.pdf.

60. Suzanne Monyak, "When the Law Recognizes Animals as People," *New Republic*, February 2, 2018, newrepublic.com/article/146870/law-recognizes-animals-people.

61. "We can trace our genealogy to the origins of the universe . . . And therefore rather than us being masters of the natural world, we are part of it. We want to live like that as our starting point. And that is not an anti-development, or anti-economic use of the river but to begin with the view that it is a living being, and then consider its future from that central belief." Gerrard Albert, quoted in Eleanor Ainge Roy, "New Zealand River Granted Same Legal Rights as Human Being," *Guardian*, March 16, 2017, www.theguardian.com /world/2017/mar/16/new-zealand-river-granted-same-legal-rights-as-human-being.

62. Catherine J. Iorns Magallanes, "Nature as an Ancestor: Two Examples of Legal Personality for Nature in New Zealand," *VertigO*, September 2015, journals.openedition.org/vertigo /16199?lang=en.

63. Ker Than, "All Species Evolved from Single Cell, Study Finds," *National Geographic*, May 14, 2010, news.nationalgeographic.com/news/2010/05/100513-science-evolution-darwin -single-ancestor.

64. Dr. Seuss, *The Lorax* (New York: Random House, 1971).

65. Michael LaChat, "AI and Ethics: An Exercise in Moral Imagination," *AI Magazine*, Vol. 7.2 (1986), DOI: doi.org/10.1609/aimag.v7i2.540.

66. "Credit is due to the combined machine learning and social science communities for starting the FAT/ML organization, which since 2014 has held excellent technical workshops annually on Fairness, Accountability, and Transparency in Machine Learning and maintains a list of scholarly papers. Credit is additionally due to the Microsoft Research FATE group in NYC for adding the 'E' for ethics to FAT." Jeannette Wing, "Data for Good: FATES, Elaborated," Columbia University, January 23, 2018, datascience.columbia.edu/FATES-Elaborated.

67. "Asilomar AI Principles," Future of Life, accessed September 8, 2018, futureoflife.org /ai-principles.

68. Sundar Pichai, "AI at Google: Our Principles," Google, June 7, 2018, blog.google/technology /ai/ai-principles.

69. Alex Campolo, Madelyn Sanfilippo, Meredith Whittaker, and Kate Crawford, "AI Now 2017 Report," Yale Information Society Project and Data & Society, Cornell University, AI Now Institute, accessed September 18, 2018, ainowinstitute.org/AI_Now_2017 _Report.pdf.

70. Meredith Whittaker, Kate Crawford, Roel Dobbe, Genevieve Fried, Elizabeth Kaziunas, Varoon Mathur, Sarah Myers West, Rashida Richardson, Jason Schultz, and Oscar Schwartz, "AI Now 2018 Report," AI Now Institute, accessed December 21, 2018, ainow institute.org/AI_Now_2018_Report.pdf.

71. John Patzakis, "GDPR Provides a Private Right of Action. Here's Why That's Important," Discovery Law and Tech, blog, February 28, 2018, blog.x1discovery.com/2018/02/28 /gdpr-provides-a-private-right-of-action-heres-why-thats-important.

72. Thomas Whiteside, "Cutting Down," *New Yorker*, December 19, 1970, www.newyorker .com/magazine/1970/12/19/the-fight-to-ban-smoking-ads.

73. Edmund Andrews, "Steven Callander: How to Make States 'Laboratories of Democracy,'" Insights by Stanford Business, Stanford Graduate School of Business, May 19, 2015, www .gsb.stanford.edu/insights/steven-callander-how-make-states-laboratories-democracy.

74. Will Knight, "The Dark Secret at the Heart of AI," *MIT Technology Review*, April 11, 2017, www.technologyreview.com/s/604087/the-dark-secret-at-the-heart-of-ai.

75. Gar Alperovitz, with the assistance of Sanho Tree, Edward Rouse Winstead, Kathryn C. Morris, David J. Williams, Leo C. Maley, Thad Williamson, and Miranda Grieder, *The Decision to Use the Atomic Bomb and the Architecture of an American Myth* (New York: Alfred A. Knopf, 1995); Karl T. Compton, "If the Atomic Bomb Had Not Been Used," *Atlantic*, December 1946, www.theatlantic.com/magazine/archive/1946/12/if-the-atomic-bomb -had-not-been-used/376238.

76. "Mr. President, I feel I have blood on my hands." J. Robert Oppenheimer, "Freedom and Necessity in the Sciences," 1958–1959 Dartmouth College Lecture Series and the Independent Reading Program, Dartmouth College, April 14, 1959, www.dartmouth.edu /~library/digital/collections/lectures/oppenheimer/index.html.

77. "AK-47 Designer Kalashnikov Wrote Penitent Letter," CBS News, January 14, 2014, www .cbsnews.com/news/ak-47-designer-kalashnikov-wrote-penitent-letter.

78. Ethan Zuckerman, "The Internet's Original Sin," *Atlantic*, August 14, 2014, www.the atlantic.com/technology/archive/2014/08/advertising-is-the-internets-original-sin/376041.

79. Dan Robitzski, "To Build Trust in Artificial Intelligence, IBM Wants Developers to Prove Their Algorithms Are Fair," Futurism, August 22, 2018, futurism.com/trust-artificial -intelligence-ibm.

80. Paul Scharre, *Army of None: Autonomous Weapons and the Future of War* (New York: W. W. Norton & Company, 2018).

81. Pamela Cohn, Alastair Green, Meredith Langstaff, and Melanie Roller, "Commercial Drones Are Here: The Future of Unmanned Aerial Systems," McKinsey & Company, December 2017, www.mckinsey.com/industries/capital-projects-and-infrastructure/our-insights/commercial -drones-are-here-the-future-of-unmanned-aerial-systems.

82. Flynn Coleman, "Beyond Killer Robots," Medium, September 21, 2016, medium.com /@flynncoleman/beyond-killer-robots-cdb71d7aa1e0.

83. Mary Wareham, "Support Grows for Killer Robots Ban," Human Rights Watch, September 5, 2018, www.hrw.org/news/2018/09/05/support-grows-killer-robots-ban.

84. Hayley Evans, "Lethal Autonomous Weapons Systems at the First and Second U.N. GGE Meetings," Lawfare, April 9, 2018, www.lawfareblog.com/lethal-autonomous-weapons -systems-first-and-second-un-gge-meetings.

85. "Killer Robots: The Case for Human Control," Human Rights Watch, April 11, 2016, www.hrw.org/news/2016/04/11/killer-robots-case-human-control.

86. Marta Kosmynam, Fitzroy Hepkins, and Jose Martinez, "Heed the Call: A Moral and Legal Imperative to Ban Killer Robots," Human Rights Watch, August 21, 2018, www.hrw .org/report/2018/08/21/heed-call/moral-and-legal-imperative-ban-killer-robots#.

87. Neil Davison, "Autonomous Weapon Systems Under International Humanitarian Law," International Committee of the Red Cross, January 3, 2018, www.icrc.org/en/document /autonomous-weapon-systems-under-international-humanitarian-law.

88. "Pathways to Banning Fully Autonomous Weapons," United Nations Office for Disarmament Affairs, October 23, 2017, www.un.org/disarmament/update/pathways-to-banning -fully-autonomous-weapons.

89. Mattha Busby, Anthony Cuthbertson, "'Killer Robots' Ban Blocked by U.S. and Russia at UN Meeting," *Independent UK*, September 3, 2018, www.independent.co.uk/life -style/gadgets-and-tech/news/killer-robots-un-meeting-autonomous-weapons-systems -campaigners-dismayed-a8519511.html.

90. "The Biological Weapons Convention," United Nations Office for Disarmament Affairs, accessed September 8, 2018, www.un.org/disarmament/wmd/bio.

91. Billy Perrigo, "A Global Arms Race for Killer Robots Is Transforming the Battlefield," *Time*, April 9, 2018, time.com/5230567/killer-robots.

92. "Autonomous Weapons: An Open Letter from AI & Robotics Researchers," Future of Life Institute, accessed September 18, 2018, futureoflife.org/open-letter-autonomous-weapons.

93. Cameron Jenkins, "AI Innovators Take Pledge Against Autonomous Killer Weapons," NPR, July 18, 2018, www.npr.org/2018/07/18/630146884/ai-innovators-take-pledge -against-autonomous-killer-weapons.

94. Brad Smith, "The Need for a Digital Geneva Convention," Microsoft on the Issues, Microsoft, February 14, 2017, blogs.microsoft.com/on-the-issues/2017/02/14/need-digital -geneva-convention.

95. Cybersecurity Tech Accord, accessed February 25, 2019, cybertechaccord.org.

96. Scharre, *Army of None: Autonomous Weapons and the Future of War.*

97. "The Toronto Declaration: Protecting the Rights to Equality and Non-Discrimination in Machine Learning Systems," Access Now, May 16, 2018, www.accessnow.org/the-toronto -declaration-protecting-the-rights-to-equality-and-non-discrimination-in-machine-learning -systems.

98. Paul Farmer and Gustavo Gutierrez, *In the Company of the Poor: Conversations with Dr. Paul Farmer and Fr. Gustavo Gutierrez* (New York: Orbis Books, 2013).

99. AI4All, "High Schoolers Lead the Way with AI Research," *Medium,* May 17, 2018, medium.com/ai4allorg/high-schoolers-lead-the-way-with-ai-research-5757469bf8e.

CHAPTER 5: THE PERNICIOUS THREATS OF INTELLIGENT MACHINES

1. "War in the Fifth Domain," *Economist*, July 1, 2010, www.economist.com/briefing/2010 /07/01/war-in-the-fifth-domain.

2. Mariarosaria Taddeo and Luciano Floridi, "Regulate Artificial Intelligence to Avert Cyber Arms Race," *Nature*, April 16, 2018, www.nature.com/articles/d41586-018-04602 -6#ref-CR5.

3. Evan Osnos, David Remnick, and Joshua Yaffa, "Trump, Putin, and the New Cold War," *New Yorker*, March 6, 2017, www.newyorker.com/magazine/2017/03/06/trump -putin-and-the-new-cold-war.

4. Rebecca Smith, "Russian Hackers Reach U.S. Utility Control Rooms, Homeland Security Officials Say; Blackouts Could Have Been Caused After the Networks of Trusted Vendors Were Easily Penetrated," *Wall Street Journal*, July 23, 2018, www.wsj.com/articles/russian -hackers-reach-u-s-utility-control-rooms-homeland-security-officials-say-1532388110.

5. Pavel Polityuk, Oleg Vukmanovic, and Stephen Jewkes, "Ukraine's Power Outage Was a Cyber Attack: Ukrenergo," Reuters, January 18, 2017, www.reuters.com/article /us-ukraine-cyber-attack-energy/ukraines-power-outage-was-a-cyber-attack-ukrenergo -idUSKBN1521BA.

6. Damien Sharkov, "Russian Accused of Massive $1.2 Billion NOTPETYA Cyberattack," *Newsweek*, February 15, 2018, www.newsweek.com/russia-accused-massive-12-billion-cyber -attack-807867.

7. David E. Sanger, "Obama Order Sped Up Wave of Cyberattacks Against Iran," *New York Times*, June 1, 2012, www.nytimes.com/2012/06/01/world/middleeast/obama-ordered -wave-of-cyberattacks-against-iran.html.

8. Nir Kshetri, "Diffusion and Effects of Cyber-Crime in Developing Economies," *Third World Quarterly*, Vol. 31, No. 7 (2010): 1057–1079, www.jstor.org/stable/27896600.

9. Heidi Zhou-Castro, "U.S. Military 'Close' to Sending Cyber Soldiers to Battlefields," Al Jazeera, December 14, 2017, www.aljazeera.com/news/2017/12/military-close-sending-cyber -soldiers-battlefields-171214111539505.html.

10. Edith Hamilton, "Chapter IV: The Earliest Heroes," in Part One of *Mythology* (New York: Little Brown, 1942).

11. "The book's subtitle—*The Modern Prometheus*—also contains an important mythological clue: Prometheus brings fire to the mortals and unleashes dire consequences in the process, granting them the ability to burn down the world. The novel provides the perfect lens through which to examine scientific innovation." Jacob Brogan, "Why *Frankenstein* Is Still

Relevant, Almost 200 Years After It Was Published," *Slate*, January 2, 2013, www.slate.com/articles/technology/future_tense/2017/01/why_frankenstein_is_still_relevant_almost_200_years_after_it_was_published.html.

12. Hamilton, *Mythology*, Part Three.

13. Hamilton, *Mythology*, Part Two, Ch. 3–4.

14. Joachim Neugroschel, ed., *The Golem* (New York: W. W. Norton & Company, 2006).

15. Kate Moore, *The Radium Girls: The Dark Story of America's Shining Women* (Illinois: Sourcebooks, Inc., 2017).

16. James Dao, "Drone Pilots Are Found to Get Stress Disorders Much as Those in Combat Do," *New York Times*, February 23, 2013, www.nytimes.com/2013/02/23/us/drone-pilots-found-to-get-stress-disorders-much-as-those-in-combat-do.html.

17. "Boston Dynamics' Robots Can Now Go for a Jog Outside and Avoid Obstacles," May 10, 2018, CNBC, video, 00:56, www.cnbc.com/2018/05/10/boston-dynamics-spotmini-and-atlas-robots-have-some-new-tricks.html.

18. Adrienne LaFrance, "An Artificial Intelligence Developed Its Own Non-Human Language," *Atlantic*, June 15, 2017, www.theatlantic.com/technology/archive/2017/06/artificial-intelligence-develops-its-own-non-human-language/530436.

19. Kenneth Neil Cukier and Viktor Mayer-Schöenberger, "The Rise of Big Data: How It's Changing the Way We Think About the World," *Foreign Affairs*, Vol. 92, No. 3 (May/June 2013): 28–40, www.jstor.org/stable/23526834.

20. "How 5 Tech Giants Have Become More Like Governments Than Companies," October 26, 2017, NPR, *Fresh Air*, 35:15, www.npr.org/2017/10/26/560136311/how-5-tech-giants-have-become-more-like-governments-than-companies.

21. Shoshana Zuboff, *The Age of Surveillance Capitalism: The Fight for a Human Future at the New Frontier of Power* (New York: PublicAffairs, 2019).

22. Paul Mozur and John Markoff, "Is China Outsmarting America in A.I.?" *New York Times*, May 27, 2017, www.nytimes.com/2017/05/27/technology/china-us-ai-artificial-intelligence.html.

23. Christy Pettey and Rob van der Meulen, "Gartner Says Global Artificial Intelligence Business Value to Reach $1.2 Trillion in 2018," Gartner Inc., April 25, 2018, www.gartner.com/en/newsroom/press-releases/2018-04-25-gartner-says-global-artificial-intelligence-business-value-to-reach-1-point-2-trillion-in-2018.

24. Sam Shead, "DARPA Plans to Spend $2 Billion Developing New AI Technologies," *Forbes*, September 7, 2018, www.forbes.com/sites/samshead/2018/09/07/darpa-plans-to-spend-2-billion-developing-new-ai-technologies/#41ba71da3ae1.

25. Julian E. Barnes and Josh Chin, "The New Arms Race in AI," *Wall Street Journal*, March 2, 2018, www.wsj.com/articles/the-new-arms-race-in-ai-1520009261.

26. Edward Geist and Andrew J. Lohn, "By 2040, Artificial Intelligence Could Upend Nuclear Stability," Rand Corporation, April 24, 2018, www.rand.org/news/press/2018/04/24.html.

27. Alexis C. Madrigal, "Drone Swarms Are Going to Be Terrifying and Hard to Stop," *Atlantic*, March 7, 2018, www.theatlantic.com/technology/archive/2018/03/drone-swarms-are-going-to-be-terrifying/555005.

28. "AI technology like generative adversarial networks (GANs), a deep-learning system [Ian Goodfellow] developed, can create fake images and learn to make them more believable. As a result, it's going to be easier to fool even more people." Jackie Snow, "AI Could Set Us

Back 100 Years When It Comes to How We Consume News," *MIT Technology Review*, November 7, 2017, www.technologyreview.com/s/609358/ai-could-send-us-back-100-years-when-it-comes-to-how-we-consume-news.

29. "Transhumanism is a class of philosophies of life that seek the continuation and acceleration of the evolution of intelligent life beyond its currently human form and human limitations by means of science and technology, guided by life-promoting principles and values." Max More, *Transhumanism: Toward a Futurist Philosophy* (Extropy, 1990).

30. Kai-Fu Lee, "AI Could Devastate the Developing World," Bloomberg Quint, September 17, 2018, www.bloombergquint.com/opinion/artificial-intelligence-threatens-jobs-in-developing-world#gs.JEbCVRU.

31. Sarah Knapton, "Artificial Intelligence is Greater Concern than Climate Change or Terrorism, Says New Head of British Science Association," *Telegraph UK*, September 6, 2018, www.telegraph.co.uk/science/2018/09/05/artificial-intelligence-greater-concern-climate-change-terrorism.

32. Dylan Love, "By 2045 'The Top Species Will No Longer Be Humans,' and That Could Be a Problem," Business Insider, July 5, 2014, www.businessinsider.com/louis-del-monte-interview-on-the-singularity-2014-7.

33. Jonnie Penn, "AI Thinks Like a Corporation—and That's Worrying," *Economist*, November 26, 2018, www.economist.com/open-future/2018/11/26/ai-thinks-like-a-corporation-and-thats-worrying.

34. David G. Victor and Kassia Yanosek, "The Next Energy Revolution: The Promise and Peril of High-Tech Innovation," Brookings, June 13, 2017, www.brookings.edu/blog/planet policy/2017/06/13/the-next-energy-revolution-the-promise-and-peril-of-high-tech-innovation.

35. Steve LeVine, "Unlocking AI Could Upend Geopolitics," Axios, July 29, 2018, www .axios.com/artificial-intelligence-industrial-revolution-geopolitics-d60e8c0e-c49b-4d7d-a 31b-20a38a63c9eb.html.

36. Ian Bogost, "Cryptocurrency Might Be a Path to Authoritarianism," *Atlantic*, May 30, 2017, www.theatlantic.com/technology/archive/2017/05/blockchain-of-command/528543.

37. John Delaney, "France, China, and the EU All Have an AI Strategy. Shouldn't the U.S.?" *Wired*, May 20, 2018, www.wired.com/story/the-us-needs-an-ai-strategy.

38. Max Tegmark, "Friendly AI: Aligning Goals," Future of Life, August 29, 2017, future oflife.org/2017/08/29/friendly-ai-aligning-goals.

39. Nicholas Carr, "Is Google Making Us Stupid?" *Atlantic*, July/August 2008, www.the atlantic.com/magazine/archive/2008/07/is-google-making-us-stupid/306868.

40. Anthony Cuthbertson, "Elon Musk and Stephen Hawking Warn of Artificial Intelligence Arms Race," *Newsweek*, January 31, 2017, www.newsweek.com/ai-asilomar-principles-artificial-intelligence-elon-musk-550525.

41. Dirk Helbing, Bruno S. Frey, Gerd Gigerenzer, Ernst Hafen, Michael Hagner, Yvonne Hofstetter, Jeroen van den Hoven, Roberto V. Zicari, and Andrej Zwitter, "Will Democracy Survive Big Data and Artificial Intelligence?" *Scientific American*, February 25, 2017, www .scientificamerican.com/article/will-democracy-survive-big-data-and-artificial-intelligence.

42. Steven Levy, "Algorithms Have Already Gone Rogue," *Wired*, October 4, 2017, www .wired.com/story/tim-oreilly-algorithms-have-already-gone-rogue.

43. Ian Sample, "Study Reveals Bot-on-Bot Editing Wars Raging on Wikipedia's Pages," *Guard-

ian, February 23, 2017, www.theguardian.com/technology/2017/feb/23/wikipedia-bot-editing
-war-study.

44. Helbing et al., "Will Democracy Survive Big Data and Artificial Intelligence?"

45. Not Flawless AI, accessed September 8, 2018, www.notflawless.ai/.

46. Julia Angwin, Jeff Larson, Surya Mattu, and Lauren Kirchner, "Machine Bias," ProPublica, May 23, 2016, www.propublica.org/article/machine-bias-risk-assessments-in-criminal-sentencing.

47. The Perpetual Line-Up, accessed September 11, 2018, www.perpetuallineup.org.

48. Ian Tucker, "'A White Mask Worked Better': Why Algorithms are Not Colour Blind," *Guardian*, May 28, 2017, www.theguardian.com/technology/2017/may/28/joy-buolamwini-when-algorithms-are-racist-facial-recognition-bias.

49. Steve Lohr, "Facial Recognition Is Accurate, if You're a White Guy," *New York Times*, February 9, 2018, www.nytimes.com/2018/02/09/technology/facial-recognition-race-artificial-intelligence.html.

50. "'When we blithely train algorithms on historical data, to a large extent we are setting ourselves up to merely repeat the past. If we want to get beyond that, beyond automating the status quo, we'll need to do more, which means examining the bias embedded in the data. The data is, after all, simply a reflection of our imperfect culture,' [Cathy] O'Neil, who now runs her own algorithm auditing firm, said via email." Eric Rosenbaum, "Silicon Valley is Stumped: Even A.I. Cannot Always Remove Bias from Hiring," CNBC, May 30, 2018, www.cnbc.com/2018/05/30/silicon-valley-is-stumped-even-a-i-cannot-remove-bias-from-hiring.html.

51. Jeff Asher and Rob Arthur, "Inside the Algorithm That Tries to Predict Gun Violence in Chicago," *New York Times*, June 13, 2017, www.nytimes.com/2017/06/13/upshot/what-an-algorithm-reveals-about-life-on-chicagos-high-risk-list.html.

52. *Precrime*, directed by Matthias Heeder, Monika Hielscher (Germany: Kloos & Co, Medien GmbH, 2017).

53. "This report found that black individuals, as with so many aspects of the justice system, were the most likely to be scrutinized by facial recognition software in cases. It also suggested that software was most likely to be incorrect when used on black individuals—a finding corroborated by the FBI's own research." Ali Breland, "How White Engineers Built Racist Code—and Why it's Dangerous for Black People," *Guardian*, December 4, 2017, www.theguardian.com/technology/2017/dec/04/racist-facial-recognition-white-coders-black-people-police.

54. *Tell Me More* Staff, "Light and Dark: The Racial Biases That Remain in Photography," NPR, April 16, 2014, www.npr.org/sections/codeswitch/2014/04/16/303721251/light-and-dark-the-racial-biases-that-remain-in-photography.

55. Joy Buolamwini, "When the Robot Doesn't See Dark Skin," *New York Times*, June 21, 2018, www.nytimes.com/2018/06/21/opinion/facial-analysis-technology-bias.html.

56. Harrison Rudolph, Laura M. Moy, and Alvaro M. Bedoya, "Not Ready for Takeoff: Face Scans at Airport Departure Gates," Georgetown Law Center on Privacy & Technology, December 21, 2017, www.airportfacescans.com.

57. "Open Letter to Amazon Against Police and Government use of Rekognition," International Committee for Robot Arms Control, accessed September 10, 2018, www.icrac.net/open-letter-to-amazon-against-police-and-government-use-of-rekognition.

58. Tovia Smith, "More States Opting To 'Robo-Grade' Student Essays by Computer," NPR,

June 30, 2018, www.npr.org/2018/06/30/624373367/more-states-opting-to-robo-grade
-student-essays-by-computer.

59. "Could AI Robots Develop Prejudice on Their Own?" Cardiff University, September 6,
2018, www.sciencedaily.com/releases/2018/09/180906123325.htm.

60. Tim Collins, "Rise of the Racist Robots: Artificial Intelligence Can Quickly Develop Prejudice on Its Own, Scientists Say," *Daily Mail*, September 7, 2018, www.dailymail.co.uk
/sciencetech/article-6143535/Artificial-Intelligence-develop-racism-own.html.

61. Kris Holt, "AI Robots Can Develop Prejudices, Just Like Us Mere Mortals," Engadget,
September 6, 2018, www.engadget.com/2018/09/06/robots-prejudice-study-mit-cardiff.

62. Stuart Fox, "Evolving Robots Learn to Lie to Each Other," *Popular Science*, August 18, 2009,
www.popsci.com/scitech/article/2009-08/evolving-robots-learn-lie-hide-resources-each
-other.

63. Mihir Zaveri, "St. Louis Uber and Lyft Driver Secretly Live-Streamed Passengers, Report
Says," *New York Times*, July 22, 2018, www.nytimes.com/2018/07/22/technology/uber
-lyft-driver-live-stream-passengers-nyt.html.

64. "Missouri Recording Law," Digital Media Law Project, accessed October 20, 2018, www
.dmlp.org/legal-guide/missouri-recording-law.

65. Daniel J. Solove, "Privacy and Power: Computer Databases and Metaphors for Information Privacy," *Stanford Law Review*, Vol. 53 (December 14, 2000): 1393, papers.ssrn.com
/sol3/papers.cfm?abstract_id=248300.

66. Vanessa Romo, "Facebook To Users: You May Want to Update Your Privacy Settings Again."
NPR, June 7, 2018, www.npr.org/2018/06/07/618076844/facebook-to-users-you-may
-want-to-update-your-privacy-settings-again.

67. James Snell and Nicola Menaldo, "Web Scraping in an Era of Big Data 2.0," Bloomberg
Law, June 8, 2016, www.bna.com/web-scraping-era-n57982073780.

68. Wendy Davis, "Craigslist Sides with LinkedIn in Battle over Users' Data," Mediapost,
October 12, 2017, www.mediapost.com/publications/article/308668/craigslist-sides-with
-linkedin-in-battle-over-user.html.

69. D. J. Pangburn, "Bots are Scraping Your Public Data for Cash Amid Murky Laws and
Ethics," Fast Company, www.fastcompany.com/40456140/bots-are-scraping-your-public
-data-for-cash-amid-murky-laws-and-ethics-linkedin-hiq.

70. Ian Sample, "Joseph Stiglitz on Artificial Intelligence: 'We're Going Towards a More Divided
Society,'" *Guardian*, September 8, 2018, www.theguardian.com/technology/2018/sep/08
/joseph-stiglitz-on-artificial-intelligence-were-going-towards-a-more-divided-society.

71. Erik Wander, "Infographic: How Much Privacy People Will Give Up for Personalized Experiences," Adweek, January 28, 2018, www.adweek.com/digital/infographic-how-much
-privacy-people-will-give-up-for-personalized-experiences.

72. Sherry Turkle, "Stop Googling. Let's Talk," *New York Times*, September 26, 2015,
www.nytimes.com/2015/09/27/opinion/sunday/stop-googling-lets-talk.html.

73. "China Invents the Digital Totalitarian State," *Economist*, December 17, 2016, www
.economist.com/briefing/2016/12/17/china-invents-the-digital-totalitarian-state.

74. Cari Romm, "Battling Ageism with Subliminal Messages," *Atlantic*, October 22, 2014, www
.theatlantic.com/health/archive/2014/10/battling-ageism-with-subliminal-messages/381762.

75. Yuval Noah Harari, "Why Technology Favors Tyranny," *Atlantic*, October 2018, www

.theatlantic.com/magazine/archive/2018/10/yuval-noah-harari-technology-tyranny
/568330.

76. Andrew Tarantola, "How Artificial Intelligence Can Be Corrupted to Repress Free Speech," Engadget, January 20, 2017, www.engadget.com/2017/01/20/artificial-intelligence-can-repress-free-speech.

77. James A. Millward, "What It's Like to Live in a Surveillance State," New York Times, February, 3, 2018, www.nytimes.com/2018/02/03/opinion/sunday/china-surveillance-state-uighurs.html.

78. Steve Stecklow, "Facebook Removes Burmese Translation Feature after Reuters Report," Reuters, September 6, 2018, www.reuters.com/article/us-facebook-myanmar-hate-speech/facebook-removes-burmese-translation-feature-after-reuters-report-idUSKCN1LM200.

79. Craig Timberg and Elizabeth Dwoskin, "Twitter is Sweeping Out Fake Accounts Like Never Before, Putting User Growth at Risk," Washington Post, July 6, 2018, www.washingtonpost.com/technology/2018/07/06/twitter-is-sweeping-out-fake-accounts-like-never-before-putting-user-growth-risk.

80. "Cognitive Offloading: How the Internet is Increasingly Taking over Human Memory," Science Daily, August 16, 2016, www.sciencedaily.com/releases/2016/08/160816085029.htm.

81. Paul Mozur, "Inside China's Dystopian Dreams: A.I., Shame and Lots of Cameras," New York Times, July 8, 2018, www.nytimes.com/2018/07/08/business/china-surveillance-technology.html.

82. Adam Greenfield, "China's Dystopian Tech Could Be Contagious," Atlantic, February 14, 2018 www.theatlantic.com/technology/archive/2018/02/chinas-dangerous-dream-of-urban-control/553097.

83. Helbing, et al., "Will Democracy Survive Big Data and Artificial Intelligence?"

84. Miles Brundage et al., "The Malicious Use of Artificial Intelligence: Forecasting, Prevention, and Mitigation Future," Future of Humanity Institute, University of Oxford, Centre for the Study of Existential Risk, University of Cambridge, Center for a New American Security, Electronic Frontier Foundation, OpenAI, February 2018, img1.wsimg.com/blobby/go/3d82daa4-97fe-4096-9c6b-376b92c619de/downloads/1c6q2kc4v_50335.pdf.

85. Todd Spangler, "Jordan Peele Teams with BuzzFeed for Obama Fake-News Awareness Video," Variety, April 17, 2018, variety.com/2018/digital/news/jordan-peele-obama-fake-news-video-buzzfeed-1202755517.

86. "Waging War with Disinformation," Economist, January 25, 2018, www.economist.com/special-report/2018/01/25/waging-war-with-disinformation.

87. Richard Kemeny, "AIs Created Our Fake Video Dystopia but Now They Could Help Fix It," Wired, July 10, 2018, www.wired.co.uk/article/deepfake-fake-videos-artificial-intelligence.

88. Michael Horowitz, Paul Scharre, Gregory C. Allen, Kara Frederick, Anthony Cho, and Edoardo Saravalle, "Artificial Intelligence and International Security," Center for a New American Security, July 10, 2018, www.cnas.org/publications/reports/artificial-intelligence-and-international-security.

89. Nicholas Thompson, "Emmanuel Macron Talks to Wired about France's AI Strategy," Wired, March 31, 2018, www.wired.com/story/emmanuel-macron-talks-to-wired-about-frances-ai-strategy.

90. Katie Langin, "Fake News Spreads Faster Than True News on Twitter—Thanks to Peo-

ple, Not Bots," *Nature*, March 8, 2018, www.sciencemag.org/news/2018/03/fake-news -spreads-faster-true-news-twitter-thanks-people-not-bots.

91. Neil Irwin, "Researchers Created Fake News. Here's What They Found," *New York Times*, January 18, 2017, www.nytimes.com/2017/01/18/upshot/researchers-created-fake-news -heres-what-they-found.html.

92. Adobe Voco, "'Photoshop-for-Voice' Causes Concern," BBC, November 7, 2016, www .bbc.com/news/technology-37899902.

93. Sebastian Ruder, "NLP's ImageNet Moment has Arrived," Gradient, July 8, 2018, thegradient.pub/nlp-imagenet.

94. Olivia Solon, "The Future of Fake News: Don't Believe Everything you Read, See or Hear," *Guardian*, July 26, 2017, www.theguardian.com/technology/2017/jul/26/fake-news -obama-video-trump-face2face-doctored-content.

95. Carnegie Mellon University, "Beyond Deep Fakes: Transforming Video Content into Another Video's Style, Automatically," Science Daily, accessed October 20, 2018, www .sciencedaily.com/releases/2018/09/180911083145.htm.

96. Nicky Woolf, "How to Solve Facebook's Fake News Problem: Experts Pitch their Ideas," *Guardian*, November 29, 2016, www.theguardian.com/technology/2016/nov/29 /facebook-fake-news-problem-experts-pitch-ideas-algorithms.

97. Federico Guerrini, "Will Technological Unemployment Fuel Modern Slavery in Southeast Asia?" *Forbes*, July 14, 2018, www.forbes.com/sites/federicoguerrini/2018/07/14/will -technological-unemployment-fuel-modern-slavery/#242589d532d8.

98. Livia Gershon, "The Automation Resistant Skills We Should Nurture," BBC, July 26, 2017, www.bbc.com/capital/story/20170726-the-automation-resistant-skills-we-should-nurture.

99. Free the Slaves, accessed September 10, 2018, www.freetheslaves.net.

100. "Human Trafficking and Technology. A Framework for Understanding the Role of Technology in the Commercial Sexual Exploitation of Children in the U.S. Microsoft Research Connections," Europa, 2011, ec.europa.eu/anti-trafficking/publications/human-trafficking -and-technology-framework-understanding-role-technology-commercial_en.

101. "Software that Detects Human Trafficking," *Economist*, May 3, 2018, www.economist .com/science-and-technology/2018/05/03/software-that-detects-human-trafficking.

102. Tyler Cowen, *Average Is Over: Powering America Beyond the Age of the Great Stagnation* (New York: Dutton, 2013).

103. "If the employment impact falls at the 38 percent mean of these forecasts, Western democracies likely could resort to authoritarianism as happened in some countries during the Great Depression of the 1930s in order to keep their restive populations in check. If that happened, wealthy elites would require armed guards, security details, and gated communities to protect themselves, as is the case in poor countries today with high income inequality. The United States would look like Syria or Iraq, with armed bands of young men with few employment prospects other than war, violence, or theft." Darrell M. West, "Will Robots and AI Take Your Job? The Economic and Political Consequences of Automation," Brookings Institution, blog, April 18, 2018, www.brookings.edu/blog/techtank/2018/04/18 /will-robots-and-ai-take-your-job-the-economic-and-political-consequences-of-automation.

104. "We all live in the digital poorhouse. We have always lived in the world we built for the poor. We create a society that has no use for the disabled or the elderly, and then are cast

aside when we are hurt or grow old. We measure human worth based only on the ability to earn a wage, and suffer in a world that undervalues care and community. We base our economy on exploiting the labor of racial and ethnic minorities, and watch lasting inequities snuff out human potential. We see the world as inevitably riven by bloody competition and are left unable to recognize the many ways we cooperate and lift each other up. But only the poor lived in the common dorms of the county poorhouse. Only the poor were put under the diagnostic microscope of scientific clarity. Today, we all live among the digital traps we have laid for the destitute." Virginia Eubanks, *Automating Inequality: How High-Tech Tools Profile, Police, and Punish the Poor* (New York: St. Martin's Press, 2018).

105. Matthew Hutson, "AI Researchers Allege that Machine Learning is Alchemy," *Science*, May 3, 2018, www.sciencemag.org/news/2018/05/ai-researchers-allege-machine-learning -alchemy.

106. Ian Hogarth, "AI Nationalism," personal blog, June 13, 2018, www.ianhogarth.com /blog/2018/6/13/ai-nationalism.

107. Nicholas Wright, "How Artificial Intelligence Will Reshape the Global Order," *Foreign Affairs*, July 10, 2018, www.foreignaffairs.com/articles/world/2018-07-10/how-artificial -intelligence-will-reshape-global-order.

108. Douglas Frantz, "We've Unleashed AI. Now We Need a Treaty to Control It," *Los Angeles Times*, July 16, 2018, http://www.latimes.com/opinion/op-ed/la-oe-frantz-artificial -intelligence-treaty-20180716-story.html.

109. Horowitz, et al., "Artificial Intelligence and International Security."

110. Henry A. Kissinger, "How the Enlightenment Ends," *Atlantic*, June 2018, www.theatlantic.com /magazine/archive/2018/06/henry-kissinger-ai-could-mean-the-end-of-human-history/559124.

111. Ibid.

112. A. Aneesh, *Virtual Migration, The Programming of Globalization* (North Carolina: Duke University Press, 2006).

CHAPTER 6: THE TRANSCENDENT PROMISE OF INTELLIGENT MACHINES

1. R. M. Allen, "Earthquake Hazard Mitigation: New Directions and Opportunities," University of California Berkeley, rallen.berkeley.edu/pub/2007allen1/AllenTreatise2007.pdf.

2. Darrell M. West and John R. Allen, "How Artificial Intelligence is Transforming the World," Brookings Intitution, April 24, 2018, www.brookings.edu/research/how-artificial -intelligence-is-transforming-the-world.

3. Michael Chui, Martin Harrysson, James Manyika, Roger Roberts, Rita Chung, Pieter Nel, and Ashley van Heteren, "Applying Artificial Intelligence for Social Good," McKinsey Global Institute Discussion Paper, accessed December 21, 2018, www.mckinsey.com /featured-insights/artificial-intelligence/applying-artificial-intelligence-for-social-good.

4. Rose Eveleth, "Academics Write Papers Arguing over How Many People Read (And Cite) Their Papers," *Smithsonian Magazine*, March 25, 2014, www.smithsonianmag.com /smart-news/half-academic-studies-are-never-read-more-three-people-180950222.

5. Semantic Scholar, accessed December 21, 2018, www.semanticscholar.org.

6. Iris.ai, accessed September 24, 2018, iris.ai.

7. Vinod Khosla, "Technology Will Replace 80% of What Doctors Do," *Fortune*, December 4, 2012, fortune.com/2012/12/04/technology-will-replace-80-of-what-doctors-do.

8. "A.I. Making a Difference in Cancer Care," CBS News, October 7, 2016, www.cbsnews .com/news/artificial-intelligence-making-a-difference-in-cancer-care.

9. Gaurav Sharma and Alexis Carter, "Artificial Intelligence and the Pathologist: Future Frenemies?" *Archives of Pathology & Laboratory Medicine*, Vol. 141, No. 5 (May 2017): 622–623.

10. Sophie Chapman, "China Uses AI to Treat Lung Cancer," Healthcare Global, November 20, 2017, www.healthcareglobal.com/technology/china-uses-ai-treat-lung-cancer.

11. Hope Reese, "The Way We Use Mammograms is Seriously Flawed but AI Could Change That," Quartz, September 6, 2018, qz.com/1367216/mammograms-are-seriously-flawed -the-way-we-use-them-now-ai-could-change-that.

12. Jane Kirby, "Artificial Intelligence Better than Scientists at Choosing Successful IVF Embryos," *Independent UK*, July 4, 2017, www.independent.co.uk/news/health/ai-ivf -embryos-better-scientists-selection-a7823736.html.

13. Topol has opined, "The potential is perhaps the biggest in any type of technology we've ever had in the field of medicine . . . Computing capability can transcend what a human being could ever do in their lifetime." Meg Tirrell, "From Coding to Cancer: How AI is Changing Medicine," CNBC, May 11, 2017, www.cnbc.com/2017/05/11/from-coding-to -cancer-how-ai-is-changing-medicine.html.

14. Timothy Revell, "AI Will Be Able to Beat Us at Everything by 2060, Say Experts," *New Scientist*, May 31, 2017, www.newscientist.com/article/2133188-ai-will-be-able-to-beat-us -at-everything-by-2060-say-experts.

15. "What is Genomic Medicine?" National Human Genome Research Institute, accessed December 4, 2018, www.genome.gov/27552451/what-is-genomic-medicine.

16. Siddhartha Mukherjee, "A.I. Versus M.D.," *New Yorker*, April 3, 2017, www.newyorker .com/magazine/2017/04/03/ai-versus-md.

17. Sarah Crespi, "Watch Robot Made of DNA Swing its Arm," *Science*, January 18, 2018, www.sciencemag.org/news/2018/01/watch-robot-made-dna-swing-its-arm.

18. Atomwise, accessed September 24, 2018, www.atomwise.com.

19. EKSO, accessed September 24, 2018, eksobionics.com.

20. Ginger.io, accessed September 24, 2018, ginger.io.

21. Yuichi Mori, Shin-ei Kudo, Tyler M. Berzin, Masashi Misawa, and Kenichi Takeda, "Computer-Aided Diagnosis for Colonoscopy," *Endoscopy*, 49 (2017): 813–819, DOI: 10.1055/s-0043-109430.

22. Kyruus, accessed September 24, 2018, www.kyruus.com.

23. Open Water, accessed September 24, 2018, www.openwater.cc.

24. Octumetrics, accessed September 24, 2018, www.ocumetics.com.

25. AI Serve, accessed September 24, 2018, www.aiserve.co.

26. Anybots, accessed September 24, 2018, www.anybots.com.

27. Rebecca Ruiz, "What It's Like to Talk to an Adorable Chatbot about Your Mental Health," Mashable, June 8, 2017, mashable.com/2017/06/08/mental-health-chatbots/#HmgFDZ mM.Pq9.

28. Matt Simon, "Catching Up with Pepper, the Surprisingly Helpful Humanoid Robot," *Wired*, April 13, 2018, www.wired.com/story/pepper-the-humanoid-robot.

29. Norman Winarsky, "What AI-Enhanced Health Care Could Look Like in 5 Years," Ven-

ture Beat, July 23, 2017, venturebeat.com/2017/07/23/what-ai-enhanced-healthcare-could -look-like-in-5-years.

30. Corinne Purtill, "Robots Will Probably Help Care for You When You're Old," Quartz, September 11, 2018, qz.com/1367213/robots-could-save-the-world-from-its-aging-problem.

31. And anyone who has read chapter 5 (or seen the TV show *Westworld*) knows that this also has the potential to backfire if we decide to act on and reinforce our deepest fears and aggressions instead.

32. Kris Newby, "Compassionate Intelligence," Stanford Medicine, Summer 2018, stanmed .stanford.edu/2018summer/artificial-intelligence-puts-humanity-health-care.html.

33. Tom Simonite, "Machine Learning Opens Up New Ways to Help People with Disabilities," *MIT Technology Review*, March 23, 2017, www.technologyreview.com/s/603899 /machine-learning-opens-up-new-ways-to-help-disabled-people.

34. Chris Kornelis, "AI Tools Help the Blind Tackle Everyday Tasks," *Wall Street Journal*, May 28, 2018, www.wsj.com/articles/ai-tools-help-the-blind-tackle-everyday-tasks-1527559620.

35. Jonah Engel Bromwich, "An App to Aid the Visually Impaired," *New York Times*, July 3, 2015, www.nytimes.com/2015/07/05/nyregion/an-app-to-aid-the-visually-impaired.html.

36. Zach Wichter, "Are You Ready to Fly Without a Human Pilot?" *New York Times*, July 16, 2018, www.nytimes.com/2018/07/16/business/airplanes-unmanned-flight-autopilot.html.

37. Oliver Balch, "Driverless Cars Will Make Our Roads Safer, Says Oxbotica Co-Founder," *Guardian*, April 13, 2017, www.theguardian.com/sustainable-business/2017/apr/13 /driverless-cars-will-make-our-roads-safer-says-oxbotica-co-founder.

38. Smart Cane, accessed September 24, 2018, assistech.iitd.ernet.in/smartcane.php.

39. Jess Vilvestre, "Bionic Eyes Are Coming, and They'll Make Us Superhuman," Futurism, November 13, 2016, futurism.com/bionic-eyes-are-coming-and-theyd-make-us-superhuman.

40. Sharon Begley, "With Brain Implants, Scientists Aim to Translate Thoughts into Speech," *Scientific American*, November 20, 2018, www.scientificamerican.com/article /with-brain-implants-scientists-aim-to-translate-thoughts-into-speech.

41. Simonite, "Machine Learning Opens Up New Ways to Help People with Disabilities."

42. "Artificial Intelligence Helps Build Brain Atlas of Fly Behavior," Howard Hughes Medical Institute, July 13, 2017, www.sciencedaily.com/releases/2017/07/170713155037.htm.

43. Alison Snyder, "An AI Learns to Predict a Scene from Just One Image," Axios, June 14, www.axios.com/an-ai-learns-to-predict-scene-from-one-image-8e6c4831-40f7-4949 -af2d-07fb7e838467.html.

44. Katie Nodjimbadem, "The Heroic Effort to Digitally Reconstruct Lost Monuments," *Smithsonian*, March 2016, www.smithsonianmag.com/history/heroic-effort-digitally -reconstruct-lost-monuments-180958098.

45. Sean Martin, "Scientists Closer to Cloning T-Rex after Discovering Remains of Pregnant Dinosaur," Express UK, March 18, 2016, www.express.co.uk/news/science/653117 /Scientists-closer-to-CLONING-T-Rex-after-discovering-remains-of-pregnant-dinosaur.

46. Kyle Wiggers, "11th-Century Glyphs Classified through AI Research Project," Venture Beat, September 4, 2018, venturebeat.com/2018/09/04/11th-century-glyphs-classified -through-ai-research-project.

47. Virtual reality replaces our reality with an alternate, simulated one. On the other hand, "augmented reality (AR) is a technology that layers computer-generated enhancements

atop an existing reality in order to make it more meaningful through the ability to interact with it. AR is developed into apps and used on mobile devices to blend digital components into the real world in such a way that they enhance one another, but can also be told apart easily." "Virtual Reality vs. Augmented Reality," Augment, accessed September 24, 2018, www.augment.com/blog/virtual-reality-vs-augmented-reality.

48. Phil Patton, *Made in U.S.A.: The Secret Histories of the Things that Made America* (New York: Grove, 1992).

49. Frederic Lardinois, "Google's AutoDraw Uses Machine Learning to Help You Draw Like a Pro," Techcrunch, April 11, 2017, techcrunch.com/2017/04/11/googles-autodraw -uses-machine-learning-to-help-you-draw-like-a-pro.

50. Rama Allen, "AI Will Be the Art Movement of the 21st Century," Quartz, March 5, 2018, qz.com/1023493/ai-will-be-the-art-movement-of-the-21st-century.

51. Dani Deahl, "Google's NSynth Super is an AI-backed Touchscreen Synth," Verge, March 13, 2018, www.theverge.com/circuitbreaker/2018/3/13/17114760/google-nsynth -super-ai-touchscreen-synth.

52. Ron Gilmer, "Cary Fukunaga, 'Maniac,' and How Netflix's Algorithm Is Becoming Entertainment's Skynet," Collider, September 20, 2018, collider.com/cary-fukunaga -maniac-netflix-algorithm.

53. Nick Stockton, "What's Up with That: Your Best Thinking Seems to Happen in the Shower," *Wired*, August 5, 2014, www.wired.com/2014/08/shower-thoughts.

54. "Sleep, Learning, and Memory," Harvard Medical, accessed September 25, 2018, healthysleep.med.harvard.edu/healthy/matters/benefits-of-sleep/learning-memory.

55. Niraj Chokshi, "The Trappist Monk Whose Calligraphy Inspired Steve Jobs—and In-fluenced Apple's Designs," *Washington Post*, March 8, 2016, www.washingtonpost.com /news/arts-and-entertainment/wp/2016/03/08/the-trappist-monk-whose-calligraphy -inspired-steve-jobs-and-influenced-apples-designs.

56. Claudia Roth Pierpont, "How New York's Postwar Female Painters Battled for Recognition," *New Yorker*, October 8, 2018, www.newyorker.com/magazine/2018/10/08/how-new-yorks -postwar-female-painters-battled-for-recognition.

57. Emotional intelligence (known as EQ or EI) is the ability to identify and manage both your own emotions as well as the emotions of others, and the term was coined by Peter Salovey and John D. Mayer in 1990; Andrea Ovans, "How Emotional Intelligence Be-came a Key Leadership Skill," *Harvard Business Review*, April 28, 2015, hbr.org/2015/04 /how-emotional-intelligence-became-a-key-leadership-skill.

58. Megan Beck and Barry Libert, "The Rise of AI Makes Emotional Intelligence More Im-portant," *Harvard Business Review*, February 15, 2017, hbr.org/2017/02/the-rise-of-ai-makes -emotional-intelligence-more-important.

59. Jeremy Kahn, "U.K. Sees $837 Billion Gain on Artificial Intelligence by 2035," Bloomberg, October 14, 2017, www.bloomberg.com/news/articles/2017-10-14/u-k-targets -ai-for-630-billion-pound-economic-bump-by-2035.

60. Edward L. Deci and Richard M. Ryan, "The 'What' and 'Why' of Goal Pursuits: Hu-man Needs and the Self-Determination of Behavior," *Psychological Inquiry*, Vol. 11, No. 4 (2000): 227–268, selfdeterminationtheory.org/SDT/documents/2000_DeciRyan_PI WhatWhy.pdf.

61. Richard M. Ryan and Edward L. Deci, *Self-Determination Theory: Basic Psychological Needs in Motivation, Development, and Wellness* (New York: Guilford Press, 2017).

62. Avantgarde Analytics, accessed September 25, 2018, www.avntgrd.com.

63. Factmata, accessed September 25, 2018, factmata.com/about.html.

64. Kyle Wiggers, "Microsoft's AI for Earth Innovation Grant Gives Data Scientists Access to AI Tools," Venture Beat, July 16, 2018, venturebeat.com/2018/07/16/microsofts-ai-for-earth-innovation-grant-gives-data-scientists-access-to-ai-tools.

65. UNICEF, "Child given world's first drone-delivered vaccine in Vanuatu," December 18, 2018, accessed December 26, 2018, www.unicef.org/press-releases/child-given-worlds-first-drone-delivered-vaccine-vanuatu-unicef.

66. "Civilian Drones," *Economist*, June 8, 2017, www.economist.com/technology-quarterly/2017-06-08/civilian-drone.

67. David Grossman, "Drones to Deliver Blood and Medicine to Rural America," *Popular Mechanics*, August 2, 2016, www.popularmechanics.com/technology/infrastructure/a22164/drones-to-start-delivering-medicine-to-rural-america.

68. Aryn Baker, "Zipline's Drones Are Saving Lives," *Time*, May 31, 2018, time.com/longform/ziplines-drones-are-saving-lives.

69. Karen Allen, "Using Drones to Save Lives in Malawi," BBC News, March 15, 2016, www.bbc.com/news/world-africa-35810153.

70. "Latest GSMA Report Highlights Success of Mobile Money with over 690 Million Accounts Worldwide," GSMA.com, press release, www.gsma.com/newsroom/press-release/latest-gsma-report-highlights-success-mobile-money-690-million-accounts-worldwide.

71. Mallory Locklear, "Microsoft's AI Tech Will Aid Humanitarian Efforts," Engadget, September 24, 2018, www.engadget.com/2018/09/24/microsoft-ai-humanitarian-efforts.

72. Peter Holley, "The World Bank's Latest Tool for Fighting Famine: Artificial Intelligence," *Washington Post*, September 23, 2018, www.washingtonpost.com/technology/2018/09/23/world-banks-latest-tool-fighting-famine-artificial-intelligence.

73. Anna X. Wang, Caelin Tran, Nikhil Desai, David Lobell, and Stefano Ermon, "Deep Transfer Learning for Crop Yield Prediction with Remote Sensing Data," COMPASS '18 Proceedings of the 1st ACM SIGCAS Conference on Computing and Sustainable Societies, No. 50 (2018), DOI:10.1145/3209811.3212707.

74. Doreen S. Boyd, Bethany Jackson, Jessica Wardlaw, Giles M. Foody, Stuart Marsh, and Kevin Bales, "Slavery from Space: Demonstrating the Role for Satellite Remote Sensing to Inform Evidence-Based Action Related to UN SDG Number 8," ISPRS *Journal of Photogrammetry and Remote Sensing*, Vol. 142 (August 2018): 380–388, doi.org/10.1016/j.isprsjprs.2018.02.012.

75. Doran Larson, "Why Scandinavian Prisons Are Superior," *Atlantic*, September 24, 2013, www.theatlantic.com/international/archive/2013/09/why-scandinavian-prisons-are-superior/279949; Antony Funnell, "Internet of Incarceration: How AI Could Put an End to Prisons as We Know Them," *Future Tense*, August 4, 2017, mobile.abc.net.au/news/2017-08-14/how-ai-could-put-an-end-to-prisons-as-we-know-them/8794910.

76. Jackie Bischof, "AI is Helping Humans Do a Better Job Bringing Poachers to Justice," Quartz, September 3, 2018, qz.com/africa/1376612/ai-is-helping-humans-do-a-better-job-bringing-poachers-to-justice.

77. Lucas Joppa, "Protecting Biodiversity with Artificial Intelligence," Microsoft blog, January 30, 2017, blogs.microsoft.com/green/2017/01/30/protecting-biodiversity-with -artificial-intelligence.

78. "Regulation of Drones: South Africa," Library of Congress, accessed September 25, 2018, www.loc.gov/law/help/regulation-of-drones/south-africa.php.

79. Atlan Space, accessed September 25, 2018, www.atlanspace.com.

80. GiveDirectly, accessed September 25, 2018, givedirectly.org.

81. Jonathan Donner, "Research Approaches to Mobile Use in the Developing World: A Review of the Literature," *The Information Society: An International Journal*, Vol. 24 Issue 3 (2008): 140–159, doi.org/10.1080/01972240802019970.

82. Andrew Czyzewski, "Five AI Breakthroughs That Could Change the Face of Science," Imperial College London, December 26, 2017, www.imperial.ac.uk/news/183586/five -ai-breakthroughs-that-could-change.

83. Elizabeth Gibney, "AI Helps Unlock 'Dark Matter' of Bizarre Superconductors," *Nature*, September 14, 2018, www.nature.com/articles/d41586-018-06144-3.

84. AI 4 Good, accessed September 24, 2018, ai4good.org/2017/01/ai-agriculture.

85. Babusi Nyoni, "How Artificial Intelligence Can Be Used to Predict Africa's Next Migration Crisis," United Nations High Commissioner for Refugees, February 10, 2017, www .unhcr.org/innovation/how-artificial-intelligence-can-be-used-to-predict-africas-next -migration-crisis.

86. Rana el Kaliouby, "Ethics in Artificial Intelligence Could Be the Next Big Movement. 5 Ways to Make it Happen," *Inc.*, November 15, 2017, www.inc.com/rana-el-kaliouby /why-artificial-intelligence-ethics-is-next-go-green.html.

87. Chris Baraniuk, "Artificial Intelligence Decodes Islamic State Strategy," BBC News, August 6, 2015, www.bbc.com/news/technology-33804287.

88. John Naughton, "Why a Computer Could Help You Get a Fair Trial," *Guardian*, August 13, 2017, www.theguardian.com/technology/commentisfree/2017/aug/13/why-a-computer -could-help-you-get-a-fair-trial.

89. John Maynard Keynes, "Economic Possibilities for our Grandchildren," *Essays in Persuasion* (New York: W. W. Norton & Company, 1963), 358–373.

90. Jessica Stillman, "21 Future Jobs the Robots Are Actually Creating," *Inc.*, December 6, 2017, www.inc.com/jessica-stillman/21-future-jobs-robots-are-actually-creating.html.

91. Victor Tangermann, "Google's AI Can Predict When a Patient Will Die," Futurism, June 18, 2018, futurism.com/googles-ai-predict-when-patient-die.

92. Dom Galeon, "Expert: Human Immortality Could Be Acquired through AI," Futurism, April 21, 2017, futurism.com/expert-human-immortality-could-be-acquired-through-ai.

93. Dan Robitzski, "This Scientist Predicted He Would Live to 150. Now He's Not So Sure," Futurism, July 11, 2018, futurism.com/artificial-intelligence-longevity-alex-zhavoronkov.

94. Dan Tynan, "Augmented Eternity: Scientists Aim to Let Us Speak from Beyond the Grave," *Guardian*, June 23, 2016, www.theguardian.com/technology/2016/jun/23/artificial -intelligence-digital-immortality-mit-ryerson.

CHAPTER 7: THE ECONOMICS AND THE POLITICS

1. "Of all bankruptcy filings, the over 55 crowd accounted for 33.7% (2013–2016) up from

8.2% in 1991." Michael Hiltzik, "Bankruptcy is Hitting More Older Americans, Pointing to a Retirement Crisis in the Making," *Los Angeles Times*, August 6, 2018, www.latimes .com/business/hiltzik/la-fi-hiltzik-bankruptcy-seniors-20180806-story.html.

2. "Health spending is projected to grow 1.0 percentage point faster than Gross Domestic Product (GDP) per year over the 2017–26 period; as a result, the health share of GDP is expected to rise from 17.9 percent in 2016 to 19.7 percent by 2026." National Health Expenditure Projections 2017–2026: Forecast Summary, www.cms.gov/Research-Statistics-Data -and-Systems/Statistics-Trends-and-Reports/NationalHealthExpendData/Downloads /ForecastSummary.pdf.

3. Margot E. Salomon, "The Future of Human Rights," *Global Policy*, Wiley Online, Vol. 3, Issue 4 (November 2012).

4. Robert H. Frank, "Why Single-Payer Health Care Saves Money," *New York Times*, July 7, 2017, www.nytimes.com/2017/07/07/upshot/why-single-payer-health-care-saves-money.html.

5. Annie Lowrey, *Give People Money: How a Universal Basic Income Would End Poverty, Revolutionize Work, and Remake the World* (New York: Crown, 2018).

6. Friedrich Engels, *The Condition of the Working Class in England in 1844 with Preface Written in 1892*, trans. Florence Kelley Wischnewetzky (London: Swan Sonnenschein & Co., 1892).

7. NPR Staff, "We Went from Hunter-Gatherers to Space Explorers, But Are We Happier?" NPR, *All Things Considered*, February 7, 2015, www.npr.org/2015/02/07/383276672/from -hunter-gatherers-to-space-explorers-a-70-000-year-story.

8. "[…] a new round of 'enclosures' that have expropriated millions of agricultural producers from their land, and the mass pauperization and criminalization of workers, through a policy of mass incarceration recalling the 'Great Confinement' described by Michel Foucault in his study of history of madness. We have also witnessed the worldwide development of new diasphoric movements accompanied by the persecution of migrant workers, again reminiscent of the 'Bloody Laws' that were introduced in 16th and 17th-century Europe to make vagabonds available for local exploitation. Most important for this book has been the Intensification of violence against women, including, in some countries (e.g., South Africa and Brazil), the return of witch-hunting." Silvia Federici, *Caliban and the Witch* (New York: Autonomedia, 2004), 11.

9. Yuval Noah Harari, "The Rise of the Useless Class," TED Ideas, February 24, 2017, ideas .ted.com/the-rise-of-the-useless-class.

10. Erik Brynjolfsson and Andrew McAfee, *The Second Machine Age: Work, Progress, and Prosperity in a Time of Brilliant Technologies* (New York: W. W. Norton & Company, 2014).

11. Rachel Nuwer, "Will Machines Eventually Take on Every Job?" BBC Future, August 6, 2015, www.bbc.com/future/story/20150805-will-machines-eventually-take-on-every-job.

12. James Manyika, Jacques Bughin, Jonathan Woetzel, "Jobs Lost, Jobs Gained: Workforce Transitions in a Time of Automation," McKinsey Global Institute, McKinsey & Company, December 2017, www.mckinsey.com/featured-insights/future-of-work/jobs-lost-jobs -gained-what-the-future-of-work-will-mean-for-jobs-skills-and-wages.

13. "~50% of current work activities are technically automatable by adapting currently demonstrated technologies. 6 of 10 current occupations have more than 30% of activities that are technically automatable." Ibid.

14. Michael Chui, James Manyika, and Mehdi Miremadi, "Four Fundamentals of Workplace Automation," McKinsey Quarterly, November 2015, www.mckinsey.com/business-functions /digital-mckinsey/our-insights/four-fundamentals-of-workplace-automation.

15. Carl Benedikt Frey and Michael A. Osborne, "The Future of Employment: How Susceptible are Jobs to Computerisation?" Oxford Martin School, September 17, 2013, www .oxfordmartin.ox.ac.uk/downloads/academic/The_Future_of_Employment.pdf.

16. "ABI Research Forecasts Almost One Million Businesses Worldwide Will Adopt AI Technologies by 2022," ABI Research, New York, June 20, 2017, www.abiresearch.com/press /abi-research-forecasts-almost-one-million-business.

17. Katja Grace, John Salvatier, Allan Dafoe, Baobao Zhang, Owain Evans, "When Will AI Exceed Human Performance? Evidence from AI Experts," Future of Humanity Institute, Oxford University, Department of Political Science, Yale University, May 3, 2018, arxiv .org/pdf/1705.08807.pdf.

18. "The AI system updates what it knows about the world without needing to be retrained and re-learn everything all over again. Basically, the system is able to transfer and apply its existing knowledge to the new environment. The end result is a sort of spectrum or continuum showing how it understands various qualities of an object." Dan Robitzski, "New Artificial Intelligence Does Something Extraordinary—It Remembers," Futurism, August 31, 2018, futurism.com/artificial-intelligence-remember-agi.

19. Nick Srnicek and Alex Williams, *Inventing the Future: Postcapitalism and a World Without Work* (New York: Verso Books, 2015).

20. Ian Lowrie, "On Algorithmic Communism," *Los Angeles Review of Books*, January 8, 2016, lareviewofbooks.org/article/on-algorithmic-communism.

21. George Marshall, *Don't Even Think About It: Why Our Brains Are Wired to Ignore Climate Change* (New York: Bloomsbury USA, 2014).

22. Ibid., 141, 208.

23. Alexa Frank, Kelly Connors, Michelle Cho, "How Design Thinking Can Help Tackle Gender Bias in the Workplace," Deloitte Insights, May 6, 2018, www2.deloitte.com /insights/us/en/topics/value-of-diversity-and-inclusion/design-thinking-business-gender -bias-workplace.html.

24. David Rotman, "How Technology Is Destroying Jobs," *MIT Technology Review*, June 12, 2013, www.technologyreview.com/s/515926/how-technology-is-destroying-jobs.

25. "Though California's economy—the world's eighth-largest—is strong in many sectors, the state has the highest poverty rate in the country, if cost of living is factored in. The situation in Silicon Valley helps explain why. About 20 to 25 percent of the population works in the high-tech sector, and the wealth is concentrated among them. This relatively small but prosperous group is driving up the cost of housing, transportation, and other living expenses. At the same time, much of the employment growth in the area is happening in retail, restaurant, and manual jobs, where wages are stagnant or even declining. It's a simple formula for income inequality and poverty. But the nature of technology itself seems to have made it worse. According to Chris Benner, a regional economist at the University of California, Davis, there has been no net increase in jobs in Silicon Valley since 1998; digital technologies inevitably mean you can generate billions of dollars from a low em-

ployment base." David Rotman, "Technology and Inequality," *MIT Technology Review*, October 21, 2014, www.technologyreview.com/s/531726/technology-and-inequality.

26. "Global wealth grew an estimated 66 percent (from $690 trillion to $1,143 trillion in constant 2014 U.S. dollars at market prices). But inequality was substantial, as wealth per capita in high-income OECD countries was 52 times greater than in low-income countries." Glenn-Marie Lange, Quentin Wodon, and Kevin Carey, "The Changing Wealth of Nations 2018: Building a Sustainable Future" (Washington, D.C.: World Bank, 2018), openknowledge.worldbank.org/handle/10986/29001.

27. Bryan Lufkin, "There's a Problem with the Way We Define Inequality," BBC, July 7, 2017, www.bbc.com/future/story/20170706-theres-a-problem-with-the-way-we-define-inequality.

28. Marianne Ferber and Julie A. Nelson, *Beyond Economic Man: Feminist Theory and Economics* (Chicago: University of Chicago Press, 1993).

29. Harry J. Frankfurt, *On Inequality* (New Jersey: Princeton University Press, 2015).

30. Larry Elliott, "World's 26 Richest People Own as Much as Poorest 50%, Says Oxfam," *Guardian*, January 20, 2019, www.theguardian.com/business/2019/jan/21/world-26-richest-people -own-as-much-as-poorest-50-per-cent-oxfam-report.

31. Gabriel Zucman, "Global Wealth Inequality," National Bureau of Economic Research Working Paper, No. 25462 (January 2019), www.nber.org/papers/w25462.

32. Esmé E. Deprez, "Income Inequality," Bloomberg, September 21, 2018, www.bloomberg .com/quicktake/income-inequality.

33. "Neoclassical economics is an approach to economics that relates supply and demand to an individual's rationality and his ability to maximize utility or profit. Neoclassical economics also uses mathematical equations to study various aspects of the economy." Investopedia, accessed September 2, 2008, www.investopedia.com/terms/n/neoclassical.asp.

34. Daniel Kahneman, *Thinking, Fast and Slow* (New York: Farrar, Straus and Giroux, 2011), 103.

35. Kate Raworth, *Doughnut Economics: Seven Ways to Think Like a 21st-Century Economist* (Chelsea Green Publishing, 2017).

36. Nermeen Shaikh, "Amartya Sen: A More Human Theory of Development," Asia Society, December 6, 2004, asiasociety.org/amartya-sen-more-human-theory-development; Amartya Sen, *Development as Freedom* (New York: Alfred A. Knopf, 1999).

37. Kai Schultz, "In Bhutan, Happiness Index as Gauge for Social Ills," *New York Times*, January 17, 2017, www.nytimes.com/2017/01/17/world/asia/bhutan-gross-national-happiness -indicator-.html.

38. "Invisible hand is a metaphor for how, in a free market economy, self-interested individuals operate through a system of mutual interdependence to promote the general benefit of society at large." "What Does 'Invisible Hand' Mean?" Investopedia, www.investopedia .com/terms/i/invisiblehand.asp.

39. Katrine Marçal, *Who Cooked Adam Smith's Dinner? A Story About Women and Economics*, trans. Saskia Vogel (New York: Pegasus Books, 2016).

40. Kate Raworth, Exploring Doughnut Economics, accessed September 1, 2018, www .kateraworth.com/doughnut.

41. "Depicting rational economic man as an isolated individual—unaffected by the choices of others—proved highly convenient for modelling the economy, but it was long questioned

even from within the discipline. At the end of the nineteenth century, the sociologist and economist Thorstein Veblen berated economic theory for depicting man as a 'self-contained globule of desire,' while the French polymath Henri Poincaré pointed out that it overlooked 'people's tendency to act like sheep.' He was right: we are not so different from herds as we might like to imagine. We follow social norms, typically preferring to do what we expect others will do and, especially if filled with fear or doubt, we tend to go with the crowd." Raworth, *Doughnut Economics: Seven Ways to Think Like a 21st-Century Economist.*

42. George Monbiot, "Finally, a Breakthrough Alternative to Growth Economics—the Doughnut," *Guardian*, April, 12, 2017, www.theguardian.com/commentisfree/2017/apr /12/doughnut-growth-economics-book-economic-model.

43. Steven Poole, "The Death of Homo Economicus review—Why Does Capitalism Still Exist?" *Guardian*, September 28, 2017, www.theguardian.com/books/2017/sep/28/death -homo-economicus-peter-fleming-review.

44. Dennis Overbye, "The Eclipse that Revealed the Universe," *New York Times*, July 31, 2017, www.nytimes.com/2017/07/31/science/eclipse-einstein-general-relativity.html.

45. David Whyte, *Life at the Frontier: Leadership Through Courageous Conversation* (Many Rivers Press, 2004).

46. "The Conversational Nature of Reality," On Being with Krista Tippett, transcript, April 6, 2016, onbeing.org/programs/david-whyte-the-conversational-nature-of-reality.

47. "Public schools were not only created in the interests of industrialism—they were created in the image of industrialism. In many ways, they reflect the factory culture they were designed to support. This is especially true in high schools, where school systems base education on the principles of the assembly line and the efficient division of labor. Schools divide the curriculum into specialist segments: some teachers install math in the students, and others install history. They arrange the day into standard units of time, marked out by the ringing of bells, much like a factory announcing the beginning of the workday and the end of breaks. Students are educated in batches, according to age, as if the most important thing they have in common is their date of manufacture. They are given standardized tests at set points and compared with each other before being sent out onto the market. I realize this isn't an exact analogy and that it ignores many of the subtleties of the system, but it is close enough." Ken Robinson, *The Element: How Finding Your Passion Changes Everything* (New York: Penguin, 2009).

48. Paul Reber, "What is the Memory Capacity of the Human Brain?" *Scientific American*, May 1, 2010, www.scientificamerican.com/article/what-is-the-memory-capacity.

49. "EU Member States Sign Up to Cooperate on Artificial Intelligence," Europa, April 10, 2018, ec .europa.eu/digital-single-market/en/news/eu-member-states-sign-cooperate-artificial -intelligence.

50. Owen Churchill, "China's AI Dreams," *Nature*, January 17, 2018, www.nature.com/articles /d41586-018-00539-y; Zachary Cohen, "US Risks Losing Artificial Intelligence Arms Race to China and Russia," CNN, www.cnn.com/2017/11/29/politics/us-military-artificial -intelligence-russia-china/index.html.

51. David E. Sanger, "Pentagon Announces New Strategy for Cyberwarfare," *New York Times*, April 23, 2015, www.nytimes.com/2015/04/24/us/politics/pentagon-announces-new-cyber warfare-strategy.html.

52. Tom O'Connor, "U.S. Is Losing to Russia and China in War for Artificial Intelligence,

Report Says," *Newsweek*, November 29, 2017, www.newsweek.com/us-could-lose-russia
-china-war-artificial-intelligence-726603.

53. Nicole Perlroth, Michael Wines, and Matthew Rosenberg, "Russian Election Hacking Efforts, Wider Than Previously Known, Draw Little Scrutiny," *New York Times*, September
1, 2017, www.nytimes.com/2017/09/01/us/politics/russia-election-hacking.html.

54. "Jamie Susskind in Conversation with Helen Lewis on How Tech Is Transforming Our
Politics," Acast, August 16, 2018, www.acast.com/intelligencesquared/jamiesusskindin
conversationwithhelenlewisonhowtechistransformingourpolitics.

55. "A Fourth Estate, of Able Editors, springs up, increases and multiplies; irrepressible, incal-
culable. New Printers, new Journals, and ever new (so prurient is the world), let our Three
Hundred curb and consolidate as they can!" Thomas Carlyle, *French Revolution: A History*
(London: Chapman & Hall, 1837), Book 1.VI. Consolidation.

56. "Republicans watch Fox while Democrats watch MSNBC; creationists see fossils as evidence of God, evolutionary biologists see fossils as evidence of evolution; doomsayers see
signs of the end of the world, and the rest of us see just another day. Simply put, our
ideologies and personal dogmas dictate our realities." Samuel McNerney, "Confirmation
Bias and Art," *Scientific American*, July 17, 2011, blogs.scientificamerican.com/guest-blog
/confirmation-bias-and-art.

57. George Lakoff, "A Modest Proposal: #ProtectTheTruth," personal blog, January 13, 2018,
georgelakoff.com/2018/01/13/a-modest-proposal-protectthetruth.

58. Maurits Meijers and Harmen van der Veer, "Hungary's Government is Increasingly Auto-
cratic. What is the European Parliament Doing About It?" *Washington Post*, May 3, 2017,
www.washingtonpost.com/news/monkey-cage/wp/2017/05/03/hungary-is-backsliding
-what-is-the-european-parliament-doing-about-this.

59. GDP per capita is $59,531.7 and climbing. The World Bank, accessed September 1, 2018,
data.worldbank.org/indicator/NY.GDP.PCAP.CD.

60. Infrastructure Report Card: Dams, American Society of Civil Engineers, 2017, www
.infrastructurereportcard.org/cat-item/dams.

61. Devon Haynie, "Report: The U.S. is the World's 7th Largest Executioner," U.S. News, April
10, 2017, www.usnews.com/news/best-countries/articles/2017-04-10/report-the-us-is-the
-worlds-7th-largest-executioner.

62. This statistic does not count those who seek temporary shelter. "US Homeless People
Numbers Rise for First Time in Seven Years," BBC News, December 6, 2017, www.bbc
.com/news/world-us-canada-42248999.

63. Alex Horton, "Perhaps Tired of Winning, the United States Falls in World Happiness
Rankings—Again," *Washington Post*, March 14, 2018, www.washingtonpost.com/news
/worldviews/wp/2018/03/14/perhaps-tired-of-winning-the-united-states-falls-in-world
-happiness-rankings-again.

64. Shannon Pettypiece, "Trump Signs $1.5 Trillion Tax Cut in First Major Legislative Win,"
Bloomberg, December 22, 2017, www.bloomberg.com/news/articles/2017-12-22/trump
-signs-1-5-trillion-tax-cut-in-first-major-legislative-win.

65. "The Future of Robotics and Artificial Intelligence in Europe," European Commission,
Europa, February 16, 2017, ec.europa.eu/digital-single-market/en/blog/future-robotics
-and-artificial-intelligence-europe.

66. Sarah Lyall, "Who Strikes Fear into Silicon Valley? Margrethe Vestager, Europe's Antitrust Enforcer," *New York Times*, May 5, 2018, www.nytimes.com/2018/05/05/world/europe /margrethe-vestager-silicon-valley-data-privacy.html.

67. Robert Herz, "The Pros and Cons of Quarterly Reporting," Compliance News, March 8, 2016, www.complianceweek.com/blogs/robert-herz/the-pros-and-cons-of-quarterly-reporting.

68. Lee Drutman, "How Corporate Lobbyists Conquered American Democracy," *Atlantic*, April 20, 2015, www.theatlantic.com/business/archive/2015/04/how-corporate-lobbyists -conquered-american-democracy/390822.

69. Anand Giridharadas, *Winners Take All: The Elite Charade of Changing the World* (New York: Knopf Doubleday, 2018).

70. Matthew Ingram, "What's Driving Fake News Is an Increase in Political Tribalism," *Fortune*, January 13, 2017, fortune.com/2017/01/13/fake-news-tribalism.

71. Michael Casey and Paul Vigna, *The Truth Machine: The Blockchain and the Future of Everything* (London: St. Martin's Press, 2018).

72. David E. Sanger, "Tech Firms Sign 'Digital Geneva Accord' Not to Aid Governments in Cyberwar," *New York Times*, April 17, 2018, www.nytimes.com/2018/04/17/us/politics /tech-companies-cybersecurity-accord.html.

73. "For Artificial Intelligence to Thrive, it Must Explain Itself," *Economist*, February 15, 2018.

74. "Overall, Theory of Mind involves understanding another person's knowledge, beliefs, emotions, and intentions and using that understanding to navigate social situations." Brittany N. Thompson, "Theory of Mind: Understanding Others in a Social World," *Psychology Today*, July 3, 2017, www.psychologytoday.com/us/blog/socioemotional-success/201707 /theory-mind-understanding-others-in-social-world.

75. "The San Francisco-based organization, which has granted $1 million to 'innovators' working on gun-safety technology, says that with help from the technology industry, it is possible 'to make firearms safer for gun owners, their families, and their communities.'" Don Reisinger, "How Technology May Make Guns Safer," *Fortune*, December 3, 2015, fortune.com/2015/12/03/safe-gun-tech.

76. Hossein Rahnama, "Augmented Eternity and Swappable Identities," MIT Media Lab, accessed December 20, 2018, www.media.mit.edu/projects/augmented-eternity/overview.

77. Roy Scranton, *Learning to Die in the Anthropocene* (San Francisco: City Lights Publishers, 2015), 16.

78. Zack Friedman, "This 27-Year-Old California Mayor Wants to Pay Residents $500 Cash Per Month," *Forbes*, November 10, 2017, www.forbes.com/sites/zackfriedman/2017/11 /10/stockton-universal-basic-income.

79. "Sikkim will Become the First Indian State to Introduce Universal Basic Income," *India Today*, January 10, 2019, www.indiatoday.in/education-today/gk-current-affairs/story /sikkim-to-become-first-state-to-introduce-universal-basic-income-1427662-2019-01-10.

80. Michalis Nikiforos, Marshall Steinbaum, and Gennaro Zezza, "Modeling the Macroeconomic Effects of a Universal Basic Income," Roosevelt Institute, August 29, 2017, rooseveltinstitute.org/modeling-macroeconomic-effects-ubi/.

81. Alex Goik, "Is Universal Basic Income as Radical as You Think?" Medium, March 19, 2018, medium.com/s/free-money/universal-basic-income-an-idea-as-radical-as-you-think -29f21472764a.

82. Atossa Araxia Abrahamian, "Saving the Sacred Cow," *The Nation*, May 3, 2018, www .thenation.com/article/can-yanis-varoufakis-save-europe.

83. Yanis Varoufakis, "The Universal Right to Capital Income," Project Syndicate, October 31, 2016, www.project-syndicate.org/commentary/basic-income-funded-by-capital-income-by -yanis-varoufakis-2016-10?barrier=accesspaylog.

84. Arjun Kharpal, "Bill Gates Wants to Tax Robots, but the EU Says, 'No Way, No Way,'" CNBC Markets, June 2, 2017, www.cnbc.com/2017/06/02/bill-gates-robot-tax-eu.html.

85. James K. Boyce and Peter Barnes, "How to Pay for Universal Basic Income," Evonomics, November 28, 2016, evonomics.com/how-to-pay-for-universal-basic-income.

86. Ibid.

87. Ellen Brown, "How to Fund a Universal Basic Income Without Increasing Taxes or Inflation," ellenbrown.com, October 3, 2017, ellenbrown.com/2017/10/03/how-to-fund -a-universal-basic-income-without-increasing-taxes-or-inflation.

88. "Further, a UBI would likely give people the financial security to be more creative and less risk-averse with their entrepreneurial projects; which is, of course, important for the vitality of any economy." Johnny Hugill and Matija Franklin, "The Wisdom of a Universal Basic Income," Behavioral Scientist, October 19, 2017, behavioralscientist.org/wisdom -universal-basic-income.

89. Margot Sanger-Katz, "Elizabeth Warren and a Scholarly Debate Over Medical Bankruptcy That Won't Go Away," *New York Times*, June 6, 2018, www.nytimes.com/2018/06/06 /upshot/elizabeth-warren-and-a-scholarly-debate-over-medical-bankruptcy-that-wont-go -away.html.

90. Casey Hynes, "The Long Game: How Developing Countries Can Get Microfinance Right," *Forbes*, April 14, 2017, www.forbes.com/sites/chynes/2017/08/14/to-alleviate-poverty -microfinance-institutions-must-work-on-much-longer-time-scales/#41415c6754fe.

91. "Almost everything will work again if you unplug it for a few minutes, including you." Anne Lamott, "12 Truths I Learned from Life and Writing," April 2017, TED, 15:55, www.ted.com/talks/anne_lamott_12_truths_i_learned_from_life_and_writing.

92. "Artificial Intelligence at Google: Our Principles," ai.google/principles.

93. Andrea Shalal, "Researchers to Boycott South Korean University over AI Weapons Work," Reuters, April 4, 2018, www.reuters.com/article/tech-korea-boycott/researchers-to-boycott -south-korean-university-over-ai-weapons-work-idUSL2N1RH0KM.

94. Cameron Jenkins, "AI Innovators Take Pledge Against Autonomous Killer Weapons," NPR, July 18, 2018, www.npr.org/2018/07/18/630146884/ai-innovators-take-pledge-against-autonomous -killer-weapons.

95. Brent Hecht, Lauren Wilcox, Jeffrey P. Bingham, Johannes Schöning, Ehsan Hoque, Jason Ernst, Yonatan Bisk, Luigi De Russis, Lana Yarosh, Bushra Anjumm, Danish Contractor, and Cathy Wu, "It's Time to Do Something: Mitigating the Negative Impacts of Computing through a Change to the Peer Review Process," ACM Future of Computing Academy, March 29, 2018, acm-fca.org/2018/03/29/negativeimpacts.

96. Russ Mitchell, "Self-Driving Cars May Ultimately Be Safer than Human Drivers. But After a Pedestrian's Death, Will the Public Buy It?" *Los Angeles Times*, March 21, 2018, www .latimes.com/business/autos/la-fi-hy-robot-car-safety-pr-20180321-story.html.

97. Anna Rosling Rönnlund, Hans Rosling, and Ola Rosling, *Factfulness: Ten Reasons We're*

Wrong About the World—and Why Things Are Better Than You Think (New York: Flatiron Books, 2018), 103.

98. Andrew J. Hoffman, "A Climate of Mind," *Stanford Social Innovation Review*, Winter 2015, ssir.org/book_reviews/entry/a_climate_of_mind.

99. "Tech Leaders Call for Autonomous Weapons Ban," Al Jazeera, July 18, 2018, www.al jazeera.com/news/2018/07/tech-leaders-call-autonomous-weapons-ban-180718074827 797.html.

CHAPTER 8: SEARCHING FOR THE DIGITAL SOUL

1. Jonathan Corum, "100 Images from Cassini's Mission to Saturn," *New York Times*, September 15, 2017, www.nytimes.com/interactive/2017/09/14/science/cassini-saturn-images.html.

2. Jeremy Hsu, "Why 'Uncanny Valley' Human Look-Alikes Put Us on Edge," *Scientific American*, April 3, 2012, www.scientificamerican.com/article/why-uncanny-valley-human-look -alikes-put-us-on-edge.

3. Anna-Lisa Vollmer, Robin Read, Dries Trippas, and Tony Belpaeme, "Children Conform, Adults Resist: A Robot Group Induced Peer Pressure on Normative Social Conformity," *Science Robotics*, Vol. 3, Issue 21 (August 15, 2018), robotics.sciencemag.org/content/3/21 /eaat7111.full.

4. Oliver Milman, "Anthropomorphism: How Much Humans and Animals Share Is Still Contested," *Guardian*, January 15, 2016, www.theguardian.com/science/2016/jan/15 /anthropomorphism-danger-humans-animals-science.

5. Adam Waytz, Nicholas Epley, and John T. Cacioppo, "Social Cognition Unbound: Insights Into Anthropomorphism and Dehumanization," *Current Directions in Psychological Science*, February 2010, 19(1): 58–62, doi: 10.1177/0963721409359302.

6. Marc Bekoff and Jessica Pierce, "Honor and Fairness Among Beasts at Play," *American Journal of Play*, 1.4 (2009): 451–475.

7. Ibid.

8. Jessica Pierce and Marc Bekoff, "Wild Justice Redux: What We Know About Social Justice in Animals and Why It Matters," *The Humane Society Institute for Science and Policy Animal Studies Repository*, 25.2 (2012): 122–139.

9. "Last year, Patricia Ganea, a psychologist at Toronto University, ran a series of experiments on three- to five-year-olds in which they were given information about animals in straight factual form and then in a more fantastical anthropomorphized way. She found that the children were likely to attribute human characteristics to other animals and were less likely to retain factual information about them when told they lived their lives as furry humans." Oliver Milman, "Anthropomorphism: How Much Humans and Animals Share is Still Contested."

10. Michael S. Gazzaniga, *The Consciousness Instinct: Unraveling the Mystery of How the Brain Makes the Mind* (New York: Farrar, Straus and Giroux, 2018), 5.

11. Nova Spivack, "Why Machines Will Never be Conscious," October 17, 2006, www .novaspivack.com/science/why-machines-will-never-be-conscious.

12. "Learning and plasticity are thus central to consciousness, to the extent that experiences only occur in experiencers that have learned to know they possess certain first-order states and that have learned to care more about certain states than about others. This is what I

call the 'Radical Plasticity Thesis.'" Axel Cleeremans, "The Radical Plasticity Thesis: How the Brain Learns to be Conscious," *Frontiers in Psychology*, February 25, 2011, www.ncbi .nlm.nih.gov/pmc/articles/PMC3110382.

13. Christopher Hooton, "A Robot Has Passed a Self-Awareness Test," *Independent UK*, July 17, 2015, www.independent.co.uk/life-style/gadgets-and-tech/news/a-robot-has-passed -the-self-awareness-test-10395895.html.

14. Stanislas Dehaene, Hakwan Lau, and Sid Kouider, "What Is Consciousness, and Could Machines Have It?" *Science*, Vol. 358, Issue 6362 (October 27, 2017): 486–492, science .sciencemag.org/content/358/6362/486; Charles Q. Choi, "How Do You Make a Conscious Robot?" *Real Clear Science*, October 27, 2017, www.realclearscience.com/articles /2017/10/27/how_do_you_make_a_conscious_robot_110432.html.

15. Dan Robitzski, "Artificial Consciousness: How to Give a Robot a Soul," Futurism, June 25, 2018, futurism.com/artificial-consciousness.

16. Ibid.

17. Stephen Wolfram, "Something Very Big Is Coming: Our Most Important Technology Project Yet," personal blog, November 13, 2013, blog.stephenwolfram.com/2013/11/something-very -big-is-coming-our-most-important-technology-project-yet.

18. Byron Reese, "Voices in AI—Episode 1: A Conversation with Yoshua Bengio," Gigaom .com, October 2, 2017, gigaom.com/2017/10/02/voices-in-ai-episode-1-a-conversation -with-yoshua-bengio.

19. Jan Faye, "Copenhagen Interpretation of Quantum Mechanics," Stanford Encyclopedia of Philosophy, May 3, 2002, plato.stanford.edu/entries/qm-copenhagen.

20. Jack Nicas, "How Google's Quantum Computer Could Change the World," *Wall Street Journal*, October 16, 2017, www.wsj.com/articles/how-googles-quantum-computer-could -change-the-world-1508158847.

21. Ibid.

22. Elsevier, "Discovery of Quantum Vibrations in 'Microtubules' Inside Brain Neurons Supports Controversial Theory of Consciousness," Science Daily, January 16, 2014, www .sciencedaily.com/releases/2014/01/140116085105.htm.

23. Subhash Kak, "Indian Foundations of Modern Science," Medium, July 24, 2018, medium .com/@subhashkak1/indian-foundations-of-modern-science-72259046700f.

24. Gazzaniga, *The Consciousness Instinct: Unraveling the Mystery of How the Brain Makes the Mind*, 185, 187.

25. Brenden M. Lake, Tomer D. Ullman, Joshua B. Tenenbaum, and Samuel J. Gershman, "Building Machines That Learn and Think Like People," *Behavioral and Brain Sciences*, Vol. 40 (2017): 10, doi.org/10.1017/S0140525X16001837.

26. Dehaene, Lau, and Kouider, "What is Consciousness, and Could Machines Have It?"

27. J. Kevin O'Regan, "How to Build a Robot That Is Conscious and Feels, Minds & Machines," Springer Netherlands, June 7, 2012, link.springer.com/article/10.1007/s11023-012-9279-x.

28. "(1) A body that responds to stimuli; (2) a method of communication; and (3) an algorithm that attempts (with little success) to deduce the reasons and motivations for these communications." Hugh Howey, "How to Build a Self-Conscious Machine," *Wired*, October 4, 2017, www.wired.com/story/how-to-build-a-self-conscious-ai-machine.

29. Will Knight, "Curiosity May Be Vital for Truly Smart AI," *MIT Technology Review*, May

23, 2017, www.technologyreview.com/s/607886/curiosity-may-be-vital-for-truly-smart-ai; Matthew Hutson, "How Researchers are Teaching AI to Learn like a Child," *Science*, May 24, 2018, www.sciencemag.org/news/2018/05/how-researchers-are-teaching-ai-learn-child.

30. Joseph Campbell, *The Hero with a Thousand Faces* (New York: Pantheon Books, 1949).

31. Octavia Butler, *Dawn* (New York: Grand Central Publishing, 1987), 39.

32. Christof Koch, "What Is Consciousness?" *Scientific American*, June 2, 2017, www.scientific american.com/article/what-is-consciousness.

33. Joan Podrazik, "What Is the Soul? Eckhart Tolle, Wayne Dyer and Others Define It," Huffington Post, December 25, 2012, www.huffingtonpost.com/2012/12/25/what-is-the -soul-eckhart-tolle-wayne-dyer_n_2333335.html.

34. "Ancient Theories of Soul," Stanford Encyclopedia of Philosophy, accessed September 12, 2018, plato.stanford.edu/entries/ancient-soul/#3.

35. R. D. Archer-Hind, ed. and trans., *The Timaeus of Plato* (Salem, NH: Ayers Co., 1988).

36. René Descartes, "Cartesian dualism," *Meditations on First Philosophy, 1596–1650* (Indianapolis: Hackett Publishing Co., 1993).

37. Joseph E. LeDoux, PhD, Donald H. Wilson, MD, and Michael S. Gazzaniga, PhD, "A Divided Mind: Observations on the Conscious Properties of the Separated Hemispheres," *Annals of Neurology*, November 2, 1977, onlinelibrary.wiley.com/doi/abs/10.1002/ana .410020513.

38. "Men ought to know that from nothing else but the brain come joys, delights, laughter and sports, and sorrows, griefs, despondency, and lamentations. And by this, in an especial manner, we acquire wisdom and knowledge, and see and hear, and know what are foul and what are fair, what are bad and what are good, what are sweet, and what unsavory; some we discriminate by habit, and some we perceive by their utility. By this we distinguish objects of relish and disrelish, according to the seasons; and the same things do not always please us. And by the same organ we become mad and delirious, and fears and terrors assail us, some by night, and some by day, and dreams and untimely wanderings, and cares that are not suitable, and ignorance of present circumstances, desuetude, and unskillfulness. All these things we endure from the brain, when it is not healthy, but is more hot, more cold, more moist, or more dry than natural, or when it suffers any other preternatural and unusual affection. And we become mad from its humidity. For when it is more moist than natural, it is necessarily put into motion, and the affection being moved, neither the sight nor hearing can be at rest, and the tongue speaks in accordance with the sight and hearing." Hippocrates, *On the Sacred Disease*, trans. Francis Adams, classics.mit.edu /Hippocrates/sacred.html.

39. Pali: "non-self" or "substanceless." "Anatta," Britannica, accessed September 3, 2018, www.britannica.com/topic/anatta.

40. "Atman means 'eternal self'. The atman refers to the real self beyond ego or false self. It is often referred to as 'spirit' or 'soul' and indicates our true self or essence which underlies our existence." Gavin Flood, "Hindu Concepts," BBC, August 24, 2009, www.bbc.co.uk /religion/religions/hinduism/concepts/concepts_1.shtml.

41. Graham Harvey, *Animism: Respecting the Living World* (New York: Columbia University Press, 2005), 42; New World Encyclopedia, accessed September 12, 2018, www.new worldencyclopedia.org/entry/Animism.

42. "Soul, to Brown, is 'not as an essence apart from the physical self, but the net sum of those encounters in which embodied humans relate to and commune with God (who is spirit) or one another in a manner that reaches deeply into the essence of our creaturely, historical, and communal selves.'" Brandon Ambrosino, "What Would it Mean for AI to Have a Soul?" BBC, June 18, 2018, www.bbc.com/future/story/20180615-can-artificial-intelligence-have-a-soul-and-religion.

43. Daniel Dennett, *From Bacteria to Bach and Back: The Evolution of Minds* (New York: W. W. Norton & Company, 2018).

44. Daniel Dennett, "'A Perfect and Beautiful Machine': What Darwin's Theory of Evolution Reveals About Artificial Intelligence," *Atlantic*, June 22, 2012, www.theatlantic.com/technology/archive/2012/06/a-perfect-and-beautiful-machine-what-darwins-theory-of-evolution-reveals-about-artificial-intelligence/258829.

45. "Turing himself is one of the twigs on the Tree of Life, and his artifacts, concrete and abstract, are indirectly products of the blind Darwinian processes in the same way spider webs and beaver dams are . . ." Dennett, *From Bacteria to Bach and Back: The Evolution of Minds*.

46. John Searle, "How Do You Explain Consciousness," March 2014, TED, 18:34, www.ted.com/talks/david_chalmers_how_do_you_explain_consciousness/transcript.

47. Steve Volk, "Down the Quantum Rabbit Hole," *Discover*, accessed November 23, 2018, discovermagazine.com/bonus/quantum.

48. Robitzski, "Artificial Consciousness: How to Give a Robot a Soul."

49. Ibid.

50. Aristotle, *The Nicomachean Ethics*, trans. W. D. Ross, and Lesley Brown (New York: Oxford University Press, 2009).

51. "William James himself always insisted that consciousness was not a 'thing' but a 'process.'" Oliver Sacks, *River of Consciousness* (New York: Knopf, 2017).

52. Ibid., 8.

53. Jorge Luis Borges, "A New Refutation of Time," *Sur*, Vol. 115 (1944).

54. Janine M. Benyus, *Biomimicry: Innovation Inspired by Nature* (New York: Harper Perennial, 2002).

55. Elizabeth Kolbert, "Why Facts Don't Change Our Minds," *New Yorker*, February 27, 2017, www.newyorker.com/magazine/2017/02/27/why-facts-dont-change-our-minds.

56. Donald R. Griffin, *Animal Minds: Beyond Cognition to Consciousness* (University of Chicago Press, 2001), 2.

57. Rodney A. Brooks, "Intelligence Without Representation," MIT Artificial Intelligence Laboratory, September 1987, people.csail.mit.edu/brooks/papers/representation.pdf.

58. "We declare the following: 'The absence of a neocortex does not appear to preclude an organism from experiencing affective states. Convergent evidence indicates that non-human animals have the neuroanatomical, neurochemical, and neurophysiological substrates of conscious states along with the capacity to exhibit intentional behaviors. Consequently, the weight of evidence indicates that humans are not unique in possessing the neurological substrates that generate consciousness. Nonhuman animals, including all mammals and birds, and many other creatures, including octopuses, also possess these neurological substrates.'" Philip Low, and Jaak Panksepp, Diana Reiss, David Edelman, Bruno

Van Swinderen, and Christof Koch, eds., "The Cambridge Declaration of Consciousness," Francis Crick Memorial Conference on Consciousness in Human and Non-Human Animals, Churchill College, University of Cambridge, July 7, 2012, fcmconference.org/img /CambridgeDeclarationOnConsciousness.pdf.

59. John D. Wilsey, *American Exceptionalism and Civil Religion: Reassessing the History of an Idea* (Illinois: IVP Academic, 2015).

60. Graham Harman, *Object-Oriented Ontology: A New Theory of Everything* (London: Pelican, 2018).

61. Timothy Morton, *Hyperobjects: Philosophy and Ecology After the End of the World* (Minneapolis: University of Minnesota Press, 2013).

62. Alan Watts, *The Book: On the Taboo Against Knowing Who You Are* (New York: Collier, 1966), 97.

63. Richard E. Cytowic, "Reality Lies Beyond What We Can Perceive," *Psychology Today*, May 2, 2017, www.psychologytoday.com/us/blog/the-fallible-mind/201705/reality-lies-beyond -what-we-can-perceive.

64. Philip Pullman, *His Dark Materials* (New York: Alfred A. Knopf, 2007).

65. Simon Worrall, "How 40,000 Tons of Cosmic Dust Falling to Earth Affects You and Me," *National Geographic*, January 28, 2015, news.nationalgeographic.com /2015/01/150128-big-bang-universe-supernova-astrophysics-health-space-ngbooktalk.

66. Kara Rogers, "7 Vestigial Features of the Human Body," Britannica, www.britannica .com/list/7-vestigial-features-of-the-human-body.

67. Axel Cleeremans, "The Radical Plasticity Thesis: How the Brain Learns to Be Conscious," *Frontiers in Psychology*, February 25, 2011, www.ncbi.nlm.nih.gov/pmc/articles /PMC3110382.

68. T. M. Scanlon, *What We Owe to Each Other* (Belknap Press, 2000).

69. Jeremy Bentham, *Introduction to the Principles of Morals and Legislation* (New York: Hafner Publishing Co., 1948).

70. Philip Goff, "Panpsychism is Crazy, but it's Also Most Probably True," Aeon, March 1, 2017, aeon.co/ideas/panpsychism-is-crazy-but-its-also-most-probably-true.

71. Godehard Brüntrup and Ludwig Jaskolla, eds., "Panpsychism: Contemporary Perspectives," Oxford University Press, 2017, ndpr.nd.edu/news/panpsychism-contemporary-perspectives.

72. Keith Frankish and Aeon, "Why Panpsychism Is Probably Wrong," *Atlantic*, September 20, 2016, www.theatlantic.com/science/archive/2016/09/panpsychism-is-wrong/500774.

73. Philip Goff, "Is the Universe a Conscious Mind?" Aeon, February 8, 2018, aeon.co/essays /cosmopsychism-explains-why-the-universe-is-fine-tuned-for-life.

74. Bernardo Kastrup, Adam Crabtree, and Edward F. Kelly, "Could Multiple Personality Disorder Explain Life, the Universe and Everything?" *Scientific American*, June 18, 2018, blogs.scientificamerican.com/observations/could-multiple-personality-disorder-explain -life-the-universe-and-everything.

75. "Vera Rubin (1928–2016)," National Science Foundation, accessed March 8, 2019, www .nsf.gov/news/special_reports/medalofscience50/rubin.jsp.

76. "In the example of Walt Whitman we find someone who rejected such binary opposites, whether between North versus South, science versus art, and even the love of man versus woman. He reminds us that to celebrate others is to celebrate ourselves,

even during our darkest hour. In 1892, while bedridden from a paralytic stroke and barely able to hold a pen to paper, this great 'poet of science' offered a final paean to his early inspiration in a work entitled Darwinism—(then Furthermore). Meantime, the highest and subtlest and broadest truths of modern science wait for their true assignment and last vivid flashes of light—as Democracy waits for its." Eric Michael Johnson, "We Contain Multitudes: Walt Whitman, Charles Darwin, and the Song of Empathy," *Scientific American*, July 19, 2013, blogs.scientificamerican.com /primate-diaries/the-song-of-empathy.

77. "When Victor imagines the two creatures looking upon each other for the first time, he calls to mind Jean-Paul Sartre's classic notion that humans learn selfhood when we are first seen by the 'other.' In *Being and Nothingness*, Sartre argues that we cannot have a self until we are recognized by an other, which allows us to see both the other in ourselves and the selfhood in others. Victor typically cannot imagine the two creatures having selves at all. So he suggests they will be 'repulsed' rather than find sympathy in one another's eyes." David Guston, ed., *Frankenstein: Annotated for Scientists, Engineers, and Creators of All Kinds* (Cambridge: MIT Press, 2017).

78. Emily Dickinson, *I Dwell in Possibility. The Poems of Emily Dickinson*, ed. R. W. Franklin (Massachusetts: Harvard University Press, 1999), www.poetryfoundation.org/poems/52197 /i-dwell-in-possibility-466.

79. "Wendell Wallach and Colin Allen offer us a different way to think about emerging properties in AI. In their book *Artificial Moral Agents*, which considers the possibility of ethical AI, Wallach and Allen compare the discovery of flight with the discovery of human beings' properties of consciousness. The earliest attempts at human flight, they note, consisted in humans behaving like birds; after all, humans knew birds could fly, so they figured their best shot of flying was to imitate the feathered creatures. Years later, however, we know that birds weren't the best models for human flight. 'It doesn't matter how you do it, so long as you get airborne and stay airborne for a decent amount of time,' conclude Wallach and Allen. There's not just one solution to flight. It 'can be manifested by a wide range of different systems made out of lots of different materials.'" Ambrosino, "What Would it Mean for AI to Have a Soul?"

80. Claudia Kalb, "What Makes a Genius?" *National Geographic*, May 2017, www.national geographic.com/magazine/2017/05/genius-genetics-intelligence-neuroscience-creativity -einstein.

CHAPTER 9: THE ADJACENT POSSIBLE

1. Paul Ratner, "In 1973, an MIT Computer Predicted When Civilization Will End," Big Think, August, 23, 2018, bigthink.com/paul-ratner/in-1973-an-mit-computer-predicted -the-end-of-civilization-so-far-its-on-target.

2. Sometimes also called the Holocene extinction or the Anthropocene extinction. Damian Carrington, "Earth's Sixth Mass Extinction Event Under Way, Scientists Warn," *Guardian*, July 10, 2017, www.theguardian.com/environment/2017/jul/10/earths-sixth-mass-extinction -event-already-underway-scientists-warn.

3. J. K. Rowling, "The Marauder's Map," Pottermore, accessed September 4, 2018, www .pottermore.com/writing-by-jk-rowling/the-marauders-map.

4. Steven Johnson, *Where Good Ideas Come from: The Natural History of Innovation* (New York: Riverhead, 2010).

5. Joseph Weizenbaum, "ELIZA—a Computer Program for the Study of Natural Language Communication Between Man and Machine," *Communications of the ACM*, Vol. 9, Issue 1 (January 1966), dl.acm.org/citation.cfm?id=365168.

6. Emiko Jozuka, "The Sad Story of Eric, the UK's First Robot Who Was Loved Then Forsaken," Motherboard, May 19, 2016, motherboard.vice.com/en_us/article/pgkkpm /the-sad-story-of-eric-the-uks-first-robot-who-was-loved-then-forsaken.

7. Keiichi Furukawa, "Honda's Asimo Robot Bows Out but Finds New Life," Nikkei Asian Review, June 28, 2018, asia.nikkei.com/Business/Companies/Honda-s-Asimo-robot-bows -out-but-finds-new-life.

8. Matthew Hutson, "Scientists Imbue Robots with Curiosity," *Science*, May 31, 2017, www .sciencemag.org/news/2017/05/scientists-imbue-robots-curiosity.

9. Carlo Ratti, "Futurecraft," Proceedings of the 2016 ACM Conference on Designing Interactive Systems, Brisbane, Australia, June 4–8, 2016, dusp.mit.edu/publication /futurecraft.

10. Damian Przybyła, "Reflection on the Future of Design," PCDN, accessed September 20, 2018, pcdnetwork.org/blogs/futuredesign.

11. Frank White, *The Overview Effect. Space Exploration and Human Evolution* (New York: Houghton Mifflin, 1987).

12. Ronald J. Garan Jr., *The Orbital Perspective: Lessons in Seeing the Big Picture from a Journey of 71 Million Miles* (California: Berrett-Koehler, 2015); "Psychologists Study Intense Awe Astronauts Feel Viewing Earth from Space," Science Daily, April 19, 2016, www .sciencedaily.com/releases/2016/04/160419120055.htm.

13. Frank White, *The Overview Effect. Space Exploration and Human Evolution*.

14. Elizabeth Landau, "'Pale Blue Dot' Images Turn 25," Jet Propulsion Laboratory, NASA, February 13, 2015, voyager.jpl.nasa.gov/news/details.php?article_id=43.

15. "Look again at that dot. That's here. That's home. That's us." Carl Sagan, *Pale Blue Dot: A Vision of the Human Future in Space* (Ballantine Books, 1997).

16. John Malouff, "Children Learn Empathy Growing Up, but Can We Train Adults to Have More of It?" The Conversation, January 10, 2017, theconversation.com /children-learn-empathy-growing-up-but-can-we-train-adults-to-have-more-of-it -68153.

17. Sourya Acharya and Samarth Shukla, "Mirror Neurons: Enigma of the Metaphysical Modular Brain," *Journal of Natural Science, Biology and Medicine*, July–December 2012, www.ncbi.nlm.nih.gov/pmc/articles/PMC3510904.

18. C. Daniel Batson, "The Empathy-Altruism Hypothesis," *Oxford Scholarship Online*, May 2011, DOI: 10.1093/acprof:oso/9780195341065.001.0001.

19. Steven R. Quartz, "The Neuroscience of Heroism," *New York Times*, April 21, 2013, www.nytimes.com/roomfordebate/2013/04/21/the-bystanders-who-could-be-heroes/the -neuroscience-of-heroism.

20. Sunaura Taylor, *Beasts of Burden: Animal and Disability Liberation* (New York: The New Press, 2017), 52.

21. Ibid.; Cathryn Bailey, "On the Backs of Animals: The Valorization of Reason in Contem-

porary Animal Ethics," *Ethics and the Environment*, Vol. 10, No. 1 (Spring, 2005): 1–17, DOI: 10.1353/een.2005.0012.

22. Nathan J. Robinson, "Now Peter Singer Argues that It Might Be Okay to Rape Disabled People," *Current Affairs*, April 4, 2017, www.currentaffairs.org/2017/04/now-peter-singer -argues-that-it-might-be-okay-to-rape-disabled-people.

23. Joshua Rothman, "Are Disability Rights and Animal Rights Connected?" *New Yorker*, June 5, 2017, www.newyorker.com/culture/persons-of-interest/are-disability-rights-and -animal-rights-connected.

24. James F. McGrath, "Robots, Rights and Religion," *Religion and Science Fiction*, 2011, digitalcommons.butler.edu/facsch_papers/197.

25. Rana el Kaliouby, "We Need Computers with Empathy," *MIT Technology Review*, October 20, 2017, www.technologyreview.com/s/609071/we-need-computers-with-empathy.

26. Jessica Amortegui, "'AI Must Be Built with Empathy,' Microsoft CEO Satya Nadella Says During UK Release of Book," Microsoft Reporter, October 6, 2017, news.microsoft .com/en-gb/2017/10/06/ai-must-be-built-with-empathy-microsoft-ceo-satya-nadella-says -during-uk-release-of-book-hit-refresh; "Are You Using Apple's Secret Skill at Work?" *Forbes*, February 2, 2017, www.forbes.com/sites/womensmedia/2017/02/02/are-you-using-apples -secret-skill-at-work/#32652b18952e.

27. Cade Metz, "Apple Buys AI Startup That Reads Emotions in Faces," *Wired*, January 7, 2016, www.wired.com/2016/01/apple-buys-ai-startup-that-reads-emotions-in-faces.

28. Deep Empathy, accessed September 20, 2018, deepempathy.mit.edu.

29. Gapminder, accessed September 2018, www.gapminder.org/dollar-street/matrix.

30. David Allegretti, "Meet the Woman Teaching Empathy to AI," *Vice*, May 29, 2018, www .vice.com/en_au/article/ywe33m/this-woman-believes-ai-can-be-taught-empathy.

31. Clara Moskowitz, "Human-Robot Relations: Why We Should Worry," Live Science, February 18, 2013, www.livescience.com/27204-human-robot-relationships-turkle.html.

32. Sherry Turkle, *Reclaiming Conversation: The Power of Talk in a Digital Age* (New York: Penguin, 2016), 232.

33. Sherry Turkle, "There Will Never Be an Age of Artificial Intimacy," *New York Times*, August 11, 2018, www.nytimes.com/2018/08/11/opinion/there-will-never-be-an-age-of -artificial-intimacy.html.

34. Olivia Goldhill, "Empathy Makes Us Immoral, Says a Yale Psychologist," Quartz, July 9, 2017, qz.com/1024303/empathy-makes-us-immoral-says-a-yale-psychologist.

35. Brendan M. Lynch, "Study Finds Our Desire for 'Like-Minded Others' Is Hard-Wired," University of Kansas, February 23, 2016, news.ku.edu/2016/02/19/new-study-finds -our-desire-minded-others-hard-wired-controls-friend-and-partner.

36. Daniel Goleman, *Social Intelligence: The New Science of Human Relationships* (New York: Random House Publishing Group, 2006).

37. Jonathan Gottschall, *The Storytelling Animal: How Stories Make Us Human* (New York: Houghton Mifflin Harcourt, 2012).

38. Paul J. Zak, "Why Your Brain Loves Good Storytelling," *Harvard Business Review*, October 28, 2014, hbr.org/2014/10/why-your-brain-loves-good-storytelling.

39. Cody C. Delistraty, "The Psychological Comforts of Storytelling," *Atlantic*, November, 2, 2014, www.theatlantic.com/author/cody-c-delistraty.

40. Alison Flood, "Robots Could Learn Human Values by Reading Stories, Research Suggests," *Guardian*, February 18, 2016, www.theguardian.com/books/2016/feb/18/robots -could-learn-human-values-by-reading-stories-research-suggests.

41. Liz Bury, "Reading Literary Fiction Improves Empathy, Study Finds," *Guardian*, October 8, 2013, www.theguardian.com/books/booksblog/2013/oct/08/literary-fiction-improves -empathy-study.

42. Maryanne Wolf, *Reader, Come Home* (New York: Harper Collins, 2018).

43. Keith Oatley, *Such Stuff as Dreams: The Psychology of Fiction* (New York: John Wiley & Sons, 2011).

44. Tom Jacobs, "Reading Literary Fiction Can Make You Less Racist," Pacific Standard, March 10, 2014, psmag.com/social-justice/reading-literary-fiction-can-make-less-racist -76155.

45. Chimamanda Ngozi Adichie, "The Danger of a Single Story," July 2009, TEDGlobal, 18:43, www.ted.com/talks/chimamanda_adichie_the_danger_of_a_single_story.

46. Kidd and Castano's research shows that reading popular works doesn't have the same effect as long-form literary fiction. David Comer Kidd and Emanuele Castano, "Reading Literary Fiction Improves Theory of Mind," *Science*, Vol. 342, Issue 6156 (October 5, 2013): 377–380, DOI: 10.1126/science.1239918.

47. Maja Djikic, Keith Oatley, Sara Zoeterman, and Jordan B. Peterson, "On Being Moved by Art: How Reading Fiction Transforms the Self," *Creativity Research Journal*, Vol. 21, Issue 1 (2009): 24–29, doi.org/10.1080/10400410802633392.

48. McMaster University, "The Art of Storytelling: Researchers Explore Why We Relate to Characters," ScienceDaily, September 13, 2018, www.sciencedaily.com/releases /2018/09/180913113822.htm.

49. Keith Oatley and Maja Djikic, "How Reading Transforms Us," *New York Times*, December 19, 2014, www.nytimes.com/2014/12/21/opinion/sunday/how-writing-transforms-us .html.

50. Jon Henley, "Philip Pullman: 'Loosening the Chains of the Imagination,'" *Guardian*, August 23, 2013, www.theguardian.com/lifeandstyle/2013/aug/23/philip-pullman-dark -materials-children.

51. Steven Pinker, *The Better Angels of Our Nature: Why Violence Has Declined* (New York: Viking Books, 2011).

52. "The Strange, Beautiful, Subterranean Power of Fairy Tales," A forum moderated by Kate Bernheimer, Center for Fiction, Issue 3, accessed September 12, 2018, www.centerforfiction .org/why-fairy-tales-matter.

53. Kidd and Castano, "Reading Literary Fiction Improves Theory of Mind."

54. Andrew Maynard, "Sci-fi Movies Are the Secret Weapon That Could Help Silicon Valley Grow Up," The Conversation, November 15, 2018, theconversation.com/sci-fi -movies-are-the-secret-weapon-that-could-help-silicon-valley-grow-up-105714.

55. Margaret Atwood, "Margaret Atwood on What 'The Handmaid's Tale' Means in the Age of Trump," *New York Times*, March 20, 2017, www.nytimes.com/2017/03/10/books /review/margaret-atwood-handmaids-tale-age-of-trump.html.

56. Jill Galvan, "Entering the Posthuman Collective in Philip K. Dick's 'Do Androids Dream

of Electric Sheep?'" *Science Fiction Studies*, Vol. 24, No. 3 (November 1997): 413–429, www.jstor.org/stable/4240644.

57. Eliot Peper, "Why Business Leaders Need to Read More Science Fiction," *Harvard Business Review*, July 14, 2017, hbr.org/2017/07/why-business-leaders-need-to-read-more-science-fiction.

58. Brian Nichiporuk, "Alternative Futures and Army Force Planning: Implications for the Future Force Era," RAND Corporation, 2005, www.rand.org/content/dam/rand/pubs/monographs/2005/RAND_MG219.pdf.

59. Emmanuel Tsekleves, "Science Fiction as Fact: How Desires Drive Discoveries," *Guardian*, August 13, 2015, www.theguardian.com/media-network/2015/aug/13/science-fiction-reality-predicts-future-technology.

60. Neil Gaiman, *The View from the Cheap Seats: Selected Nonfiction* (New York: William Morrow, 2016).

61. Zak, "Why Your Brain Loves Good Storytelling."

62. "Oatley and his York University colleague Raymond Mar suggest that the process of taking on another's consciousness in reading fiction and the nature of fiction's content—where the great emotions and conflicts of life are regularly played out—not only contribute to our empathy, but represent what the social scientist Jèmeljan Hakemulder called our 'moral laboratory.'" Wolf, *Reader Come Home*; Jèmeljan Hakemulder, *The Moral Laboratory: Experiments Examining the Effects of Reading* (Amsterdam, Netherlands: John Benjamins, 2000).

63. "Human Empathy & Interconnectedness," Joseph Campbell, 1986, YouTube, accessed September 19, 2018, www.youtube.com/watch?v=_CGb-p_0gvY.

64. Karen Armstrong, "Do unto Others," *Guardian*, November 14, 2008, www.theguardian.com/commentisfree/2008/nov/14/religion.

65. Krista Tippett, "The Happiest Man in the World," *On Being*, November 12, 2009, onbeing.org/programs/matthieu-ricard-happiest-man-world.

66. Karen Armstrong and Archbishop Desmond Tutu, "Compassion Unites the World's Faiths," CNN, November 10, 2009, www.cnn.com/2009/OPINION/11/10/armstrong.tutu.charter.compassion/index.html.

67. Alison Flood, "Robots Could Learn Human Values by Reading Stories, Research Suggests," *Guardian*, February 18, 2016, www.theguardian.com/books/2016/feb/18/robots-could-learn-human-values-by-reading-stories-research-suggest.

68. Craig Wigginton, "Mobile Continues Its Global Reach into All Aspects of Consumers' Lives," Deloitte Global Mobile Consumer Trends Second Edition, 2017, www2.deloitte.com/global/en/pages/technology-media-and-telecommunications/articles/gx-global-mobile-consumer-trends.html.

69. "Mobile Biometric Market Forecast to Exceed $50.6 Billion in Annual Revenue in 2022 as Installed Base Grows to 5.5 Billion Biometric Smart Mobile Devices," PR Newswire, September 14, 2017, www.prnewswire.com/news-releases/mobile-biometric-market-forecast-to-exceed-506-billion-in-annual-revenue-in-2022-as-installed-base-grows-to-55-billion-biometric-smart-mobile-devices-300519359.html.

70. Sara H. Konrath, Edward H. O'Brien, and Courtney Hsing, "Changes in Dispositional Empathy in American College Students over Time: A Meta-Analysis," *Personality and Social Psychology Review*, 15.2 (2011): 180–198, DOI: 10.1177/1088868310377395.

71. Jean M. Twenge and W. Keith Campbell, *The Narcissism Epidemic: Living in the Age of Entitlement* (New York: Atria, 2010).

72. Ap Dijksterhuis and John A. Bargh, "The Perception-Behavior Expressway: Automatic Effects of Social Perception on Social Behavior," Baillement, accessed September 20, 2018, www.baillement.com/texte-perception-behavior.pdf.

73. Chris Weller, "Silicon Valley Parents Raising Their Kids Tech Free," Business Insider, February 18, 2018, www.businessinsider.com/silicon-valley-parents-raising-their-kids-tech-free-red-flag-2018-2.

74. "Catastrophic forgetting occurs when a neural network loses the information learned in a previous task after training on subsequent tasks. This problem remains a hurdle for artificial intelligence systems with sequential learning capabilities." Joan Serrà, Dídac Surís, Marius Miron, and Alexandros Karatzoglou, "Overcoming Catastrophic Forgetting with Hard Attention to the Task," Cornell University Library, last revised May 29, 2018, arxiv.org/abs/1801.01423.

75. Dan Robitzski, "Artificial Intelligence Cho, New Artificial Intelligence Does Something Extraordinary—It Remembers," Futurism, August 31, 2018, futurism.com/artificial-intelligence-remember-agi.

76. Demis Hassabis, "The Mind in the Machine: Demis Hassabis on Artificial Intelligence," *Financial Times*, April 21, 2017, www.ft.com/content/048f418c-2487-11e7-a34a-538b4cb30025.

77. Jamie Condliffe, "Google's AI Guru Says That Great Artificial Intelligence Must Build on Neuroscience," *MIT Technology Review*, July 20, 2017, www.technologyreview.com/s/608317/googles-ai-guru-says-that-great-artificial-intelligence-must-build-on-neuroscience.

78. Dan Falk, *In Search of Time: The History, Physics, and Philosophy of Time* (New York: St. Martin's Griffin, 2010).

79. Ibid.

80. William A. Roberts, "Mental Time Travel: Animals Anticipate the Future," *Current Biology*, Vol. 17, Issue 11 (June 5, 2007): R418–R420, doi.org/10.1016/j.cub.2007.04.010.

81. Kevin Charles Fleming, "Our Stories Bind Us," *Pacific Standard*, January 26, 2018, psmag.com/news/our-stories-bind-us.

82. David Streitfeld, "Computer Stories: A.I. Is Beginning to Assist Novelists," *New York Times*, October 18, 2018, www.nytimes.com/2018/10/18/technology/ai-is-beginning-to-assist-novelists.html.

83. Dan Sperber and Hugo Mercier, *The Enigma of Reason* (Boston: Harvard University Press, 2017).

CHAPTER 10: A HUMAN ALGORITHM

1. Jane Goodall, *My Life with the Chimpanzees* (New York: Simon & Schuster, 1996).

2. Jane Goodall, *In the Shadow of Man* (Mariner Books; 50th Anniversary of Gombe edition, 2010).

3. Scott Feinberg, "Awards Chatter Podcast—Jane Goodall ('Jane')," *Hollywood Reporter*, August 15, 2018, www.hollywoodreporter.com/race/awards-chatter-podcast-jane-goodall-jane-1134696.

4. Victor Ottati, Erika D. Price, Chase Wilson, and Nathanael Sumaktoyo, "When Self-Perceptions of Expertise Increase Closed-Minded Cognition: The Earned Dogmatism

Effect," *Journal of Experimental Social Biology*, Vol. 61 (November 2015): 131–138, www .sciencedirect.com/science/article/pii/S0022103115001006.

5. Federico García Lorca, "Floating Bridges," in *Suites* (Los Angeles: Green Integer, 2001).

6. Leon M. Lederman and Dick Teresi, *The God Particle* (New York: Dell, 1993).

7. Jane Varner Malhotra, "Yet to Be Solved: the Problem of God," *Georgetown Magazine*, Fall 2018, issues.washcustom.com/publication/?m=54565&l=1#{%22issue_id%22:533408 ,%22page%22:16}.

8. Ibid.

9. "The Global Religious Landscape," Pew Research Center Religion & Public Life, December 18, 2012, www.pewforum.org/2012/12/18/global-religious-landscape-exec.

10. Brian J. Grim, "How Religious Will the World Be in 2050?" World Economic Forum, October 22, 2015, www.weforum.org/agenda/2015/10/how-religious-will-the-world-be-in-2050.

11. Michael Lipka and Claire Gecewicz, "Americans Now Say They're Spiritual but Not Religious," Pew Research Center, September 6, 2017, www.pewresearch.org/fact-tank/2017 /09/06/more-americans-now-say-theyre-spiritual-but-not-religious.

12. Peter Beinart, "Breaking Faith," *Atlantic*, April 2017, www.theatlantic.com/magazine /archive/2017/04/breaking-faith/517785.

13. Shafi Musaddique, "How Artificial Intelligence Is Shaping Religion in the 21st Century," CNBC, May 11, 2018, www.cnbc.com/2018/05/11/how-artificial-intelligence-is -shaping-religion-in-the-21st-century.html.

14. Mark Harris, "Inside the First Church of Artificial Intelligence," *Wired*, November 15, 2017, www.wired.com/story/anthony-levandowski-artificial-intelligence-religion.

15. Beth Singler, "fAIth," Aeon, June 13, 2017, aeon.co/essays/why-is-the-language-of -transhumanists-and-religion-so-similar.

16. Kevin Kelly, *The Inevitable* (New York: Penguin Books; Reprint edition, 2017).

17. James Vincent, "What Algorithmic Art Can Teach Us about Artificial Intelligence," The Verge, August 21, 2018, www.theverge.com/2018/8/21/17761424/ai-algorithm-art -machine-vision-perception-tom-white-treachery-imagenet.

18. Future of Life, accessed September 20, 2018, futureoflife.org/ai-researcher-vincent-conitzer; Vincent Conitzer, Walter Sinnott-Armstrong, Jana Schaich Borg, Yuan Deng, and Max Kramer, "Moral Decision Making Frameworks for Artificial Intelligence," Proceedings of the Thirty-First AAAI Conference on Artificial Intelligence (AAAI-17) Senior Member/ Blue Sky Track, San Francisco, California, 2017, users.cs.duke.edu/~conitzer/moral AAAI17.pdf.

19. Jolene Creighton, "The Evolution of AI: Can Morality be Programmed?" Futurism, July 1, 2016, futurism.com/the-evolution-of-ai-can-morality-be-programmed.

20. Alex Beard, "How Babies Learn—and Why Robots Can't Compete," *Guardian*, April 3, 2018, www.theguardian.com/news/2018/apr/03/how-babies-learn-and-why-robots-cant-compete.

21. Karen Hao, "Giving Algorithms a Sense of Uncertainty Could Make Them More Ethical," *MIT Technology Review*, January 18, 2019, www.technologyreview.com/s/612764 /giving-algorithms-a-sense-of-uncertainty-could-make-them-more-ethical.

22. Joel Lehman, Jeff Clune, Dusan Misevic, Christoph Adami, Julie Beaulieu, et al., "The Surprising Creativity of Digital Evolution: A Collection of Anecdotes from the Evolutionary Computation and Artificial Life Research Communities," ResearchGate, March 13, 2018,

www.researchgate.net/publication/323694489_The_Surprising_Creativity_of_Digital
_Evolution_A_Collection_of_Anecdotes_from_the_Evolutionary_Computation_and
_Artificial_Life_Research_Communities.

23. David Deutsch, "Philosophy Will Be the Key that Unlocks Artificial Intelligence," *Guardian*, October 3, 2012, www.theguardian.com/science/2012/oct/03/philosophy-artificial
-intelligence.